CONVERSATIONS WITH
MARK FROST

TWIN PEAKS, HILL STREET BLUES, AND THE EDUCATION OF A WRITER

CONVERSATIONS WITH
MARK FROST

TWIN PEAKS, HILL STREET BLUES, AND THE EDUCATION OF A WRITER

DAVID BUSHMAN

Book interior designed by Scott Ryan
Front design: Blake Morrow
Back cover design: Mark Karis
Mark Frost portraits by Blake Morrow
blakemorrow.ca
Edited by E. J. Kishpaugh

Published in the USA by Fayetteville Mafia Press
Columbus, Ohio

Contact Information
Email: fayettevillemafiapress@gmail.com
Website: fayettevillemafiapress.com

ISBN: 9781949024104
eBook ISBN: 9781949024111

CONTENTS

Acknowledgments

First and foremost, thanks to *Mark Frost*, for generously sharing his time and insights. I've long admired his work; now I have deep, deep respect for his intellect, conscience, and integrity as well.

John Thorne and *Christian Hartleben* were *hugely* generous with their insights, expertise, and editorial comments. To my mind, these are perhaps the two greatest experts on the subjects of *Twin Peaks*, Mark Frost, and David Lynch, and this book would not have been possible without them.

Scott Ryan at *The Blue Rose* magazine, another *Twin Peaks* savant, is an exceptional friend and business partner whose guidance and support were of monumental importance to this project, and I cannot thank him enough.

Every Fayetteville Mafia Press book owes gratitude to *Janet Cole* and *Jason Jarnagin*, but this one especially. They are great friends and supporters, and it is hard to fail with them in your corner.

Thanks to *Blake Morrow* for his generosity, professionalism, and artistic vision, and to *E. J. Kishpaugh* for her relentlessness and expertise. And boundless thanks to *Mark Karis* for the eleventh-hour rescue (not to mention his typically brilliant work). And speaking of rescues, hat tips to *Mischa Cronin*, and *Marita Albinson* and *Tosaka Thao* from the Guthrie Theater.

Thanks also to *Scott Frost* for his time and insights, and to *John Walsh*, a kind and generous man whom I had the great pleasure of meeting and befriending because of his connection to Mark Frost. RIP, John.

The *Twin Peaks* fan community is extraordinary. I have benefited greatly from their research and encouragement many, many times over the years. Special mention to ***Pieter Dom, Brad Dukes, Ben Durant, Mark Givens***, and ***Bryon Kozaczka***.

Many thanks also to ***Jane Klain*** and ***Maria Pagano*** of The Paley Center for Media.

As always, deepest thanks to the three most important people in my world: ***Mariam, Alex,*** and ***Scout***.

Introduction

Rarely—never?—do we hear the phrase "Mark Frost's *Twin Peaks*." And why not? Though he is clearly a master yarn spinner with a sharp intellect, a distinctive sense of humor, an infatuation with mythology and the occult, and—above all—profound empathy and soulfulness, Frost is never credited as the auteur of *Twin Peaks*. And yet a convincing argument can be made that he is the heart and soul of *Twin Peaks*, and that without his participation the series never would have resonated so fervidly with the legions of fans who have embraced and obsessed over it.

Hopefully, this book is that argument.

In 2015, when I first sat down to write *Twin Peaks FAQ: All That's Left to Know About a Place Both Wonderful and Strange*, I was 99.9 percent certain that David Lynch had been 99.9 percent responsible for the genius of *Twin Peaks*.

I was wrong.

In my defense, I was wrong because almost everyone on the planet had been telling me that David Lynch was the true genius behind *Twin Peaks*. Article after article, book after book, podcast after podcast raved about "David Lynch's *Twin Peaks*"—often without so much as mentioning the contributions of Mark Frost, who not only had cocreated the series, but also wrote or rewrote nearly every episode and ran the first two seasons of the show on a daily basis.

For example: a recent three-page *Sunday Times of London* article on Lynch and the impact of *Twin Peaks* on television declared, "It's hard to imagine the delirious plotting of *Breaking Bad*, the gruesome glee of *Dexter* or even the harsh realism of *The Wire* without Lynch's inspired precursor."

Lynch's inspired precursor.

In *Television Rewired: The Rise of the Auteur Serie*s, Martha P. Nochimson wrote that David Lynch "made his anger with the script [for the season two finale of *Twin Peaks*, written by Frost, Harley Peyton, and Robert Engels] explicit in our phone conversation on January 18, 2018: 'I hate it. They don't understand the Red Room at all.'"

The problem with this assertion is that it assumes Lynch has sole proprietorship of the meaning of the Red Room. Though in fact he did create it (for the European ending to the pilot), Frost, Peyton, and Engels bore responsibility for nurturing it over the course of two seasons, plus constructing an entire mythology around it—one that would accommodate, or even drive, the narrative—whenever Lynch wasn't around.

Which was often. Lynch popped in and out of the original series—he was barely present at all for season one (instead, he was off making *Wild at Heart*); during season two he appeared in five episodes as FBI Regional Bureau Chief Gordon Cole (he had supplied Cole's voice in two episodes of season one, but didn't appear on screen until season two). All told Lynch directed six episodes of the original series, including the two most celebrated—the pilot and the series finale. He famously threw out chunks of the finale's script and improvised what many people—critics, scholars, fans, and Mark Frost himself—consider perhaps the most thrilling (if perhaps inscrutable) series ending of all time.

In fact, Frost—inspired by his interest in spirituality and the occult—devised much of the intricate mythology of *Twin Peaks* with the assistance of Peyton and Engels, often by finding ways to integrate Lynch's largely visceral, narratively underdeveloped concepts into a cohesive and coherent story (well, mostly, anyway). After all, Frost is above all a storyteller.

Of course, David Lynch is a brilliant artist. Many of the most enduring and disquieting images associated with the first two seasons of *Twin Peaks*—the dancing dwarf, the Red Room, the evil spirit Bob, the One-Armed Man, the Chalfonts/Tremonds—are products of Lynch's contorted (and I mean that in the nicest way possible) imagination.

But the original *Twin Peaks* is far more than a compilation of those iconic moments. So much of the show's allure derives not from the recesses of our unconscious, but from the *heart*. Think about it. Harry S. Truman resolutely waits for Dale Cooper to emerge from the Black Lodge. The tortured love of Norma Jennings and Ed Hurley. Cooper and Hawk ponder the afterlife, then escort a devastated Leland Palmer off the Great Northern dance floor. Major Briggs shares the details of a dream with Bobby over a slab of pie. Doc Hayward tells Donna how lucky he is to be her father.

All these iconic moments, and so many more like them, tug at us every bit as potently as creamed corn and the Owl Cave ring, just in a different way.

Twin Peaks is the sum part of its surreality *and* its humanity; take away either one and you have a show without anywhere near the impact.

It's worth noting that the most prevalent complaint among those *Twin Peaks* fans who don't revere *Fire Walk With Me*—the theatrical prequel that Mark Frost had no hands-on involvement with whatsoever—is a perceived lack of warmth. The same can be said about Peaks fans who *admired* the intuitive brilliance of season three (which Frost and Lynch cowrote, but Lynch directed in its entirety) but didn't *love* it; they couldn't shake the feeling that *something* was amiss.

No one will ever fully and clearly demarcate the individual contributions to *Twin Peaks* between Mark Frost and David Lynch, and there's no implication here that Lynch didn't supply plenty of emotional power of his own. But the two *combined* to produce magic.

Frost's career—and not just with respect to *Twin Peaks*—hasn't gotten nearly the attention it deserves. He has created, written, and produced television programming for five decades, from the hoary days of three-network hegemony to what many now cite as a new Golden Age of television (which, it can be persuasively argued, *Twin Peaks* pioneered). Frost cut his teeth in the seventies at the famous Universal factory, working alongside industry titans like Steven Bochco, Richard Levinson & William Link, Roy Huggins, and Stephen J. Cannell; after that Bochco brought him over to *Hill Street Blues*, one of the most important narrative dramas in American television history, produced by MTM, one of the most important independent television production companies.

He walked away from a lucrative Hollywood career in search of purpose and creative fulfillment, focusing instead on documentaries and theater—in Minneapolis.

He wrote and directed a provocative feature film that, for reasons beyond his control, barely registered commercially, but was warmly embraced by some of the nation's most prominent critics.

At the height of his success, he took yet another creative gamble by producing a series of half-hour documentaries—"docu-poetry," he called them—for prime-time commercial television.

He switched paths midcareer, focusing on novels and nonfiction books instead—partly to reassert artistic control over his work, partly because he preferred the solitary professional life of a book writer.

And later in life, *he* approached David Lynch with the audacious idea not only to resurrect *Twin Peaks*, but to do it in a way that was inventive and ingenious and evocative of the new era—because what does *Twin Peaks* stand for if not that?

Conclusions?

One, Frost likes to work. And while not everything has been critically or popularly embraced, he has unquestionably accumulated an impressive body of work, and demonstrated an exceptional gift for exploiting—in multiple media—generic conventions to explore profound, culturally resonant issues with intelligence, eloquence, and wit.

Two, Mark Frost is hugely responsible for the artistic success of *Twin Peaks*, as well as the passionate devotion of the show's fan base.

Three, his contributions are woefully underappreciated.

Four, he has insisted throughout his career on taking creative risks, rather than repeating himself.

Five, Frost's work reflects a deep capacity for empathy and a devotion to humanism; it is perhaps his defining characteristic as an artist.

Six, he is hugely appreciative and respectful of his admirers and fans.

And seven, he has—*along with* David Lynch—changed the landscape of television, and for that, we should all be grateful.

Hence, this book. It's about time we said thanks.

***

The transcripts that follow are the records of twenty-two phone interviews conducted specifically for the purposes of this book over a period of fifteen months, from February 2018 to October 2019. A typical interview lasted about one hour—sometimes more, sometimes less. We had one off-the-record in-person meeting, at a restaurant in New York City.

That this book exists at all is a function of the fact that I reached out to Mark Frost, who was initially reluctant.

Throughout our conversations, Frost was never more passionate than when we were discussing *ideas*—political, philosophical, social, and artistic. I sometimes had trouble keeping up, having to immerse myself in the works of Joseph Campbell, Carl Jung, Annie Besant, Jiddu Krishnamurti, Colin Woodard, and countless others, just to respond meaningfully to his comments.

No complaints there.

৵

1

"Someday I'm Going to Be a Writer"

(Growing Up)

Mark Frost has television in his blood, you might say. At the time of his birth—on November 25, 1953, in Brooklyn, New York—his father (Warren, who would go on to play a major on-screen role in *Twin Peaks*, as Will "Doc" Hayward) was floor director on *The Philco Television Playhouse*, a crown jewel of the so-called Golden Age of live TV drama. Among the fabled writers who passed through *Philco's* doors—so, the antecedents to people like Frost, Vince Gilligan, Amy Sherman-Palladino, Joss Whedon, David Simon, and all the other great contemporary TV drama authors—were Paddy Chayefsky, Robert Alan Aurthur, Horton Foote, and Gore Vidal.

The Frosts never stayed in one place for long; over the next two decades, they'd move to, from, and/or within New York, California, and Minnesota. Like Nick Carraway in *The Great Gatsby*—"I was within and without"—Mark Frost figured out how to blend in, but, in his own words, "felt like an outsider in almost every instance."

Clues to Frost's thematic preoccupations, strengths, and choices as a writer over the past five decades are sprinkled throughout this deep dive into his early years—a vivid imagination, a flair for storytelling, a strong moral conscience, a distrust of authority, and an acute sense of empathy, especially for the marginalized.

We begin at the beginning: on November 25, 1953.

***

Mark, let's start off by talking about what your childhood was like. You were born in Brooklyn because your dad was working in live

television at that point, is that right?

My dad was the floor director and later stage manager for *Philco Playhouse*, so his job was right there in Manhattan. My mother's family had an apartment on 56th Street, and we lived there for a while, moved out to Brooklyn Heights, and finally to Westbury, Long Island, when I was about two or three. We moved to California in 1958, when live television started to die in New York and most of the industry shifted to the West Coast. That prompted our leaving.

Dad went out six weeks ahead of us. He had a job on a detective show called *The Lineup*, in the story department. He found a place for us to live, then we flew out, my mom, my brother, Scott, and I, in the summer of '58, same year the Dodgers moved from Brooklyn to LA. I was already into baseball at that point, and they sold me on the idea of moving by saying, "Well, the Dodgers are going, so we're going to go too." That helped me make the transition.

Lindsay, your sister, wasn't born yet?

Lindsay was not born. She's nine years younger than I am.

Your dad wasn't acting or directing at this point? He was working only on the production side?

That was his way in. My dad had grown up in a small town in Vermont, with parents of very modest means, and was looking at life as a carpenter, a blue-collar existence in Essex Junction. He'd been born in Newburyport, Massachusetts. The family moved to the Bronx for a few years and ultimately moved to Vermont. The height of the Depression. His father was just trying to scrape together a living as a traveling salesman, Willy Loman, on the road a lot. Dad's mother ran a nursery school in the basement of her home for over fifty years, a beloved figure in their little town. She lived to a hundred. They dedicated the children's section of their library in town to her, and we helped support that later in her life.

I don't think he was looking forward to a whole lot. The thirties were tough times. When the war broke out, he was about to turn seventeen and tried to find a way to enlist. The Army wouldn't take him at that age, but he found out the Navy would if you had signed permission from your parents, so he went across the street to the Navy recruiting office. Ended up stationed on a destroyer escort called the USS *Borum*. The escort was a new class of ship, a scaled-down high-speed destroyer used in U-boat warfare and escorting convoys, so their reputation was as submarine killers. He was a chief petty officer, galley hand, and gunner.

One of their first active deployments was D-Day. The armada that crossed the channel was supposed to be led by a line of minesweepers, but they were short a few, so they threw in some of their escorts. That was how he experienced D-Day, front line of the invasion. They saw one of their sister ships go down about a mile portside when it hit a mine, and they parked two, three miles off Omaha Beach, shelling the Germans for the next week and a half. As the battle moved inland, they ferried the wounded back and forth to Southampton. It was pretty hot, and they saw a lot of action.

He spent the rest of the war patrolling the North Atlantic. After V. E. Day, they were redeployed to the Pacific. They were on their way— they'd almost made it to the Panama Canal—when Truman dropped the bomb on Japan. The war ended, and they came back to Norfolk.

After that, he returned home, took advantage of the G. I. Bill and entered Middlebury College, an hour south of where he'd grown up. He saw a play there and was persuaded to try out for one, *The Admirable Crichton*, which had been a hit on Broadway, and got cast in a small part. He caught the bug right away and said, "This is what I want to do with my life."

He met my mom that same year. They were in an acting class together. Love at first sight. They spent summers doing summer stock around New England and upstate New York and got married their junior year.

My mom was a budding actress, a very pretty ingénue, so that was going to be their life, and this shared dream ultimately led them to New York. They had both tried out—my mom told me the story this way—for the Royal Academy in London; she was accepted, and he wasn't, a fateful moment in her career because she didn't want to go without him, so they stayed in New York. He eventually got his foot in the door behind the camera in live television, but never gave up the idea of acting. When my brother and I came along Mom dropped it and, in the way of the fifties, became the homemaker and not the career woman.

Did your mom have any television credits from her days in New York?

No, she felt one career was going to be all they could support. The uncertainty of the profession had already set in. I don't remember her working at all until we got to Los Angeles, where she took "civilian" jobs. The first I remember was working the retail counter at Sears Roebuck. She later began a teaching career that became the main focus of her professional life.

They were bohemians in that sense. Theater gypsies. They loved that lifestyle, and it determined the course of their lives. They were perfectly happy being nomadic in their search for work, which led to us moving as often as we did when I was young. But they truly loved the theater. It was the world they wanted to live in and one both would return to later. Dad was doing acting and straight jobs to support us, too, selling real estate to fund that side of his life. I remember at five or six years old seeing him on *Perry Mason* on television—he did a couple of episodes. The best part he had was in a Debbie Reynolds and Tony Randall vehicle, *The Mating Game*, playing a harried IRS officer, and that was as close as he got to breaking through. It was a good part, and he was good in it, invited to the premiere and all that.

But for whatever reason, it didn't happen for him, and when our sister was born, the pressure of providing for a family came into play. So he sold real estate but decided that wasn't the way he wanted to live his life. In 1965, at forty, he said, "I want to go back to the theater," so he got a master's at Occidental College in Pasadena in theater arts. That's when I first remember actively becoming interested in what he was doing. He was directing and teaching classes, and he'd let me sit in on rehearsals and keep the book for actors. It was a magical world to me. I was fascinated by the set designs he did for the productions he worked on, building sets in miniature. This was a glimpse behind the curtain for me of a compelling culture, of making shows come to life.

You didn't see any of that during the *Philco* years?

I have vague memories of walking around backstage, stumbling on all these black lighting and electric cables, seeing cameras and watching people doing things in front of them.

But not meeting Paddy Chayefsky or any of the great television writers who essentially were antecedents for yourself?

Had I been a little bit older, I might have and would remember it, and I had those experiences a few years later, but not in New York. Once we moved to LA, after the cop show my dad was working on didn't pan out, he got a job at CBS Television City—first in the drapes department, eventually in the story department. By then, I was in first grade, and we were living in Silver Lake, not far from where they were building Dodger Stadium, which I was keenly interested in. We used to check out the progress of Chavez Ravine as it went up. My dad took us to opening day when it opened in 1962 [April 10]. I still have the program from that first game. That was a big deal.

Your dad operated the drapes? So I guess you know where I'm going with this?

They wrangled drapes for all their shows, and when you think of all those game shows and variety shows, that's a lot of drapes.

Did Nadine's obsession with drapes in *Twin Peaks* have anything to do with that?

That wasn't a conscious factor. But it's an interesting question.

I heard somewhere that you actually appeared on Art Linkletter's show yourself, as a kid.

In first grade, I got picked as one of two kids from my school—Elysian Heights Elementary School—to be on *Art Linkletter's House Party*. My first personal taste of show business. They sent a car, a limo, to school to pick us up and take us to Television City, where they taped the show—I knew the place because I'd visited Dad at work—and we were escorted to the kids' dressing room. Linkletter came in. They'd done preinterviews with us, and he double-checked all the answers with us. A really friendly, animated, happy guy who made you feel comfortable, and I felt immediately at home in that environment. I just said, "Yeah, this is kind of cool. We're going to make a show."

They led us out and sat us on these high stools, which put us closer to eye level with Linkletter, and we're hearing things. The curtains were drawn, but you could hear a murmur of the audience, applause occasionally, as the rest of the show was going on. Things were happening, red lights going on, cameras being moved. Then suddenly the curtains parted, and there's a live studio audience that seemed to me substantial—I was little and this was a big space—and I thought, "Wow, this is amazing." I felt strangely at ease in that setting. I had a couple of good lines. Because we'd been given the answers beforehand, Art carried little cheat-sheet cue cards in case we messed up. We'd been told we were just going to repeat what we'd gone over in the green room. So Art asked me what I wanted to be when I grew up, and I said I wanted to be an astronaut. And he said, "I'm told you know some good jokes." I said, "I do," and he said, "Would you like to tell us one?" And I said, "Well, I have one about my pets," and he said, "What kind of pets?" and I said, "I have some goldfish." So he asks, "What are their names?" And I said, "Eenie, Meenie, and Miney." And he said, "Eenie, Meenie, and Miney? What happened to Mo?" And I said, "There ain't no Mo."

I got a huge laugh and went, "Oh, I think I like this." And a few weeks later I was told they wanted me to come back and do the show again. And I said a curious thing. I said, "You know, I didn't like that they asked us all the questions beforehand." It felt a little phony to me. One of the kids in our group had frozen and couldn't talk, he was terrified, and I saw Linkletter kill his mic and cue the kid with the answer, then turn his mic back on. And I just thought, "There's something weird about this." So I said, "I don't think I want to go back." It was an instinct of, "I don't want to be a child actor," I realized later. A good instinct. And so I turned them down.

We had a close family friend—a friend of my grandmother's—who was the head of casting at Desilu. Her name was Ruth Burch. A legend in the business, and I'd known her ever since we moved to LA. When I was eight, nine, ten, I used to go once a year to stay overnight and visit her. She worked right at Desilu—now Paramount—and she'd take me to work, and I'd go visit the sets of the shows they were doing. On the set of *The Andy Griffith Show*, I was astonished when I saw the jail, the set where the town drunk, Otis, was always locked up. They'd removed the back wall for a camera angle, and I went, "Otis could have walked right out of here. What kind of cell is this?" The big thrill was meeting Ron Howard, who was working that day. We talked about that years later when I got to know him. That night I watched a taping of *The Dick Van Dyke Show*. Had dinner beforehand with Ruth and Dick Van Dyke at the commissary, and Rose Marie came over. I have the fondest memories of her. She couldn't have been nicer to me, in my little blue blazer and tie and short blond buzzcut. The next year Ruth took me and my brother to visit the set of *Gilligan's Island*. Decades later, I worked on the same lot, Radford Studios, in Studio City. We were hanging out by the lagoon, wandering around waiting for them to start, and Tina Louise came out of her dressing room in full Ginger makeup and hair, and I was just stunned. I could barely speak.

So you were a Ginger guy instead of Mary Ann?

I liked them both, but Ginger sure made an impact.

I want to backtrack a second. You mentioned about your father during the war being headed to the Pacific Theater when the bomb was dropped. Obviously that brings to mind *Twin Peaks*—season three, Part 8. Was that something he talked to you about ever?

My dad was, like a lot of World War II vets, very reticent to talk about the war. He'd seen a lot. It wasn't until much later in life he'd open up about it at all, more to my brother than to me. He told Scott that before he'd met our mom, while on shore leave in London, he'd met an English nurse, and they had a romance. I'm not sure how far it went, but leave ended and they wrote to each other. When he came back to London some weeks later, he learned she'd been killed in the blitz. Her house had been destroyed. Heavy experiences for a kid—eighteen, nineteen, twenty years old. And like most guys who went through these things, he came out of it with what we now think of as PTSD.

Would you describe your childhood as idyllic?

Parts were idyllic. More problematic was the degree to which they moved around, which made it chaotic. Three or four times when I'd just settled into a neighborhood and a group of friends, all of a sudden it was, "OK, pack up the car. We're moving." Once after kindergarten, again after first grade, once after fifth, again after eighth grade—that was the move to Minnesota—and then after a year in a Minneapolis suburb, we moved again. So it was hard for me to have any continuity. A couple of preschools, three elementary schools, two middle schools, two high schools. My parents were, like most in that era, more wrapped up in their own lives than they were in their kids.' Just a different parenting style, and it was a time in their lives they were struggling to find themselves, personally and professionally. They were always struggling financially. I was left to my own devices, trying to figure out life for myself, and developed a strong sense of self-sufficiency. All of which led to an intense and vivid inner life from the start.

We had an old family home—my mother's family—on a small lake in upstate New York, outside of Troy. So we were there for part of every summer until my midteens. I developed a strong, mystical connection to the place. I felt really at home around that lake, in nature, as kids often do, before your left brain takes over. Fully alive. So that became a foundational counterpoint to the challenges of moving schools and changing friends and baseball teams.

That was your grandmother's place, right? I interviewed Scott once, and he told me that she and your grandfather had divorced and that she lived in Taborton and he moved to Troy. ￭

Yes, those were my mother's parents.

Right, the Calhouns.

They divorced in the thirties. My mother's dad was a prominent obstetrician, Doug Calhoun, for whom Calhoun Memorial Hospital in *Twin Peaks* was named. The character my dad played in the show, Doc Hayward, was based in large part on him. One of the first doctors who worked with Margaret Sanger in starting Planned Parenthood. He'd been head intern at Bellevue, did a lot of pro bono work in poor neighborhoods, Harlem. Saw a lot of forceps birth, a dangerous and often destructive common practice, and started a program to eradicate it. That got him involved with Sanger pretty early, enlightened about those sorts of issues, forward-thinking. He also delivered me, which was kind of unusual for my generation.

Those summers when you went out to Taborton—

Taborton was where my grandmother lived. The house on the lake had belonged to her parents. An eighteenth-century farmhouse that my mother's grandfather, Thomas Lawson, an engineering professor at RPI, turned into a ten-room house. He built a windmill to pump water up from the lake; it's still there, a local landmark. My grandfather Calhoun moved to Troy after they divorced. He had remarried. He loved golf, and he lived near the Troy Country Club. So when we went to see him, we went into town.

You and Scott both talked about your grandmother being a great storyteller. What was that like? Did you used to gather in front of the fireplace?

She was half brilliant raconteur and half bullshit artist, and you never knew which you were going to get. An amazing woman in many ways. She'd been a concert violinist, studied at the Sorbonne in the twenties, and starting in 1933, she was chief administrator of the WPA music program. Big job. She ran that program, and later became a player in upstate Republican politics, Nelson Rockefeller's campaign manager for Rensselaer County for all of his gubernatorial and presidential runs.

Scott said she also had some interaction with Eleanor Roosevelt.

Through the WPA. That was her connection to Eleanor. She later lived in Paris for a number of years before the war, then worked for the OSS during the war in London as a translator.

With all this moving around that you were doing, did you feel like an outsider or was it easy for you to adapt socially?

There were two levels to it. One, I could always adapt but didn't necessarily feel at home. I learned how to blend in but felt like an outsider in almost every instance. That led to the beginning of a writer's consciousness— an observational eye, of watching myself in various situations—which played a big part in why I started writing as early as I did.

When you talk about the development of this inner life, how specifically does that connect to writing?

That was where my inner life found a partner, that self-expression and creativity can nurture you in that way, if you're open to it. That was the beginning of feeling comfortable in my own skin. When you're moving around, different schools, trying to fit in, you develop a hyperawareness, always trying to figure out what the system is, what's the social network, who do I need to know, who I need to avoid. So I felt a keen sense of that, by necessity, really early.

I know you were an athlete as a kid, but were you also very studious? Were you socially active?

Until sixth grade, I didn't think of myself as particularly smart. I went to school, did what they told me to, and felt like I was doing time in a minimum-security prison. I had one or two teachers I responded to, but the rest were just punching a time clock. So my life outside of school became more important. Friendships with kids in every neighborhood we lived in. The model was *Stand by Me* [the 1986 Rob Reiner film, adapted from a story by Stephen King]. A group of buddies to hang with. Life was lived outside. You got on your bike and roamed. Rarely seen by your parents. You'd leave in the morning, come home at night for dinner. That's the way it felt, both on the lake and in those California neighborhoods. Exploring the hills. Riding the tunnels of the LA river. An adventure-based life. We dug forts, played war games, which I was usually organizing. More a leader than a follower, on a small scale.

Then I got interested in stories and reading. I became fascinated by the mechanics of a typewriter when I was five or six. The idea that you could hit a key and letters appeared on a blank piece of paper seemed magical. When I was around eight, I started typing stories from the *LA Times*, just retyping on my page what I read in the paper, because I loved the feeling of watching the words appear in order, that I could somehow do that on my own. That's when I first began to feel I wanted to do this.

You started writing at what age?

They have photos of me writing stories when I was five, six, seven. But I didn't start writing my first novel until eleven.

That old, huh?

[Laughs] I was a slow starter.

Do you remember what it was about?

The whole story. As a result of visiting these TV factories, I had a more focused interest in what a television show was than most kids my age. I knew it was something people made—not something that mystically appeared in a box. Seeing my own dad on the tube brought that home. After seeing that people did this for a living, I started to closely follow some particular shows. That one that knocked me out was *The Man from U.N.C.L.E.* I'd seen a couple of early Bonds—*From Russia with Love, Goldfinger*—but here was this same kind of glamorous figure in our living room every week. I sent away for the *Man from U.N.C.L.E.* briefcase: a machine gun you could assemble, hidden knife, multiple IDs, *U.N.C.L.E.* badge. Incredible. So at eleven, I sat down and wrote a completely derivative novel about two agents who worked for the International Council for Peace and Justice. The I.C.P.J. Not as euphonious an acronym as U.N.C.L.E. I still have it—120 pages—in a box somewhere.

Were there other television shows or movies that made an impression on you?

I was a *Bonanza* fan. We'd bought a color television, and that was the first show I remember watching every week in color. *Twilight Zone*, hugely influential. *The Wild Wild West* became a favorite; every Friday we were parked in front of the set for that. For our generation, *Batman* was a phenomenon. Through our connection with that casting director, we met one of Burt Ward's [Robin's] stuntmen. Huge street cred. *Get Smart* I really keyed into. Early Mel Brooks, absolutely hilarious. *The Monkees* and *Laugh-In* were game changers. And I liked a lot of the English imports: *The Avengers*, *The Saint*, *Secret Agent* with Patrick McGoohan. *The Fugitive* became a big favorite of mine—echoes of that showed up in *Twin Peaks*—but the one that most inspired me was when

CBS ran *The Prisoner* in the summer of '68. That effectively blew the top of my head off in terms of what television could aspire to, and stayed with me forever.

I was always a moviegoer—saw my first film at Grauman's Chinese at the age of five—but Hitchcock was the first filmmaker that really captivated me: *North by Northwest, Rear Window, Psycho, Vertigo*. I just rewatched *Marnie* for the first time in decades, and it's a whole lot better than I'd remembered. A companion piece to *Vertigo*. His abuse of Tippi Hedren has colored the way that film is perceived, and it was a flop at the time, but *Marnie*'s a damn good movie.

Just to digress for a minute, on the subject of Hitchcock, I was listening to a podcast you did with Sam Esmail, the creator of *Mr. Robot*, and you quoted Hitchcock as saying there's a difference between surprise and suspense. What did he mean by that?

He actually differentiated shock and suspense. The famous example he always used was in *Sabotage*, about the hunt for terrorist bombers in London. There's a scene where a boy's on a bus, and he's unwittingly got a bomb with him in a satchel—we know it, he doesn't—and finally, the bomb goes off. Suspense came from us knowing, but not the boy. Shock would've been if we hadn't known it was there and the bomb went off. Good for fifteen seconds, but that's it. But interestingly, Hitchcock later said he made a mistake by killing the boy after the audience was emotionally invested in him. Although he said there was still great shock when the bomb went off, it killed the suspense because it left the audience so upset. He always favored informed suspense over shock—until *Psycho*, anyway. That was one of the formative moments in his development as a storyteller—always let the audience be a little ahead of where the characters are, so that you can hook them with that squirming feeling of, "Oh, no, don't let this happen!" And that in many ways was the key to his career.

What other movies made an impact when you were younger?

The Great Escape, Fail Safe, Seven Days in May made big impressions. David Lean's *Lawrence of Arabia* and *Bridge on the River Kwai*, and Kubrick's *Dr. Strangelove* really landed. Then *2001* flattened me, had an even greater impact on me than *The Prisoner* did. I actually wrote Kubrick a twenty-page letter. I later read an interview in which he said he never answered fan mail, but he mentioned getting all these letters from young people who said *2001* profoundly changed the way they thought about film and life. I was one of 'em.

As I got into later adolescence: *Bonnie and Clyde, Cool Hand Luke, The Wild Bunch, Midnight Cowboy*, which really landed, and I later [on *The Believers*] worked with [*Midnight Cowboy* director John] Schlesinger. Around that time, sophomore/junior year of high school, I got a job as an usher at The Campus Theatre in Minneapolis, an arthouse cinema on, as the name suggests, the university campus. That became my introduction to Bergman and Buñuel, and Truffaut and Fellini. Seeing Jean Renoir's *The Rules of the Game* on the big screen was life changing; I still consider it the greatest film ever made. Costa Gavras's *Z* was hugely influential, as was Haskell Wexler's *Medium Cool*, realizing film could speak with political force.

Concurrent with this, in high school I started going to the university film club, run by a wonderful guy named Al Milgrom, a dedicated cinephile who took it upon himself to introduce the Golden Age of American film to young people. My first time seeing the Marx Brothers, Buster Keaton, W. C. Fields, Chaplin on a big screen. Sixteen millimeter prints. That was also how I learned about Howard Hawks, John Ford, Frank Capra, that whole generation of American filmmakers.

It's interesting to hear you talk about *The Prisoner* and *2001*, because something they have in common with *Twin Peaks* is that they're not so much about narrative as they are experiential, especially that last episode of *The Prisoner*. A lot of times people say that with *Twin Peaks*, Mark Frost brought the narrative coherence to it and David Lynch brought the surrealism, and I think that people just make that assumption. I don't know whether it's true or not, but clearly

you have an aesthetic appreciation for that sort of surreal approach to filmmaking.

It's a simplistic way people have of putting ideas in boxes in order to tell themselves, "Oh, so that's how that works." Collaboration is always more complex and interwoven than that, and intuitive. It just happened that when we were first working on the show, we had a simpatico way of viewing things. I would say that if you're looking at the whole range of works I just mentioned, those influences are all part of my bandwidth. The point is they're just a part of it, the ground out of which my creativity developed. It's more fertile and comprehensive than people are used to considering when assessing what I've done—from immersion in the theater to Billy Wilder to Abel Gance and Maya Deren. That's a broad reach.

Getting back to your family life, did the Frosts typically all have dinner together, or was your dad usually off working?

During those years, unless Dad had an early curtain or rehearsal, we usually had dinner together.

What was the conversation like around the Frost dinner table?

Two areas. Their world was theater, movies, the arts. That was not only their professional interest; it was their secular religion. So we tended to focus on those subjects. We went to a lot of movies together, watched television together.

Other than that, it was history and politics. My dad had an uncle, his great uncle, who for ten years was Franklin Roosevelt's personal secretary, and before that, his corresponding secretary and one of his closest associates. His name was Will Hassett—a newspaperman from Vermont. My dad was his favorite nephew.

There's a great scene in Uncle Will's memoirs, which he published in 1958—he also worked as Truman's secretary for eight years after FDR died—when my dad came to visit the White House. He was a young Navy chief on day leave from Norfolk, and he happened to be there the day they were celebrating the eleventh anniversary of FDR's first inauguration. There was a big gathering in the East Room. My dad arrived, and the man who opened the door for him was the secretary of the Navy from the Joint Chiefs of Staff. Dad was seated between Supreme Court Justice William Douglas and a ranking senator. He got to meet FDR, and his eyes were like saucers, Uncle Will wrote. On my mother's side, her mother ran the WPA Music Program in the thirties. So you can see why my folks were dyed-in-the-wool Roosevelt Democrats.

They were also, not surprisingly, huge Kennedy supporters. His assassination devastated them—hit them very hard, a desolate feeling. He was buried on my tenth birthday—my birthday was canceled—and like everybody else, we were all glued to the TV that week, from Dallas to his burial at Arlington. The assassination of [Lee Harvey] Oswald by [Jack] Ruby, saw it live, the whole thing. Shaped my worldview to this day.

All of that speculation over the lone gunman and all of that, you weren't obsessed with that when you were young, were you?

That came later. But liberal politics were the center of their worldview, through their own experiences and their connection to Uncle Will. We used to see him once a summer when we went back East. He'd come down for a day to the races in Saratoga. A kind, sweet man, much older at that point, in his eighties. For my twelfth birthday, he gave me a copy of his book, the diary he kept during the war years with FDR [*Off the Record with FDR: 1942–1945*].

I don't think of your work necessarily as political, but anyone who follows you on Twitter knows how invested you are in politics.

I think yes and no. I haven't written a lot that's overtly political—aside from my movie *Storyville*, set in the world of New Orleans politics—

but I've always had an affinity for the genre.

Politics mattered in our house. During the '64 election, we lived in a very conservative town, La Crescenta, California, north of Glendale. My parents didn't feel at home in a place with such a high-visibility John Birch Society presence, that had been a hotbed of Ku Klux Klan activity as recently as the thirties. Barry Goldwater was a polarizing figure for them, and Goldwater supporters were all around us. That's when I first became aware of this great divide in our country. My sympathies have always moved more naturally toward the humanistic, FDR Great Society lens of looking at the world.

In 1967, we moved to Minnesota, where my dad worked toward his PhD in the theater department. At the end of my eighth grade, we drove to Minnesota, which was, of all the moves we made, the most wrenching and disorienting. Minneapolis in '67 was nothing like the vibrant, multicultural cosmopolitan city it is now. Back then, it was still a frigid, sleepy Midwestern town. We lived for a year in an awful suburb there. If you've seen the Coen brothers' movie *A Serious Man*, that was my ninth-grade neighborhood. A sterile, lifeless place, and the worst year of my life—our local Target was the cultural apex.

Fortunately, the next year we moved into the inner city. A vibrant, hilly tree-lined neighborhood that straddles the line between Minneapolis and St. Paul called Prospect Park—mostly university people, faculty members and their kids—and for the first time in my life, I felt completely at home. And later that year, tenth grade, I got into a high school intern program at the Guthrie Theater, which set the course of my life. In the next three years, I earned more than half the credits to graduate working at the Guthrie.

This was 1968 to '69, and that university environment and theater department was a bastion of sanity at a time when the country was coming apart at the seams. Revolutionary politics were a formative part of our daily life, and it made for a wild, tumultuous high school experience. For years, they'd run what was called University High School, for kids from faculty families, the kids in my new neighborhood. Intellectual, liberal, freethinking, but the year I got there, they merged it with a blue-collar city public high school called Marshall.

There's a little town—you may have heard of it if you're a Dylan fan, he lived there when he went to the U of M—called Dinkytown, just off campus, where students and faculty hang. This blue-collar high school was on one side of Dinkytown, the building we used for University High classes was on the other, with Dinkytown smack in the middle. "Positively Fourth Street" was about Bob Dylan's time in this area. He'd lived above a drugstore, on the corner of the main intersection—it still had a soda fountain—which had already become a landmark.

My high school was a mix of fifty percent conservative blue-collar kids, twenty-five percent University High "hippies," and 400 African American kids they bussed in that year from the north side, another culture superimposed on this one spot. That was a volatile environment, and things did not go smoothly. Constant fights, a knifing, once a kid drove his car through the front doors. Crazy, all of this happening against the backdrop of constant protests at the university campus, a half mile away, about the [Vietnam] war. There were days you could smell the tear gas in the air.

What about religion? Was that a part of your life growing up?

No.

Did you ever go to church?

My mom was raised Presbyterian. Her father was Scottish, two generations removed, and she had a churchgoing impulse. When I was a kid, she began going to Unitarian church, so my brother and I went for a year or two of Sunday school. Dad was a determined, defiant agnostic, which I later figured came from the war; hard for him to buy in after the things he'd seen. I remember him being profoundly offended by the hypocrisy of televangelists—scam artists preaching to raise money, he used to say. And I remember thinking he was right—I had an early instinct for what made a good story—that what I was hearing in Sunday school sounded like a bunch of hooey. So, no, we weren't religious, but in the back of my mind, maybe through a connection to nature, I sensed I might be inherently spiritual, not at all the same thing.

You mentioned before that you read a lot. Were there books that had a particularly strong influence on you?

For the same reasons—moving around so much, having to make different friends—my constant was books. My parents had a large library but different tastes. I discovered in sixth grade I could actually buy my own books, which I started to do. I got hooked early on the Hardy Boys. A big favorite of mine was *The Travels of Jaimie McPheeters*, a young-adult novel about a boy who travels out West with his family in the nineteenth century. I was drawn to Civil War stories. I liked big books. Sir Walter Scott and James Fenimore Cooper at eleven. I checked out *Ben-Hur* at the library and worked my way through that, by Lew Wallace, who'd been a Civil War general. Robert Louis Stevenson, Jack London, H. G. Wells, Jules Verne, Dumas—they all thrilled me.

You asked me if I thought of myself as studious. In fifth grade, they gave us the first standardized test to measure academic standing, and I tested in a way that hadn't surfaced in class, because I'd never been that interested in what they were teaching. But when we moved after fifth grade, I was placed in an accelerated-learning class, and that made a big difference. I was suddenly with a group of motivated learners, and we had a teacher, Frank Weber, who was kind and caring and loved teaching, and anybody in that class would say he was one of those teachers who held up the light for them. So with Frank Weber's guidance, my reading took a huge step forward, and I started tackling all sorts of genres. He introduced me to Ray Bradbury, who I inhaled. Robert Heinlein, Ursula K. Le Guin. He also introduced me to journalism and the sports writing of Jim Murray, one of the great columnists of all time, who worked for the *LA Times*. He opened my mind to a whole other world, and he was the first one I told, "Someday I'm going to be a writer."

I had a great experience when my last book came out. I was at a wonderful bookstore called Vroman's in Pasadena, and a guy who worked at the store introduced himself. I hadn't seen Eric Forrester in fifty years. He was not only one of my sixth-grade classmates, he was the catcher on my baseball team, and we had a really joyful reunion. He'd gone on to a really rich life as a professional musician and teacher at USC, and we talked about Mr. Weber and how much he'd meant to us. Mr. Weber gave me my first copy of *The Hobbit*, which had just made its way into print in the States, so that opened up a whole new area of fantasy storytelling. I began haunting the library and started a paper route to pay for my paperbacks, and I owe it all to Frank Weber. So Tolkien grabbed me, then Dickens, and as I got into the Guthrie in high school, it was playwrights—Chekhov and Shakespeare, Arthur Miller and Tennessee Williams. I tore through all of Steinbeck, Fitzgerald, Hemingway. Thornton Wilder became a favorite, plays and prose, and then newer voices. Kurt Vonnegut and Jerzy Kosinsky, Walker Percy, Saul Bellow, James Baldwin, E. L. Doctorow, Joseph Heller, John Fowles, William Styron, *The Autobiography of Malcolm X*, John Le Carré, Ian Fleming, Eric Ambler. Truman Capote, particularly *In Cold Blood*, which united nonfiction with a narrative and novelistic feel. Joyce Carol Oates, Joan Didion. Three brilliant autobiographies by people who'd been in show business have always stayed with me—Clifford Odets, Charlie Chaplin, and Frank Capra.

I know Joseph Campbell is someone you have great admiration for. He once told his students, "When you find a writer who really is saying something to you, read everything that writer has written, and you will get more education and depth of understanding out of that than reading a scrap here and a scrap there and elsewhere."

I couldn't agree more. That's the way to do it.

"Then go to people who influenced that writer, or those who were related to him, and your world builds together in an organic way that is really marvelous." Who's that writer for you, if there is one?

Campbell himself, for one. There've been so many writers I felt an affinity for and who helped shaped my worldview and feelings about living a creative life. And at various times in your life, different people speak to you. It's always changing.

I've been much more interested in nonfiction of late. Direct, real-life experience, as much as I can learn about human nature. I'm reading a new Napoleon biography, one of Julius Caesar, and another about the history of Rome, learning about what the old world thought of as "greatness." At what point do these giant figures cross over into becoming a danger to themselves and others? Did the achievements they brought to the world during their time in power last long enough to outweigh the bloodshed it cost? Fascinating subjects to consider.

2

"Alfred Hitchcock in the Corner Booth"

(Hollywood: There and Back Again)

Remember the seventies? Maybe you've repressed. Tom Wolfe famously called it the "'Me' Decade" (and, less famously, "The Third Great Awakening"), embracing the Hobbesian notion of self-preservation.

For Mark Frost, the seventies was a period of exploration, exhilaration, restlessness, experimentation, and, ultimately, realization.

Early in the decade, Frost left home in Minneapolis to attend college at Carnegie Tech (now Carnegie Mellon University) in Pittsburgh; by 1980 he had accepted a job to join the legendarily brilliant—but volatile—writers' room at NBC's *Hill Street Blues*, one of the most transformative shows in television history.

In between, Frost left college early, broke into prime-time television writing (thanks to the mentorship of writer/producer Steven Bochco, a fellow Carnegie alum) at the powerhouse Universal Studios, and abandoned Hollywood to return to Minnesota, hoping to reignite his passion for writing through work that was meaningful and fulfilling.

By the time of Frost's arrival, Universal Television was the dominant producer of prime-time television entertainment, thanks to an accumulation of hit shows over the decades including *Dragnet*, *Ironside*, *Marcus Welby, M.D.*, *McCloud*, *Columbo*, *McMillan & Wife*, *Kojak*, *The Six Million Dollar Man*—and far too many more to mention here.

Some of the most revered writers of the sixties and seventies—the age of three-network hegemony—honed their craft at Universal, including Bochco, Jack Webb (*Dragnet* and *Adam-12*), Richard Levinson & William Link (*Columbo* and *The Name of the Game*), Roy Huggins & Stephen J. Cannell (*The Rockford Files*), David Chase (*Rockford* and, many years later, but not for Universal, *The Sopranos*), Glen A. Larson (the original *Battlestar Galactica*), and Donald Bellisario (*Magnum, P.I.*).

And yet, in a defining moment, Frost renounced all this, returning to Minnesota to focus on playwriting—at significant financial loss. As he himself recounts below, multiple factors influenced this decision, among them the belief that a career churning out formulaic scripts for the Universal factory would never provide the creative fulfillment he craved. He vividly recalls an eye-opening poolside conversation at an A-list Hollywood party with Terence Young, a British film director best known for his work on the early Bond films, that helped him reach this conclusion.

Frost is like a sponge, soaking up knowledge and counsel from anyone whose intellect and values he respects. His mentors—people like Bochco, the actor Alan Arkin, the children's TV host Fred Rogers, the theatrical legend Tyrone Guthrie—have guided him both personally and professionally, a testament to his intellectual curiosity and his desire to live a principled life.

***

When it came time to apply to colleges, were you entertaining different possibilities or was your mind-set on Carnegie Mellon?

Carnegie Mellon came directly out of my experience at the Guthrie Theater. During high school, I spent more time at the Guthrie than I did at my school. This was in effect a high school apprentice/conservatory program. Citywide auditions from every high school. Over sixty of us were brought in. From the theater's perspective, it was practical: they wanted free labor. They were preparing an epic production of *Julius Caesar*, and the director wanted seventy-five extras for crowd scenes. They never would have been able to afford that many actors, so they came up with this program to use students as extras and gave us an unparalleled level of instruction in return.

By tenth grade, I'm taking movement and voice and stagecraft. I was not only in *Julius Caesar* but also *The Tempest* and *Mourning Becomes Electra*, as an extra or a stagehand. They also had a second theater, a smaller stage where they put on more experimental plays. So not only was I being exposed to the classical pantheon—Chekhov and Brecht and Shakespeare and Shaw—on the smaller stage I saw this revolution going on in American theater: LeRoi Jones and Brendan Behan and Edward Albee. It was extraordinarily stimulating.

So my peer group from tenth grade on, although I was still an athlete and playing sports at school, was this big group of theater kids and our older colleagues. The actors and staff took us under their wings. They were incredibly kind and generous. A determinative period for me. When it came time to look at colleges, the best theater conservatory program in the country was by consensus at Carnegie Mellon, or what they called Carnegie Tech. Juilliard was on the rise, but it wasn't quite at that level yet. So that was the only place I applied.

Were you thinking of acting at this point, or did you know you weren't going to be an actor?

I'd done a fair amount by that point—there and a few other theaters around town—and knew I didn't want to act for a living. I liked it, didn't love it. I particularly didn't like having to learn and remember lines. During those years at the Guthrie, I was also active in the theater department at my high school. We had a young theater teacher, and we ran it together. He staged the first off-Broadway production of *Indians*, Arthur Kopit's play about Buffalo Bill. I played the lead, and all the Twin Cities papers reviewed it. Then I directed two of my own plays, writing and directing, at the school. Just living and breathing it—writing, directing, acting, producing, sometimes all of the above. The Guthrie produced the third play I wrote as a high school tour show; I acted in it, and we toured around the state.

You weren't consumed yet by the idea of being a writer?

Writing had emerged as the lead sled dog, but I saw myself as a person of the theater, with all of these pursuits in the Venn diagram overlapping.

Was Carnegie a positive experience for you?

Yes. I spent three years there. They didn't offer playwriting for freshmen, so I came in as an acting major. The second year, I switched to directing, and it wasn't until junior year that I could switch my formal major to playwriting. Freshman year, I learned about a brilliant graduate school playwriting professor named Leon Katz. He'd come out of Yale Drama, and he went back to Yale later. The key to the rest of my time at Carnegie became my relationship with Leon Katz. He really gave me what I needed. I was lucky.

Katz was a mentor?

One hundred percent. He'd been a noted avant-garde playwright in the sixties, had a number of plays produced, wrote textbooks about drama and theater. He just passed away recently. So I heard about Leon, but he only taught grad students, and I wasn't even yet a playwriting major as an undergrad. But I thought a play I'd just written might appeal to him—about Antonin Artaud, an infamous avant-garde playwright in the 1920s.

Have you ever seen Carl Dreyer's masterpiece, *The Passion of Joan of Arc*? Artaud plays one of the leads and makes an indelible impression. Along with a few other playwrights, like Guillaume Apollinaire, and a circle of artists like Max Ernst, Artaud was part of the Dada-Surrealist movement in Paris, but he was also truly wild. In the thirties, he took off for Mexico to live with the Tarahumara Indians, an aboriginal, spiritual people. A little like what Carlos Castaneda did in the seventies, but Artaud did it fifty years earlier. So he sought out these shamans that he'd heard about, and participated in their peyote rituals; he was kicking a heroin habit at the time. The legend was that after they resisted this outsider's attempt to assimilate, he was so persistent they eventually took him in, and he studied with them and later wrote about it. So the conceit of the play was, many years after Artaud's death—he died young and tragically—I posited that the Tarahumara had created a ritual to celebrate his life and the impact he'd had, bringing his culture to them and vice versa. The play was a ritualized performance, a celebration of his life, with seven actors each portraying him at a certain point of his evolution as a human being. It was pretty out there.

So I'd written this play and just thought, "This might be the kind of thing Leon Katz would respond to." I asked for an appointment with him, walked in, and told him, "Look, I can't take classes from you, but I'm hoping you wouldn't mind giving me some feedback on this," and just plopped the play down on his desk. He called me like a week later and said, "You need to come in here right away." He asked me how old I was. I said I was eighteen and he said, "No, that can't be right. You couldn't have written this." Long story short, he said, "We're going to get your play produced, and I'm going to help you do it." And sure enough, it was produced a few months later at the University of Pittsburgh. For my remaining two years, I'd talk to him; we'd have lunch or dinner and discuss things maybe once a week. He was extraordinarily generous with his time. Even after I moved out to LA, we stayed in close contact for many years. His son Elia was a screenwriter in LA, and he became a friend as well.

Switching gears here, didn't you also work on *Mister Rogers' Neighborhood* while you were at Carnegie?

That was an important experience for me. I started my second year at Carnegie—that would have been fall of '72, all the way through spring of '74, when I left to come back to California. I had a friend who was the lighting director on the show, and they had an opening, so I worked two or three evenings a week. It was timed perfectly because we'd start work around four and go till about nine or ten. Like everyone on the crew, I got to know Fred, and he was just the loveliest guy. He was so real and present and so available. An astonishingly honest, decent human being, and really funny. It was just a pleasure to be around him.

What exactly did you do there?

I was on the lighting crew and also helped moving sets, getting the show ready for production. I spent a lot of time up in the catwalks moving instruments around. I'd studied lighting at Carnegie, so I knew a little bit about it. I joined the crew at roughly the same time as a young stand-up comic from Pittsburgh, Michael Douglas. He later changed his name because a member of SAG already had that name. That was Michael Keaton, a Pittsburgh native, and we had a blast. We became friends and had a lot of laughs, a lot of fun. I took off for LA a little bit before he did, I think, in May of '74, and he came out a little bit after that. Terrific guy and a wonderful performer who's stood the test of time and is usually the most interesting thing in whatever he's in.

He was doing miscellaneous work on the set as well?

We were both on the lighting crew, but you just pitched in and did whatever they needed. He was working his way into comedy as a stand-up. That's what we talked about a lot—moving to LA, hopes and dreams of a career in show business. Michael's spoken often about what a great influence Fred was in his life, and that's something we shared.

What were your takeaways from working on that show?

There was a calm professionalism about the way they approached the work. Very practical. The way they treated people was exemplary, as was the way they conducted themselves. Fred was a singular man. He's the kind of figure or role model we need to look to at times like this—somebody with profound decency, honesty and strength of character, his kindness to people. I watched him interact with so many people and kids. I was watching somebody who—if I didn't realize it at the time—by osmosis was becoming one of the most important role models I've had in life.

And then you had your fateful meeting at Carnegie with Charlie Haid.

During my third year—my first as a playwright—I'd written a play they were going to do as a mainstage production the next year. That spring, an alumnus, Charlie Haid, had come to town to direct a play. He'd graduated from Carnegie ten years before, and he and I hit it off immediately. We spent so much time together and he kept telling me, "You should come out to LA this summer. One of my classmates was Steven Bochco." I hadn't heard the name at that point, but Steven was a young writer then at Universal. And Charlie said, "I'll introduce you. You should come."

The more I thought about it, the more I liked the idea. I hadn't been back to LA since we'd moved away in '67, and my girlfriend at the time was from LA. She was going there for the summer, so it became an easy idea: spend the summer there and come back to Pittsburgh for my senior year. So I hitched a ride out to LA in May of '74 with a grad school couple from Berkeley, theater friends. We landed in Berkeley on the heels of the kidnapping of Patty Hearst. She'd been a neighbor of theirs; so we toured all these Hearst locations, including the bank the SLA [Symbionese Liberation Army] had shot up where Patty was photographed with a machine gun. I made my way down to LA, sleeping on a friend's couch, when the LAPD shot it out with the SLA about three miles from where I was staying, a few days after I arrived. Welcome to LA. I watched it live on TV, went outside, saw the smoke from the fire in the distance, heard the sirens. Pretty wild time.

I'd written to Bochco, and he invited me over to Universal to have lunch. Steven was a wonderful, generous guy. He was working as story editor on *McMillan & Wife* at that point, part of the three-part mystery wheel they were doing with *Columbo* and *McCloud*. We're chatting in his office, he's telling me about his life, how he got there, and in walks Peter Falk, in costume, wearing his Columbo trench coat. Wow. Then Steven takes me to lunch at the commissary and, oh, my God, there's Alfred Hitchcock in the corner booth, eating an enormous meal, alone.

He was making *Family Plot* at the time, his last picture. It felt like the old days of the Hollywood studio system, and in a way, it was the last iteration of that. Universal was a factory Lew Wasserman had created. If I remember this correctly, they produced almost half of all prime-time television at that point. Three networks, only sixty-six hours, and they were doing upwards of thirty. So the energy, the excitement of being there, and then at lunch Steven asks, "What do you want to go back to Pittsburgh for?" And I said, "Well, now that you mention it." He said, "I never went back when I left early to work out here, and I can introduce you to people. See what happens." So I said, "Why not?" Three weeks later, I booked my first gig.

And that first gig was?

It was a show called *Sunshine*.

With Billy Mumy, from *Lost in Space*, right?

Billy Mumy was on the show. Universal had done a TV movie, with Cliff DeYoung in the lead, about a young working musician whose wife dies tragically, and he's left to raise his young son alone. The John Denver song "Sunshine on My Shoulders" had become a hit, so they thought, "Let's make this a counterculture one-camera comedy-drama." Billy played his collaborator in the band. Do you have any idea who the drummer was in the band?

I don't.

It was my old buddy Special Agent Albert Rosenfield [Miguel Ferrer]. That's when we met. His first gig, my first gig.

That's amazing. I had no idea. And from that point on you were able to sustain yourself through writing?

Yes. I joined the Writers Guild and worked at Universal all that year. I wrote a couple of stories for another show—*Lucas Tanner*, starring

David Hartman as a high school teacher. And then I booked *The Six Million Dollar Man.*

You never had to wait tables? You were able to sustain yourself just through your writing?

I was making a living. All that year, I didn't have to take another job.

What did your parents say when you told them you weren't going back to Pittsburgh?

I said, "Look, I'm already doing what I went to school to learn. What do I need a degree for? I'm not going to be a teacher. And you won't have to pay for my senior year." And they said, "We can't argue with your logic."

I signed with a wonderful agent—a woman named Joan Scott, who ran an agency called Writers and Artists—and she paired me up with two roommates who were also clients of hers. We became fast friends and are still to this day: Michael O'Keefe and Adam Arkin.

Did you actually never go back to Pittsburgh, even to pick up your stuff? How did that work?

I eventually did go back, but just to pick up my stuff.

I know you had a connection to Bochco, but—looking at *Sunshine*, *Six Million Dollar Man*, *Lucas Tanner*—was there a specific person whom you hitched your star to?

Bochco didn't have a job to give me at that point. He was on the rise. But what he did do—the way the atmosphere there worked was very collegial. All the guys who were running shows would compare notes, talk to each other, and if somebody came along who seemed to have the goods they'd pass the word around that this is somebody you should take a look at. That's how a lot of my friends got started at Universal.

So it was more a clubhouse feeling, and once you were in that door you might work for any number of people. There were so many shows going, so many different productions, so many producers—the showbiz version of farm-team baseball, to work your way up the chain.

How did you learn how to do it, though?

Just by doing it. Bochco taught me the ropes: "Here's how this works: you go in, pitch a couple of story ideas. You're going to come in first as a freelancer." Freelance writers were much more the rule than the exception then. That was the lifeblood of series television. Guys would go—women too, but few and far between then—they'd go from show to show until they caught on and worked on one show. There was a group—I remember feeling this particularly on *Six Million Dollar Man*—of older writers who'd been there for a decade and worked their way up to staff positions who were wary of young talent. They didn't want you to come in and replace them, so it was a dance between "OK, we'll give the young guys a chance, but . . ." And I got there at the height of the youth movement in Hollywood. Not long after [Steven] Spielberg had walked on the lot, snuck into an office, pretended he was working there, and ended up directing television shows. The suits had an eye on the future, so younger writers and directors were being given more chances than ever before.

What about getting into the weeds of it, though, like writing beats and breaking scripts into acts? Was there somebody who was particularly helpful to you?

It was different with every show. The man who ran *Sunshine* was George Eckstein, who'd been around for a long time, and he was helpful. That was a half-hour show, so counting out the beats of a story wasn't as complicated. Again, I always had Bochco to go to as a kind of Dutch uncle. If I had a question, his door was open to me to call or come in and ask, "How do I handle X, Y, or Z?" Steven was also a very astute and canny political guy. He knew how studios worked. He knew how backlots worked.

You mentioned the youth movement. Was there a sort of Universal mafia of writers whom you hung out with?

There were a few guys I met. One's still a dear friend to this day, Jeff Freilich, who was working at that time on *The Hulk* and *Baretta*. He was at Universal for years. Later he became the showrunner on *Falcon Crest* and through the years has been on shows like *Burn Notice*, *Halt and Catch Fire*, *Grace and Frankie*, still working. He was there then. But the older guys who had moved already up to showrunner were [Donald] Bellisario, Glen Larson, Stephen Cannell. There were tiers of people, a hierarchical system, and at that point, I was on the entry rung. I'd just turned twenty-one that fall.

You mentioned Spielberg, and I know you met with him later on, during *Twin Peaks*, but did you have any interaction with him during your days at Universal?

No, I heard about him. This brash young guy who'd snuck onto the lot and ended up directing *Duel*, *Sugarland Express*—his first feature—and finally *Jaws*. I remember my friends Michael O'Keefe and Adam Arkin thinking, "God, that's ballsy. Maybe we should try that." But Steven was fearless that way, unstoppable. He ended up directing television episodes, and once he did *Duel*, he was on his way.

And the older guys, some of them were more generous than others in terms of mentoring?

I would say that continues to this day. It depends on how you view your career. Steven [Bochco] always pointed to the creators of *Columbo*—Richard Levinson and William Link—as the two who'd really mentored him, and Steven was that for me. You don't really need more than one.

Did you work at all with Roy Huggins, who created so many great shows—*77 Sunset Strip*, *Maverick*, *The Rockford Files*, and one of your favorites, *The Fugitive*?

I'd hear people talk about him, but I don't recall meeting him. Another guy in my age group, just starting out then, was Joel Surnow [who would go on to create *24*]. Later on, after I'd left *Hill Street*, he was running *The Equalizer*, and I wrote a couple of scripts for him when he was understaffed.

Some of the other old-timers—people like David Victor and Harve Bennett—what kind of interaction did you have with them?

I met all of them eventually. Today, we'd call them showrunners, but they were actually at a bit more of a remove. They were executive producers. George Eckstein was the first that I met, through *Sunshine*. David Victor, interestingly enough—who'd done *Marcus Welby*, he had a whole bunch of credits—turned out to be the uncle of the man who years later became my literary agent. One of the great friends and influences in my life, a true legend who we lost about a year ago named Ed Victor. I didn't learn David was Ed's uncle until ten years ago. Harve Bennett played the same role on *The Six Million Dollar Man*, but he was never in the writers' room. Below his pay grade. I probably met Harve twice. He later went on to produce the *Star Trek* movies.

I hear he was a little bit of a holy terror.

He was nice to me. I heard that later, that he was a screamer, but I never witnessed it. He was supportive of young talent in my case, but he was operating at a level far above where I was working at the time.

Did you learn anything from these guys, or did you just not have enough interaction with them?

They weren't there to teach; they were there to run shows, and they hired you because they thought you could do the job, and if you couldn't, there were other people who could. So it wasn't a university experience. Bochco was the only one who was supportive in that regard, and at that point, I wasn't working directly for Steven. He was my faculty adviser on the Universal campus, helping me understand how things worked. So I'd go in and be prepared. I knew how to pitch stories and meet with producers and story editors. The freelance market was much more vibrant then, and that was how most shows got written.

You mentioned Levinson and Link, who were largely known for their mysteries. Did you know them?

I met them with Steven, but never worked with them. They were on the lot at Universal when I was there, and were already top tier.

I interviewed Bill Link once years ago, and he was a pretty angry man.

Really? What was he angry about?

I think part of it was that age is a difficult thing to deal with in Hollywood, in terms of getting work. I remember once interviewing Allan Burns, who was the cocreator of *The Mary Tyler Moore Show*, and he said he would walk in to pitch shows to network executives who didn't even know who he was. So I think it was partly that, but I think also that he and Levinson had had some falling out with Peter Falk about the character of Columbo.

There was a notorious story like this in the nineties, I remember. Jeff Sagansky, a CBS executive I knew, had gone over to start a film division—it may have been the early days of TriStar—and there was a story about him taking a meeting with Fred Zinnemann [director of *High Noon*, *From Here to Eternity*, *Julia*, and numerous other iconic films]. Zinnemann goes into the meeting, and Sagansky says, "So tell me, what have you done?" You can imagine how the meeting went from there. That's part of why—in television, but Hollywood in general— it's like a casino, sometimes you have to know when it's time to pocket your winnings and walk away. I haven't known many people who've been able to do that, by the way.

Why do you suppose that is?

I think it's human nature. I saw this close-up with Aaron Spelling, who got used to a certain lifestyle and level of renown and had not developed what I would call an inquisitive state of mind about the rest of the world. He was too wrapped up in being Aaron Spelling. His job was demanding, took up all of his time and headspace, and before too long, you stop being a citizen of the world and become a prisoner of your own fame. I didn't have any interest in going down that road.

Getting back to the writing process at Universal, there were no writers' rooms? Everything was done by freelancers?

It wasn't the writers' room experience we later had on *Hill Street*. There'd be one or two guys who would sit down with freelancers. You pitch a few ideas; they'd say, "OK, there's something here we'd like to work with," or they'd say, "We liked your ideas but let's give you one of ours and let you run with it." It varied from show to show, but it was a simpler and less formal arrangement than what we now think of as the writers' room. And these shows were all standalone episodes. You didn't have to concern yourself with long-term story arcs or what was going on over the course of a season with a character. It was geared toward, "Let's tell a story within the world of this show," and those were clear borders—well-defined, so you didn't need to move outside them.

If I went back and looked at *Sunshine*, *Lucas Tanner*, and *The Six Million Dollar Man*, am I going to recognize those as Mark Frost scripts?

Not at all. This was impersonal work, factory work. But I was happy to be doing it and making money. I'd never had a nickel.

Just trying to ascertain when we start to see who Mark Frost is through his work. It seems like some of your thematic preoccupations—Jung, Theosophy, conspiracy theories, good

versus evil—really haven't surfaced by this point. Is that a fair statement?

With one exception. After the JFK assassination—two years later— I got a copy of the Warren Commission report. It was published in paperback, and I read every page and began to have some doubts. And then Mark Lane's response [*Rush to Judgment: A Critique of the Warren Commission's Inquiry into the Murders of President John F. Kennedy, Officer J. D. Tippit and Lee Harvey Oswald*] raised more doubts. There was a funny thing—this was with my best friend in Minneapolis. You may remember the "Paul is dead" rumors? That was the first conspiracy theory we tracked down. We were juniors in high school and started hearing that if you turned the *Sgt. Pepper* album cover upside down, the word "Beatles" spelled out in a floral display on the front was actually a phone number, and if you called the phone number, you would hear what had happened to Paul. We made that call. I don't remember who answered, but it certainly wasn't anybody interested in talking about Paul McCartney. That was the first earworm of conspiracy theories introduced to my system. So my friend Jerry Stein and I—when we went off to separate colleges, we were always writing each other about the latest in the Kennedy theories. "It's going to come out. We're going to find out who really did this."

The midseventies was really a renaissance for the sitcom, because you had Norman Lear's Tandem Productions, which produced shows like *All in the Family*, and you had MTM, which you eventually went to work for. At that point, they were still in their sitcom, pre-*Lou Grant* phase, so that was where a lot of the innovations were coming, but Universal was doing so much drama, and there seemed to be this dichotomy where some of the stuff was very generic and formulaic and then you had things like *The Bold Ones* and other quality programming.

They were like a classic Hollywood studio from the Golden Age, in that they had a variety of in-house goals: They'd do bread-and-butter series, they'd do B pictures, they would do prestige pictures. They were making huge numbers of movies of the week as well. It ran the gamut, and you found your own level in the ecosystem. For a youngster, it was really stimulating to be a part of.

You wound up staying in LA for just nine months, then went back to Minnesota to write plays. A lot of people, I think, would be surprised by that decision.

Turned out the pull of my roots in the theater was stronger than I'd thought, and I wasn't ready to abandon them.

Were you at all frustrated by the restrictions of writing for broadcast TV?

I was. I'd cut my eyeteeth on stuff that was a lot more daring and cutting-edge than prime-time fare. I also had gotten a look at the high end of Hollywood through my roommate Adam Arkin's dad, Alan, who we were close to. Alan became our surrogate dad during that year. He was a major star at that point, and we saw a lot of what Hollywood filmmaking at the higher levels looked like. It was a daunting world, filled with a lot of complicated, often crazy people as far as I could tell.

I remember going to A-list Hollywood parties, seeing people I knew from the movies. One in particular stands out. A party at producer Bert Schneider's house, from *Of Hearts and Minds* fame. Through his partnership with Bob Rafelson he was instrumental in terms of moving the industry into a new era—shows like *The Monkees*, movies like *Five Easy Pieces* and *The King of Marvin Gardens*. I found myself sitting by the pool in a conversation with Terence Young, who directed most of the early James Bond movies. Solid, no-nonsense man. In that detached way Brits have of being an eternal tourist in Hollywood, he was observing this Bacchanalian party, and said, "Look around, Mark"—we'd just met, but he was being avuncular. "See all these famous, beautiful people? We're all whores." A quote worthy of Fitzgerald at his most cynical. And I said, "Really?" And he said, "We'll do anything for money. We all have a price, and they know what it is."

And I'm looking around at the biggest names of that era, and asking myself, "If that's true, do I really want to sign up for that?" A formative moment for me. I know it sounds apocryphal, but I actually had that conversation.

When you suddenly started making money at Universal, was it difficult to deal with that in a responsible way? I'm sure there was a lot of temptation in Hollywood.

It's something you have to learn. I didn't really start making good money, by any standards, until '82 when I joined *Hill Street*. That was my first big year. You have to learn as you go. You have to pick the right people to advise you. There are a lot of operators waiting to clip you in Hollywood. You've heard stories about people who've been cleaned out by their quote-unquote business managers. So you learn that "business managers" aren't regulated in California; anybody can set up shop as one, and unfortunately, hundreds and hundreds of people get victimized every year. You learn to be careful.

I did come across a quote somewhere where you said that you, Adam, and Michael were three crazy guys running amok in Hollywood. Were those pretty wild days?

I mean, look, you're in your early twenties; you've got a little cash for the first time in your life. You're working. It's a candy store, one where a lot of people take the brakes off their moral center once they become successful. So you're witnessing a lot of strange and unusual behavior. You have to hope you've got an operational moral compass going into that experience to get you through it, and we've all compared notes and looked back on that period: What were the odds, number one, of three young guys coming out and having successful careers in a difficult business—but also the fact that we'd survive it? Because we knew a lot of people who didn't, a lot of people who fell by the wayside or into addiction at some point.

Why do you think you didn't turn into one of those people?

For me, it was growing up in the business. Growing up in the theater helped; it's a more egalitarian enterprise than network TV or movies, and there's more of a focus on what you're there to do collectively. In the theater, your intent is to entertain, but also—in some way, shape, or form—to tell something of the truth. So I never lost that predisposition. It had been reinforced by three years at Carnegie Mellon. We trained there to be working professionals, and then meeting people like Alan, who at that time was a big movie star but was also ethical and circumspect and respectful of other people. Through him, I got to see and meet a lot of other people, as well as in my own work. You slowly build an adult set of your own ethics and morality, and that's something that happens in the doing. You can't just write down a list and then go enact it. It has to be applied situationally. So it's live and learn: you make mistakes and you learn from them as you become a fully formed adult. If you're lucky, that system, that moral compass, is what allows you to get there without hurting yourself or other people.

Had you and your dad ever spoken about this world? He had some exposure to it, right?

He'd had a fair amount of it and also had his fair share of disappointment. It hadn't worked out for him. He had to go back into teaching. They left California. It's a complex world. For a young person to be thrown into that heady mix—I suppose, at some level I registered that I wasn't fully equipped to handle all this yet, at that age, working at that level. One of those unconscious, higher-self-talking-to-younger-self moments, saying, "This isn't the right time for you to be here," and I listened to that voice.

Do you remember anything about when and where you were when you made the decision that this wasn't what was going to fulfill you creatively at this point in your life, so you returned to the Midwest?

I don't know that I made up my mind all at once. It was a gradual thing. My girlfriend from Carnegie had gone to California that summer, and that was a reason for going out there. As it happened, she was also on her way to the Guthrie. She'd been accepted into a master's program at the University of Minnesota that placed actors as apprentices in the Guthrie rep company, so she was one of the reasons I went back to Minneapolis as well. It's seldom just one thing when you make a big life decision, and as I look back now, I don't regret it. It allowed me to work deeper into my craft. If I'd stayed in LA and gotten a job on the staff of *The Six Million Dollar Man* for the next two or three years or *The Bionic Woman*—which they'd offered me—I wouldn't have learned as much, instead of going back and working at the Guthrie, writing plays and finding my own voice. This was what drove, at an intuitive level, that particular decision.

I was reading in your novel *The Paladin Prophecy* where Will West first arrives in Wisconsin at the school, and he says that this is where he belongs, and I'm thinking to myself, "Is that Mark speaking about the Midwest?"

I think Will's reaction was based more on my adolescent years in the Midwest and what I found when I finally got to the Guthrie. My first time there, during my high school years, my world revolved around the Guthrie, a remarkable place that was an island of culture. At the time there was no place else like it between the coasts. The Guthrie had opened in 1963, the first regional repertory theater in the country, and it attracted great talent. One of my jobs during my second year was formative; the theater's founder, Tyrone Guthrie, had come back to direct—what turned out to be his last production there—*Uncle Vanya*. I was chosen to be one of his assistants, so I got to sit and watch him direct Chekhov, and that opened up the world of theater arts on a very deep level. There's Shakespeare and there's Chekhov and there's not a lot of other people at that level of the pantheon. And to see that production come together—the humanity and humor and pathos that he was able to bring to life—has guided me ever since. So I had a strong memory of, and fondness for, the town because of those formative years I spent there and also for the friends I've kept to this day.

Those years in Minnesota, between Universal and *Hill Street*, what

were they like? Were they difficult years financially?

Yes, from late '75 to when I went back, in spring of '81. I had planned to go back earlier, but a long writers' strike in 1980 prevented that. I did my theater work and supplemented it with odd jobs. You do what you can to pay the rent and put food on the table.

What were some of the odd jobs that you did?

I drove a school bus. I taught writing in the Minnesota state prison at Stillwater, through a Guthrie outreach program. I wrote and directed industrial films for a friend of mine who had a film company in Minneapolis. Good folks, and I really liked working with them. I did that about a year and a half. I did documentaries for a while. I did a lot of voice-overs for radio—commercials, narration, things like that—all while I was writing plays, getting them produced. The oddest of those—in the late seventies, there was a documentary about ABBA set to air on American television. It was all in Swedish, so they needed to dub in American voices, and they picked me to be the voice of either Benny or Bjorn, I don't remember which. I'd never actually dubbed something before. It was one of those dubs where you'd faintly hear him in Swedish in the background and hear the English translation in foreground.

You learn to cobble a living together. Spent a couple of horrible winters with a crappy car that wouldn't start. You had to plug your car in at night in the cold months there, so it wouldn't freeze over. That's how cold it was. It was Siberia in Minneapolis. I think of them now as character-building years, learning you can get through anything to get where you want to go, and when you have a little bit of success later, it makes it a little more satisfying.

You never had to sleep in your car or anything like that?

No, I was never homeless—just freezing—but I was living paycheck to paycheck.

You talked earlier about finding your voice, and you also talked about writing several plays when you went back. Do you remember anything about those plays, and were you still searching for your voice and your thematic preoccupations?

That's part of what any young writer's got to do. It's not something you instantly grasp and pursue, and even when you do find it, it takes years to master the craft enough to be able to facilitate it. So at that age—early to midtwenties—you're still a sponge, soaking up all these experiences, seeing good work, reading good work, and then trying to stumble your way toward finding your own.

One of the plays I'd written, a comedy called *The Nuclear Family*, was produced at the St. Nicholas Theatre in Chicago, fall of '77. David Mamet's theater. As part of their new playwrights' program, they staged a really strong production, directed by Emily Mann—my then girlfriend from the Guthrie, who went on to do lots of great work in the theater in New York and run the McCarter Theatre at Princeton. She wrote the play about Harvey Milk [*Execution of Justice*], which was a sensation on Broadway and was later made into a movie.

During these years, I also wrote some plays on commission. One with a brilliant group called the Children's Theatre Company of Minneapolis, led by a visionary director named John Donahue. I also became a resident with a group called The Playwrights' Lab, and for a while, I ran a program of my own at a place called Theatre in the Round, bringing new young plays to their audience. I wrote, directed, and produced a comedy revue based on the work of a beloved *Minneapolis Tribune* cartoonist named Richard Guindon. And throughout, I worked as a literary fellow at the Guthrie. So you're doing what's in front of you, working your way toward mastery, and figuring out what it is you want to say—and not that many writers in their twenties fully get there. It's a process.

Were you also experimenting in terms of thematic preoccupations? Was there some commonality among your works yet?

It was developmental. I made some friends with an organization at the University of Minnesota—our nickname for it was the Video Lab, but it had a fancier name—and their job was to provide documentaries to the local PBS station. Run by a guy who was fast becoming my best friend, Stephen Kulczycki, and we're close to this day. A position opened up there as a writer/producer in 1978, and I worked there for two years. That's what brought me back to filmmaking. I worked on some of their documentaries, writing things, doing voice-overs, and then I tackled one of my own.

This was my first writing-and-directing effort, *The Road Back*. A true story about a guy I knew, a former boxer named Jim Beattie, who was a friend of my family—my dad had cast him in a couple of plays. At the time, Jim was in his mid- to late thirties, and when I met him, he was running a halfway house for teenage felons who were trying to get out of the juvenile justice system. But what really grabbed me was Jim's own story. Jim in the early sixties had been a heavyweight boxer, and he was a huge man, six foot nine—a lot like Gerry Cooney. He had a devastating left hook and a ton of power, and he'd been rising through the ranks, won a lot of amateur titles and pro fights. Suddenly, a syndicate from New York wanted to sign him to an exclusive contract.

These were the days of Sonny Liston—before Cassius Clay/Muhammad Ali came along—and they wanted to find a "white knight in shining armor" to rehabilitate the image of boxing. In other words, it was a racially charged crusade. Jim was brought to New York, and they trained him at Gleason's Gym. As they do with fighters they want to promote, he worked his way up the ladder, hand-picked opponents, fighting in the [Madison Square] Garden, working his way into the top ten with the goal of getting a title shot. Then Jim discovered that the guy who owned his contract turned out to be Frank Costello, one of the senior mob bosses of New York City. Jim was a principled guy and decided, "I don't want to work for the mob. They'd own me lock, stock, and barrel." So he told them he wasn't going to fight for them anymore, after one last fight. They told him, "You can't quit. We own your contract. You can't go anywhere. We know where you live, we know where your family is."

A shot was fired at his wife while she was standing outside their brownstone—meant to scare her, not hit her—and he went into the Garden for what was going to be his last fight for them and they put Thorazine in his water bottle, and he was beaten to a pulp. So he fled New York City, took his family back to Minnesota, got a job as a traveling pharmaceutical salesman, became addicted to his own product, and in the midst of struggling with suicidal despair, he was picked to play the Great White Hope in the movie *The Great White Hope*, Jess Willard, the guy who knocks out James Earl Jones in the movie. By the time I had met Jim, he had cleaned up his life, was working his way back, and as a way to get the kids he was working with clean, he was teaching them how to box. As he got back into the gym, he realized, "Well, maybe I've still got something," and began thinking about a comeback. That's when I met him, and that's when I started filming. He was prepping for what was billed as the heavyweight championship of Minnesota, so he went back to Gleason's to train.

One of the sources I had for this: in the early 1960s, Robert Drew produced a series of classic documentary series for ABC News, and one of the shows he did was about young Jim Beattie when he was on the rise. I met with Drew, and he graciously allowed us access to all his footage from his film. So with that and shooting Jim's return to New York—I never was able to get actual footage from *The Great White Hope*, but they let me use stills—and a bunch of contemporary interviews with him, I was able to piece together his story. He ended up winning that title fight and seemed to be well on his way back to a fulfilled life.

So that was the narrative. The first time I'd worked with something that I felt was so fully formed. Writing, directing, and producing became my preoccupation for a year. By the time it aired on PBS and was well received—I'd been back in Minnesota four years at that point—I was getting really tired of Minnesota winters. I'd also gotten to that point where I felt, "I might know enough now to go back to California. I have a good calling card with the movie, I have a little more maturity, and I've learned enough about storytelling that I think I could start my career in earnest."

So I contacted Bochco, early 1980, and he was just starting work on *Hill Street Blues*. He'd had a couple of swings and misses with series of his own by that point—*Delvecchio*, with Judd Hirsch and Charlie Haid, and *Paris*, with James Earl Jones. So Steven said, "Well, I've got this new show, and it's coming on the air in the spring." He had high hopes for it, and when *Hill Street* debuted, it became an immediate critical hit but didn't pull in good numbers and looked like it might be canceled. But [NBC entertainment president] Brandon Tartikoff really went to bat for it, picked it up, and then the second season was delayed because of that writers' strike, so my trip back to LA was on hold. That strike went on for six or seven months, and when it ended, I went back to LA in spring of '81. *Hill Street* was just starting its third season, and that's when I went to work for Steven.

I came across a pretty interesting interview with you, some PBS thing called *Portrait*.

Yeah, that would have been early nineties. For a station in St. Paul, I think.

The interviewer asked if success had come easy for you, and you said that it didn't, that internally it was very difficult and it took a long time to come to terms with all the things growing up involved, and that you had some lean years before you went back to LA. What did you mean by internal difficulties and having to come to terms with the things growing up involved?

I think I meant maturing. You go through a peripatetic childhood like I did, parents moving around a lot and a fair amount of economic uncertainty for them. My dad was a struggling actor, selling real estate, and then he was a grad student and eventually built a teaching career at the University of Minnesota, but these were lean years financially. I'd left Hollywood after that first year, when things went well, but I wasn't sure I wanted to commit, having put so much time into playwriting and working in the theater. I wanted to make sure I wasn't taking the easy way out, even though it was the first time I'd ever made any money. So when I talk about the lean years it's those, '75 to '81. And at the end of them, I went, "You know, playwriting is rewarding and I love the theater, but I really do want to be able to make a living and have the freedom to do things I want to do." So that's when I went back and gave it another try.

3

"You Needed to Bring Your A Game"

(Hill Street Blues)

I n 1982, Mark Frost returned to Hollywood, again at the invitation of Steven Bochco, to join the writing staff at *Hill Street Blues*.

Though little remembered today, *Hill Street* is one of the most important shows in the history of television, especially prime-time episodic drama. A police procedural set in a troubled, never-identified inner city, it was created by Bochco and Michael Kozoll for MTM Enterprises, a dominant indie producer of the seventies and eighties, originally known for sitcoms, including *The Mary Tyler Moore Show* (Moore herself, whom the studio was named after, was one of its three founders, along with then-husband Grant Tinker and Arthur Price), but later for prestige dramas like *Hill Street*, *Lou Grant*, and *St. Elsewhere*.

Hill Street was, for its time, revolutionary—adapting soap-opera tropes (fractured narratives, continuing storylines, large ensemble casts) to prime-time "prestige drama," featuring nuanced, morally ambiguous characters and tackling difficult, topical issues with sophistication and intelligence (a throwback to the days of "Camelot TV" in the early sixties, but a far cry from what network television drama had become). A little context: When *Hill Street* premiered in January 1981, the top-rated TV dramas were *Dallas*, *Dukes of Hazzard*, *The Love Boat*, and *Little House on the Prairie*.

While *Hill Street* never did crack the top ten in overall viewership, it was a top-thirty show for three of its seven seasons. Even more importantly as far as NBC was concerned, it appealed to the young, upscale demographic coveted by advertisers. Critics showered it with praise. In its fifth season—Frost's last with the show—it ranked thirtieth overall and was the final hour in NBC's vaunted "America's Best Night of Television on Television," also including *The Cosby Show*, *Family Ties*, *Cheers*, and *Night Court*.

Over seven seasons, the show earned ninety-eight Emmy nominations and was crowned Outstanding Drama Series four times.

Contributing scripts, in addition to Bochco and Frost, were Anthony Yerkovich (*Miami Vice*), Dick Wolf (*Law & Order*), David Milch (*Deadwood*), Karen Hall (*Judging Amy*), and Pulitzer Prize winner David Mamet.

The entire pantheon of what Syracuse University's Robert Thompson has dubbed "Television's Second Golden Age"—including shows like *St. Elsewhere*, *Moonlighting*, *thirtysomething*, *LA Law*, *Picket Fences*, *China Beach*, and even Frost's own *Twin Peaks* (cocreated with David Lynch, of course)—sprang from the critical and commercial success of *Hill Street Blues*. This convinced broadcast networks that in the face of mounting pressure from alternative sources of entertainment—cable, VHS, video gaming—creative risks needed to be taken, and that patience could be rewarded for shows that were performing poorly overall (as *Hill Street* first did) but drew enviable demographics and critical applause.

Frost spent three seasons with *Hill Street*, rising from story editor to executive story editor.

It was, he says, "my graduate school, an advanced degree in understanding how television worked and how to deal with the most extreme personalities imaginable. It gave me a lot that I took forward, and I look back on it very fondly."

***

Would you say that the writers' room as we now know it started with MTM in the eighties?

As far as I know, it did, and I think we were at the forefront of it. Steven had developed this way of working with the staff, and [Bruce] Paltrow and the guys downstairs with *St. Elsewhere* were doing something similar. It felt cutting-edge, I'll put it that way. This wasn't something that had been handed down to Steven; it evolved with him through his years of experience and was refined as we went. But everybody felt much more included. He used to compare it to a pitching staff on a baseball team: you had your starters, your long relievers, you had your closers, you had situational types who could get a left-handed batter out. I'm stretching the metaphor, but it was like having a full bullpen. The whole staff worked together, and everybody played to their strengths.

Tell me how a *Hill Street* script was written. There are so many names attached to each episode, between story and teleplay.

During the off-season, we were encouraged to come back in with ideas for specific characters, specific story arcs, themes. Then we'd all sit in a room and start talking. Out of those discussions, storylines emerged that attracted our attention, and we'd play them out, bat them back and forth, see how each character fit into what was developing. We tended to write in three-episode arcs, but there'd be a few longer arcs beyond that that could last for half a season or even a full season. So you'd have constant interplay of arcs that were ending, new ones beginning, and every once in a while you'd find something really strong, a stand-alone story that dominated an episode. The best example of that was that first one [David] Milch wrote, that he won the Emmy for.

"Trial by Fury."

"Trial by Fury." The rules were there to guide us, but they weren't rigidly enforced, and the stories went where the staff's imaginations took them. You'd chart the parameters of an episode, then sit in a room and start identifying scenes. Everyone took notes. After a week or so, we were ready to beat out the story one scene at a time, for whoever was going to take the first pass on that episode. Steven recorded those sessions; we'd pop a cassette in and talk it through beat by beat by beat and act by act: cold open, roll call, and through the four acts of the hour. Then whoever was on point would go off and write their first draft.

At that point you're going off by yourself, whoever is taking the first pass?

Unless it was deeper into the season, and then it might be two people. Somebody would take the first two acts and someone else the back half of the episode. As you got closer to the end of the season, when the production monster's chasing you, snapping at your heels, it might be, "OK, you take one act, you take the second," somebody takes the third, and somebody takes the fourth. So it was a function of the exigencies of the moment how they were divvied up.

Steven was in the room but not doing much of the writing himself?

He would occasionally; he was busy. Running the show was a lot of work. So generally he was the manager, and we were the pitching staff. He might polish or rewrite as needed, but he had all that other stuff to do, that we learned about by osmosis, although that wasn't our domain at that point. Our job was to get those scripts out.

I read that Bochco said everybody on the writing staff had their own area of expertise, so Jeffrey Lewis was really well versed in legal issues, Anthony Yerkovich had this sort of quirkiness, David Milch was the street poet. Did you have one?

I loved writing Hill and Renko, because I knew Charlie Haid so well, and I got to know Michael Warren, so I knew the rhythms of that duo. Michael Conrad [Sergeant Phil Esterhaus] and the roll calls—the ornate language that he used was a good fit for me. And I liked writing for Joe Spano, Lieutenant Henry Goldblume, the liberal conscience of the squad room. I was a little more idealistic than Lewis or Milch, who took a more jaded view of the world.

In the way that Captain Furillo, the Daniel J. Travanti character, was Bochco's alter ego, would you say that Henry was yours?

He would have been the closest.

It seems like you liked writing for the more loquacious characters, like Renko and Esterhaus.

And Howard Hunter, the SWAT commander, who loved to turn a phrase. An urban variation on Miles Gloriosus, the archetypal Greek character of the vainglorious military commander. I had fun with him, too.

First as story editor and then as executive story editor, what were your specific responsibilities?

That reflected increasing responsibility about making sure stories were in shape, bringing ideas in, and helping with the overall process. There was no hard and fast division of labor. It meant that as you moved through the system and your credit advanced, you were given a little more responsibility every year.

Other shows had more rigid distributions of responsibility based on titles. For us, Steven was always the head. Tony Yerkovich was in that number two spot when I first came on in season three. That shifted when Tony left to do *Miami Vice*, so it became Jeff Lewis and David Milch. They were the senior guys. I was a rung below them. But it was teamwork, and my experience in sports helped me with that. I liked it. I enjoyed being a part of that team.

Those rooms had to be a little crazy though, with all of those personalities. I think Bochco has said that Milch, by his own definition, is a sociopath. You had a lot of really talented people in those rooms, and some real characters. What were those meetings like?

They were all sorts of things. Often a free-for-all. They were hilarious at times, they were tense at times. Milch brought a special edge to everything he was a part of. You learned to play nicely with others, but we subjected ideas to a rigorous development phase—so they stood up to logic, character, overall theme. It was a group process, but Milch was a wild card because his personal habits were so erratic and his process so chaotic. At this point, when he was starting out, he may have been a bit more under control than later in life, but then I never worked with David again afterward. I loved him. I consider him a friend, and he was fun to be around, but he was also tragically self-destructive and could be a real handful. He didn't mess with me, for some reason. I'd been around brilliant, chaotic people before, in the theater. I learned you've got to lay down strict boundaries or they will not respect you. David and I always got along really well.

Can you think of any really funny or crazy stories that happened in that writers' room?

There was a lot of gallows humor. When Mike Conrad [Esterhaus] was dying—he was a difficult guy. The cast didn't seem to like him that much. I know he didn't get along with certain of the younger actors. He did with Steven—they'd worked together before—but not everybody. He was great in the role and perfect for that part, and he died tragically young, but there might have been an office pool on how long he was going to last. I'll put it that way.

Yeah, I've read about that. Especially Kiel Martin [J. D. LaRue] and Charlie Haid used to give him a hard time.

Kiel and Charlie were handfuls in their own right. Kiel, I mean he gave Milch a run for his money. But a cast that big, you're bound to have some people bump heads, and we certainly did.

Hill Street **was a huge critical hit, and a lot of these people had been around, like Travanti and Conrad, and suddenly they become famous. The whole experience must have been hyperreal in a way.**

Those first two seasons were really good creatively, but the show didn't hit a ratings benchmark until the third season. The second season was almost an act of mercy on the part of Tartikoff and NBC. They loved the show. They knew nobody had watched it that first season, but felt if they rode it long enough, it was going to pan out. Brandon had great instincts. I got there concurrent with the show's ascendance to this cultural pinnacle. Those middle three years arguably were the high-water mark, so it was heady stuff to go to work every day on the show everybody was talking about. That translated to big numbers by the third season, and awards had really started to flow, so it was like playing for the Yankees during one of their winning-streak eras.

MTM was in general revolutionizing episodic drama at that time. What was your relationship like with the guys over at St. Elsewhere— Tom Fontana, John Masius, Bruce Paltrow, the Tinker brothers? Was there competition between you? Was it friendly?

It was friendly, collegial. I think underneath it was competitive. There wasn't a lot of time for either staff to sit around and share war stories. When you're making shows like that, you're half underwater all the time. But the interactions were always friendly. Bruce and Steven set the tone by their relationship, a jokey, competitive, almost high school kind of one-upmanship, but never mean-spirited.

Were you guys even watching each other's shows? Did you ever come in the next day and say, "Did you see what they did on St. Elsewhere last night?"

I think we felt, at least during the years I was there, that critically we had the upper hand, that we'd done it first and were winning all the Emmys. It wasn't often talked about, but it was like the Yankees and Red Sox. I remember somebody making a joke about having a story idea all typed up until we decided we could do better and they went to throw it in the trash, and somebody said, "Just leave it outside downstairs; they'll figure out a way to use it." But there was no open antagonism. It all added up to this wonderful atmosphere on the lot as a vibrant, exciting place to work. That was the closest I experienced—although I did to some extent at Universal in the seventies—to knowing what a

Golden Age movie studio must have felt like. You know, you go to the commissary and there's X, Y, and Z, and you talk about this, that, and the other thing. There were a lot of good, really talented people working at MTM during those years.

Getting back to the writers' room, were there ever any really intense creative differences that came up, about which way a story should go or which way a character should go?

That was fairly routine. It was a roomful of people with strong opinions, and they got aired out like you would in the judge's chamber of a courtroom, none of it intended for public consumption. This was the private process of a team—a clubhouse meeting would be the analogy for baseball. The big decisions were ultimately Steven's call. We'd make our cases, and sometimes the debates got passionate. But I can't think of an instance where it didn't result in a better outcome, because it forced you to test your thesis or idea under rigorous laboratory conditions. If you couldn't hold your own in that room, you were going to be relegated to the bench pretty quickly.

Sounds intense. There's that Milch quote that "There's a saying in all writers' rooms: 'It's all fear or faith. You're either trying to satisfy your guess about other people's expectations or working through the genuine and authentic possibilities of the material.'"

As always, David was wonderfully coherent about the process—and slightly less so while being in the process itself.

He obviously loved writing for Dennis Franz.

He loved working with Dennis. We had a great storyline when Dennis first played Sal Benedetto in the third season, and I worked on at least one of those. Great fun to write for, a crackerjack talent. He had that Chicago thing, that edgy presence. The same quality Dennis Farina had when I worked with him later [on *Buddy Faro*]. You knew exactly where you stood with him. He gave you what he had, he came prepared, and he was a fantastic guy off-screen as well as on. David had this, let's charitably call it a Damon Runynesque affection for the demimonde, a world he was more than a little comfortable with: con men and grifters and people on the margins, not just of civility, but criminality. He'd been there, more than any of the rest of us had. So he brought a vividness and immersion that leapt off the screen.

Would he literally be lying on his back in the writers' room dictating?

Sometimes. He had a bad back, and I remember him ending up on the floor a lot. I also remember his pants ending up around his ankles on more than a few occasions. The thing you have to remember is David was truly hilarious. So while arguing ferociously in defense of something, he'd pull his pants down and, as the British say, take the piss. His pretensions, back then, never lasted long.

Was it fun? Intimidating?

No, no, it was really fun. You had to be confident. You had to be prepared to back up what you brought in with sound reasoning and have it thought through. It was a great testing ground.

Karen Hall was the only woman on the staff, so what was it like for her?

You'd have to ask her, but it couldn't have been easy. This was a locker-room atmosphere, but she gave as good as she got. She was good at standing up for herself. I remember she and Milch bumping heads more than a few times.

Did it ever come to blows between anyone in the room? I know on set it did, between Kiel and Michael Conrad. Or was it Charlie and Michael Conrad?

Yeah, they had to be separated. All three of them were hotheaded, but it was nothing anybody took seriously, like a shouting match in a dugout, that's how we looked at it. Greg Hoblit, our producing director and an underappreciated part of the equation, handled the production side of things, and he did it brilliantly. So a lot of things that might have blown up on other shows never even reached us, because Greg was so good at smoothing them over. He directed a lot of episodes as well. We had a great stable of directors, and you could count on them to take care of business on the stage.

But no near fisticuffs in the writers' room? Sorry to be so persistent about this.

There were conflicts that usually revolved around Milch, because David's so complicated—let's use that as our rubric for him—that conflicts are inevitable. But if you could hold your own and not let him run roughshod over you, then it could be great fun to collaborate. That was my experience, but again I drew a line with him early on. As I said, you needed to bring your A game.

Do you think the show was better because of all the creative turmoil? Or do you think that just drains energy from everybody?

I think it's a razor's edge and can cut either way. It depends on the strength of the material. Sometimes it works, and sometimes it doesn't. It's not how I like to work. It's more a reflection of the showrunner's inner state, I think, than it is a process. I came from the theater, so I was used to deep examination of material and working and reworking until you had something right, so that didn't feel unusual to me. It's often cited as good for the creative process. That's probably true exactly fifty percent of the time.

Did you personally spend much time on set?

I did, because I made it clear to Steven that my interests were in more than just writing. I wanted to direct, and I wanted to produce, and so I spent a lot of time on stage and eventually directed an episode. It was a powerful learning experience for me in every way, a postgraduate degree in making a television show.

That was a difficult experience, directing the episode?

It was hard. I had directed a lot of theater, I'd directed the documentary I mentioned, but I'd never worked with this kind of train set before, and so there was a lot of on-the-job learning. Greg was excellent in helping me prep and get through it, and I've always loved working with actors, so I had fun with them. I cast Fran McDormand in a small role, one of her first jobs, as a deputy district attorney, and I brought in a talented comic named Taylor Negron, who just passed away, to play an interesting villain. You learn all sorts of things in that kind of environment: the importance of casting, the importance of network interface, how to manage all those relationships. I was a sponge during those three years.

Why would you say you haven't directed more than you have over the years?

I learned after I directed the feature I did [*Storyville*] that what I loved about directing was working with actors, crafting performances, and telling a story. It's a crushingly difficult job from a physical stamina standpoint, and for somebody used to the solitary job of writing—as my choices have reflected over the last twenty years, I much prefer writing books to anything else—it's an overpoweringly social experience. I'm too used to having time alone to think and work and write, and that's antithetical to a director's lifestyle. So that's what I discovered after I'd done it a number of times: I enjoyed it and found it satisfying, but my true calling was to do something more solitary.

You mentioned actors and how much you liked working with them, but I get the sense from reading his autobiography that Bochco didn't share that love. I remember he called Lee Grant a bitch on wheels and talked about how Peter Falk basically ruined *Columbo*. When he talks about Kiel Martin and Charlie Haid, you

don't really get the impression that he loves actors so much. But you come from a family of actors. You've acted yourself, and it sounds like you have a different opinion of actors.

Maybe I understand them better. I understand that their process is different and that they're individually different from one another, but we can't do what we do without them. Steven came from the Universal–factory school of filmmaking where actors were software, a necessary part of the process. And there were many he adored; there were some he got along with famously. But I think he'd just been through too many battles.

One of the reasons he liked the ensemble show—which he repeated with *LA Law* and to an extent with *NYPD Blue*—is that you're not at the mercy of a single personality, as you would have been with Peter Falk on *Columbo*. That can get complex quickly, and if it's not handled right, the whole enterprise can sink if that central relationship fails. And there are actors who are simply impossible to work with. When David Caruso left *NYPD Blue*, for instance. We'd first used him on *Hill Street* in a small part as an Irish gangster. He was striking, but he made Steven's life miserable on *NYPD Blue,* and he quit, thinking he was going to have a big movie career. He's not a joy to work with, to put it mildly, based on everything I've heard about him. So your mileage may vary. It just depends on who you get into business with.

You mentioned in an earlier conversation that you admired the film work of Robert Altman. Was Altman ever someone whom Bochco talked about as an influence with respect to *Hill Street*?

You mean in terms of directorial style? Overlapping dialogue? Bob Butler, who directed the pilot, took some things from Altman. There were two other things that were influential. The movie *Fort Apache, the Bronx*, which Bochco told me was an influence, and a PBS documentary called *The Police Tapes*, which later aired in an edited version on ABC. Steven definitely cited that as a major influence. During that period when I was still living in Minneapolis but knew I was going back to

Los Angeles to work on the show, I spent an afternoon with Anthony Bouza, the captain in the documentary—he'd become the police chief in Minneapolis—to pick his brain about his years in the South Bronx, what it was like to be in that kind of precinct in that time in the city. As I understood it, Steven wanted to capture that feeling with the show. Bouza was really helpful, gave me some good ideas to think about. As far as I know, those were the two most important influences. Steven relied on Butler a lot, for that handheld feel. The dialogue treatment came from the Altman school of filmmaking, the first time anybody tried anything like that on network television, so it was a breakthrough.

I remember Bouza from that film. He was incredible. A real philosopher.

Exactly right, and he was a model for Furillo, I remember Steven saying. Soft-spoken, deep-thinking, really interesting man.

There are some really provocative story arcs during your time there—just for example, you had the arc where the Linda Hamilton character gets raped, and Joe Coffey [Ed Marinaro] is having such a hard time dealing with it. Dennis Franz is there originally as Sal. You had the gay policeman, Joyce's infertility, Furillo shooting a robber. Anything you remember as your favorite story arc or a favorite scene?

A couple of things come to mind. The Linda Hamilton arc was really good. That was a strong storyline for Ed, who became a good friend of mine. We were always trying to find something for Ed; I thought he was underrated as an actor, and that fit him really well.

One that really stands out is Michael Conrad's death, and how we handled the death of Esterhaus. It was a powerful thing to go through even on a personal level for the cast. Michael was a complicated guy, and people had mixed feelings about him, but he was fun to write for and the way we dealt with his death, I thought—I can't remember if it was the first time someone had done that in a dramatic network show, but it was close to it. We all worked on that episode.

The other that jumps out at me was the death of Dominique Dunne. She was playing the part of a battered woman that eerily echoed her own life experience [Dunne was strangled to death by her ex-boyfriend in 1982, at the age of twenty-two], and she was killed not long after we had finished shooting, before any of the episodes had aired. That was particularly hard-hitting, because she was so young and talented and had such a bright life ahead of her. That hit everybody hard. I was seated next to her dad [Dominick Dunne] on a plane years later—at least twenty—and we talked about it, how it changed everybody on the show. It was a powerful conversation for both of us.

With Esterhaus's death, I think the street sweeper scene is one of the great moments in episodic drama ever, because it's so antisentimental. Do you remember where that came from?

We were all beating out the story and sitting in the room. I honestly don't remember who mentioned the street sweeper. It was a group conversation. We thought putting his ashes on the street was an appropriate gesture. It was probably Steven who came up with the idea of the street sweeper—which was, as you say, the perfect antisentimental touch for a strong, emotional moment.

We talked earlier about how you were looking for your voice, and it took you awhile to get. When did you feel confident that you found it? Did that happen on *Hill Street*?

I wouldn't say I found it definitively. What I think I'd found, by the time I ended three years on *Hill Street*, was that I'd finished my apprenticeship—I guess I'd put it that way—and I was ready to explore using my craft to find my own voice. The part of it I haven't really talked about much—this was heavily influenced by the theater and particularly Chekhov—what interested me most was humanism. Writers who were not polemic, who were willing to engage with all sides of a situation, all sides of a question, and all sorts of people without judgment. Those were the artists I was continually drawn to, whether it was in prose, or on the stage or on film. Altman was a big influence for me at that time. The film *Chinatown* had become my favorite film. I loved the idea of blurring the lines of genre to get to deeper truths, if you could find a way. *Chinatown* still stands out for me as one of the most perfect screenplays ever written, because it was engaging on so many levels of story and character and theme at the same time. It's densely rich, an insanely well-made movie on every level. Similar to *The Godfather* films, which have had a huge and lasting impact on our culture. One of my favorite phrases about writing—and I don't generally like the tendency to create aphorisms or express your feelings in pat sentences—but one of my favorite ways of thinking about art and storytelling is that "nothing is as it seems."

That is *Twin Peaks* in a nutshell, right?

That's right. Because that was my experience in life. So I was going along, looking at the world, seeing the presumptions people had about who they were and how they were moving through life. I'd grown up through the Nixon years, watching the Watergate hearings.

There's a little bit of Kilroy in my life, how I've been in weird proximity to a lot of stories. I was writing a play my sophomore year of college about John Wilkes Booth. I'd happened on the true story of Booth, how this was originally a much larger conspiracy to kidnap Lincoln and ransom him for the return of Confederate prisoners as a way of extending the war. It was a lunatic plot. Booth was a madman, but he had enlisted other people, and as far as I could tell, no one had written about it much, so I went to Washington to research it at the National Archives and visit Ford's Theatre. It was an incredible experience, seeing all this history, to go into the archives and pull open a tray and there's Lincoln's bloody collar from the night he was shot. Booth's derringer, the stovepipe hat Lincoln was wearing that night. It made history come alive in a way I hadn't experienced before, and it just so happened I was staying at a Howard Johnson's, which just so happened to be across the street from the Watergate Hotel. And this was within a week or two of the break-ins and the arrest of the Watergate burglars . . . who were staying at the same Howard Johnson's, where E. Howard Hunt was conducting their operation.

Again, this idea that nothing is as it seems. When I found this out, I went, "Gee whiz, I was right there." That harkened back to my obsession with the JFK assassination, less than ten years in the past at that point. This was around the time of the House investigating the theory that there may have been more gunshots. It was a paranoid era, and our generation was taught firmly by experience: Don't take things at face value, question authority. As a result, I'm resolutely antiauthoritarian. I guess that's all by way of saying that's how your voice comes together. There's another side to it too—a spiritual education, which was going on at the same time.

Why did you end up leaving *Hill Street* after season five?

The sequencing went like this: Steven, as you know, was fired by MTM after the fifth season, and he'd made a deal to go to Fox to create a new show [*LA Law*], and Milch and Jeffrey Lewis behind his back had agreed to stay on and run *Hill Street* for MTM. They wanted me to stick around and work on the show, but I'd done three years at that point, and I'd learned that I didn't like doing the same thing over and over again. Repetition was deadening to creativity, my own creativity, a personal quirk. I'm not judging people who do that; it just isn't right for me. I felt that after three years, if I stayed any longer, it was going to get stale, and I wouldn't be able to give it my best effort. It would be about the money and not the work. So I decided to leave.

When did you start to get the feeling that Bochco wasn't long for the job, and how did that filter down to you?

I started to pick up intimations during season five. Steven had this negotiation going on. Grant Tinker had moved to NBC [where he became chairman/chief executive officer]. Arthur Price [who became interim MTM president] was from the business side and not, well, let's say charitably, he wasn't Grant Tinker, and it was like getting a small craft warning ahead of a storm. Something was in the wind. And Steven finally took me aside one day and told me what was going on, so I realized our run was coming to an end.

What was going on?

There were financial differences with Price. He was trying to hold the line. It was an expensive show. It was probably not going to have a great life in syndication because of its extended-narrative nature, so they were trying to make as much as they could on the initial run, and that meant holding down costs. Steven wanted to maintain standards and felt to do that he had to be able to produce the show the way he had been doing it. There was little to argue with the results. But by the fifth year, the show was what it was. It was the most critically rewarded show at that point in television history, but from a businessman's standpoint, Price was saying, "That and a quarter will get me a copy of the *LA Times*. I need to make money, so I need to trim around the edges." And that just rankled Steven no end, and eventually led to them cutting him loose. The hardest thing for him was that they'd gone behind his back to talk to Lewis and Milch about taking over if Steven were to leave, and I think he felt a little Julius Caesar about that.

How did you find out that Steven had been cut loose?

He told me at the end of the year. Steven invited me to come play a round of golf at Riviera one morning. I'd already turned down the *Hill Street* guys. Steven said, "I'm going to do this new show, and if you'd like to come over and work on it, I'd love to have you." That afternoon I had a meeting with John Schlesinger to talk about a book he wanted to develop for Fox, the movie that became *The Believers*, and I wanted to give movies a try. I thought, "Well, *there's* a way to not repeat yourself." Every movie's different.

The meeting with Schlesinger went really well. They offered me the job and I had to tell Steven I was going to turn him down. I had a chance to be an associate producer on the movie, write the movie, and observe a master filmmaker at work. He [Schlesinger] basically said, "I'll let you be involved in every stage of preproduction, production, and postproduction," and he was as good as his word. It became a phenomenal experience. That was a real turning point for me.

When all is said and done, *Hill Street* was a positive experience?
Absolutely. It was my graduate school, an advanced degree in understanding how television worked and how to deal with the most extreme personalities imaginable. It gave me a lot that I took forward, and I look back on it very fondly.

When you eventually moved over to showrun at *Twin Peaks*, what specifically did you take with you from your experiences at *Hill Street*?

Everything. The entire experience I packed up into a portmanteau trunk and dragged behind me. It's a job—not to conflate its importance—but it's like the presidency. I've had people who've worked around the White House tell me nobody learns how to be president until you *are* president. There's nothing that can prepare you for it. Even with three years of working on *Hill Street*, you still have to learn your own way once you become a showrunner. So every bit of experience that you have—personally, professionally, socially, creatively—is something you take with you and need to do that job effectively. It's an enormously complex and challenging position. There's all sorts of different ways to do it, and it's very individualistic, but mine was based primarily on the experiences that I'd had during *Hill Street*.

4

"Early in Your Career, Say Yes to Everything"

(The Believers, Spielberg, Aliens, Trump)

Originally the plan for this chapter was to explore solely Frost's first foray into theatrical films, as writer/associate producer on *The Believers*, a 1987 supernatural thriller directed by Oscar winner John Schlesinger (*Midnight Cowboy*). However, the conversation wound up twisting and turning in all sorts of directions; hence, alien encounters, interdimensionality, time travel, and Donald Trump, all themes that eventually feature prominently in Frost's oeuvre.

Also surfacing here: the infamous Shaver Mystery, which pops up again in Frost's 2016 novel, *The Secret History of Twin Peaks*, and also plays a crucial part in the mythological story of a race of beings known as Lemurians, which will resonate with Frost-Lynch fans (and which Frost expounds upon in the following chapter).

Richard Sharpe Shaver gained notoriety in the 1940s as the author of a controversial series of yarns published in *Amazing Stories*, a pulp magazine edited and published by a diminutive (four-foot-tall) hunchback by the name of Ray Palmer. Shaver claimed that he personally had encountered a subterranean race of sinister beings called the Dero (for detrimental energy robots), and that he himself, in a past life, had lived among these beings under the name Mutan Mion.

Though *Amazing Stories* was a science fiction magazine, both Shaver and Palmer peddled these stories as true; the June 1947 edition of the magazine—the "All Shaver Mystery Issue"—pitched "The Shaver

Mystery" as "The Most Sensational True Story Ever Told."

The Believers, on the other hand, is blatantly fiction, loosely adapted by Frost from the 1982 novel *The Religion*, credited pseudonymously to Nicholas Condé, a hybrid of Robert Stuart Nathan (*Law & Order*) and Robert Rosenblum. Starring Martin Sheen, Helen Shaver, Jimmy Smits, Robert Loggia, and Harris Yulin, it is a horror film with socioeconomic subtext: NYPD psychologist Cal Jamison (Sheen) is summoned to treat Officer Tom Lopez (Smits), who, while infiltrating a malevolent Santerian cult, goes stark raving mad (or does he?), convinced that rogue practitioners of the (real-life) Afro-American religion are using their supernatural powers to torment him.

Spoiler alert here: the cultists are tied to a cabal of New York City one-percenters who sacrifice children in exchange for wealth, fame, and power, giving new meaning to the term "voodoo economics." These privileged monsters are led by a supercilious New York City tycoon who bears a striking resemblance to a certain public figure whom Frost has consistently lacerated over recent years, especially on Twitter.

The film, produced and distributed by Orion Pictures, cost about $13 million to shoot; principal photography commenced in June 1986, and *The Believers* opened in New York and Los Angeles a year later before expanding to 1,534 screens nationwide. According to Box Office Mojo, it wound up grossing $18.7 million domestically, ranking fifty-ninth for the year.

Reviews were mixed. For instance, *The New York Times*'s Vincent Canby derided it as an "absurd, especially cheerless movie"; Michael Wilmington of the *Los Angeles Times* said it was "one of the better-produced, more exciting and intelligent thrillers of the year."

***

How did you come to the attention of John Schlesinger or whoever it was who reached out to you to adapt *The Believers*?

I was represented by CAA [Creative Artists Agency]. They sent him a screenplay I'd written years earlier while still living in Minneapolis, based on a true-crime situation that caught my eye. Many years later [2000] it was made as a Lifetime movie directed by a friend of mine, Sollace Mitchell, *The Deadly Look of Love*, which was not my original title. [Originally called *True Romance*, it fictionalizes the 1977 murder of Susan Rosenthal, stabbed ninety-seven times in her home by June Mikulanec, later found not guilty by reasons of insanity and committed to a state hospital.] That screenplay attracted Schlesinger for a movie he was developing. We had a successful meeting, and they told me a few days later they wanted me on the project, so I was thrilled and just went with it.

One of my earliest mentors, Alan Arkin—a wonderful man, one of the great actors in American film history—gave me a great piece of advice. He said, "Early in your career, say yes to everything. In show business, you never know if something's going to come through. Odds are it won't. But if it does, you give yourself more opportunity." He saw that as a key to his success. I developed a screenplay with him that he was going to direct in 1975 based on a book called *Ox Goes North*, a wonderful story. Today you'd call it a young-adult book. We never got the movie made, but working with Alan on it was a fantastic learning experience.

What happened next with *The Believers*?

I read the book [*The Religion*] they'd optioned to adapt, and thought, "Well, it's a horror movie and it's a little twisted, but it's a chance to make a movie with John Schlesinger, you know, *Midnight Cowboy*." They'd screened it at that art house theater I worked at in 1970. Watched it a dozen times. I'd also been on the set when he was making *The Day of the Locust* in 1974. I'd gotten to know [actor] Bill Atherton, also a Carnegie grad, visited Bill on the set and saw Schlesinger at work twelve years earlier at Paramount. A legendary talent. So my interest in the project was more about the chance to work with a world-class director than it was the material.

That's interesting, because I'd point out two things about this film that I'd suggest are consistent with Mark Frost's thematic preoccupations. One might surprise you: the villain, Robert Calder, played by Harris Yulin, is clearly a wealthy, capitalist businessman

who presents some consistency with your writing and thinking since. And what's interesting is that I was going back and looking at reviews of the film, and *The Washington Post* described his character as a Donald Trump–like real estate magnate.

Well, there you go. I actually met Trump with John when we shooting in New York—1986, at a party at the director Randall Kleiser's house, a loft in the middle of Hell's Kitchen, which hadn't really gentrified yet. A Hollywood A-list party, and I'm having a conversation with John and Warren Beatty, who I'd met once before, and he and John were good friends. I look behind Beatty and see Trump come into the room. I know who he is—this buffoonish New York plutocrat—and watch him survey the room like a shark looking for a meal. His eyes fall on Beatty, and he makes a beeline over and horns in on the conversation. To his eternal credit, Beatty just shakes his hand and says, "You know, I'm talking to John here." And Trump doesn't even look phased. He goes back to scan mode, checks the room, finds another target, and takes off to horn in on another conversation. So it's funny you mention it, because I put a little of him in that character.

And *The Washington Post* picked up on it. The other thing is, it's interesting to hear you say you weren't that interested in the genre, because supernaturalism has gone on to play a rather important role in your career. Did *The Believers* in any way incite your interest in it?

I had an interest in it already, and *The Exorcist* had taken horror mainstream as a genre. But within the business, it was still a semirespectable street to work, and I didn't want to end up typecast. I was careful about that and tried to bring as many authentic touches to it as we could, so it didn't seem like a cheapie. That was something we talked about a lot. Make it as truthful as possible and culturally as authentic as possible, to show that Santeria [the Afro-American religion that figures prominently in the movie] was a powerful, positive force for some Latin communities both in the Caribbean and New York and not just an exotic oddity to exploit for cheap thrills.

Certainly that would be a hallmark of your work, transcending genre to address deeper issues.

The idea that a group of one-percenters had co-opted this religion and perverted it for their own purposes was the class story central to the piece. It makes literal what capitalism does to the underclass of society. It was a great working experience. We took a year to nail down the script, developed it at Fox. Then Fox decided not to make the movie, but John had a lot of admirers at the studios. Within three or four days, he'd set it up at Orion.

Interesting to see you set the early part of the story in Minnesota, which isn't the case in the book. Did you go back there to shoot?

No, we started in New York, spent about six weeks on New York locations, and then we moved up to Toronto.

So Toronto stands in for Minnesota?

Yes. We were one of the first projects that crossed the border to take advantage of Canadian production credits. We shot in '86, and it came out in June of '87. We had the misfortune of opening the same day as the first *Predator*, which blew us out of the water at the box office. But it gave me the chance to follow a project from start to finish—from developing a script all the way to the finished print, test screenings, working with studio and audience comments. I got to direct a lot of second unit, and even a day of looping. Spent hours with Martin [Sheen], and we had great fun together filling in noises like Foley work. There's a scene where they're removing a body bag from a barge, and we were lifting a heavy roll of carpet, grunting. I had a wonderful time with Martin on that movie. Wonderful, generous man.

After *The Believers*, your next credit is something called *Scared Stiff*, a theatrical film that was released in 1987, with Andrew Stevens and Mary Page Keller. You have an "original screenplay" credit, along with Daniel F. Bacaner and Richard Friedman, who also directed. I

know Friedman had come from *Tales from the Darkside* and went on to direct *Phantom of the Mall: Eric's Revenge* and *Doom Asylum*, so a real genre guy. How involved were you in that?

Scared Stiff was a spec script I wrote before I started working on *Hill Street*. Dan Bacaner was a friend of mine from Minnesota, who'd been a high school friend of the Coen brothers—I met them through Dan. He read the script and wanted to produce it. He'd helped raise money for Joel and Ethan [Coen] on *Blood Simple* and got credited as an executive producer.

So he had a way to finance [*Scared Stiff*] and optioned the script. I didn't have anything to do with the production. I was involved with *Hill Street* and had no time to pay attention to it, so it happened off to the side. I don't think I've ever seen the finished film. Following Arkin's Law, it was one of those early things you just say yes to.

You mentioned the Coen brothers. Did you have any connection to them yourself? Is there any sort of Minneapolis mafia out there?

I met them out here [in California] when I moved back in '81, and they were just getting started. We've been friendly over the years. At one point, they were planning to do *Fargo* as a TV series, the first time around—maybe fifteen, twenty years ago. They asked if I had any interest in helping them develop it, which I was too busy to do at the time.

Do you watch the new *Fargo*, by the way, on FX?

I like it a lot. The second season in particular is my favorite, in part because my old friend Adam Arkin worked on it, and the story arc involved that UFO angle, which I believe was based on the same UFO rash of sightings that I'd investigated back in '77, '78.

You investigated them back then or that's when they happened? We skipped right over that.

I forgot! Around the time I was doing *The Road Back*. I was working with a friend on that series of documentaries for PBS, and we both had an interest in this. We read stories in the [Minneapolis] *Star Tribune* about these startling series of events and encounters, so we drove out there to check it out on a Saturday. We were having breakfast at a cafe—I don't even remember the name of the town—and happened to bump into a ufologist who was there. There's a national organization of amateur UFO investigators—there's an acronym for it, MUFON. We bumped into this guy at breakfast who was there to look into it, and he had the names of all the witnesses and addresses and had made plans to go talk to them, so we told him we were documentary filmmakers and asked, "Would you mind if we tagged along?" and he said, "Absolutely."

So we drove around town and spoke with four or five different people who'd had startling encounters with phenomena that were really hard to explain away. This was just after *Close Encounters* had come out, so it was very much in the news and national consciousness. This cemented my interest in it as a subject—actually talking to these very down-to-earth, no-nonsense people who clearly had no reason to lie about something like this. They were not seeking publicity. They had no interest in being made fun of, yet they'd clearly gone through something that had left them utterly shaken. So it was a fascinating experience, and it led me to believe that there was something here that was hard to wrap your mind around.

What do you think now?

I tried to articulate it in *The Secret History of Twin Peaks*. I went as deep as I ever have in researching the subject writing that book and came out believing there's something universal about this. It's in every culture, and it seems to have gone back a long way in time, so it's either an ongoing psychological phenomenon that people experience internally or there's something real to it physically. I can't decide if it's one or the other, or both. It's like there's a shadow following us around as human beings.

I had an interesting conversation about it years later with Steven Spielberg when we were finishing the first season of *Twin Peaks*. Steven was a fan of the show, and his wife, Kate Capshaw, was close friends with the wife of Harley Peyton, who I'd brought in to write and produce the show. I'd written and directed the final episode of season one, and Steven invited us over to dinner. I showed him the rough cut of the episode, and he was interested in directing an episode. During the course of the evening, we got into a conversation about UFOs. I was fascinated to hear about his experiences with *Close Encounters* working closely with Allen Hynek, who'd been in charge of Project Blue Book, and what he really thought about it. He echoed my sentiment: There's definitely something there. And he thought the most likely explanation might involve time travel, with people coming back from the future to try to prevent catastrophes, particularly the development of atomic weapons. When you look at the details of some of these sightings and how many have been centered on nuclear-weapon sites, there may be something to it.

I felt I went as far as I needed to go with the subject with the work I did in *Secret History*. It was something that's always intrigued me, and if you reference the writing there, particularly the sections about Doug Milford and Major Briggs, I was able to pinpoint how I felt about it.

You had researched it in Minnesota and then sat on it for twenty to thirty years, or you were researching it all that time?

It was an interest that came and went. I included it in the second season of *Twin Peaks* in the early nineties, so it wasn't that long before I incorporated it into something, but the circularity of the conversation in a James Burke way here was part of why I liked *Fargo*, because the incident lined up with the timeline of the story they were telling that took place in the seventies, when I had my experience with those witnesses.

When you went back to research the history of UFOs for *Secret History*, what kind of research did you do?

A comprehensive, deep dive, all the way back to Project Blue Book. There's a whole raft of titles, a lot of them recent, that deal with the subject. The Whitley Strieber books came out in the eighties, which was a startling take on the subject. Others took it a step further. One that resonated in particular is called *Operation Trojan Horse* by John Keel. Another was *Witness to Roswell*.

I read *The Report on Unidentified Flying Objects* by Edward Ruppelt, which is kind of an early bible on the subject, published all the way back in 1956. That book doesn't even mention Roswell, but it does mention a lot of the stuff you get into, like the Arnold sightings, the Shaver Mystery and Ray Palmer, which raises another question: Did you come across Ray Palmer and Lemuria through your UFO research or was it the other way around? Did you come across Ray Palmer because you were interested in Lemuria, or Lemuria because you were interested in Ray Palmer? I know I am going way out of chronology here, but let's go with the flow.

Lynch and I had both heard about Lemuria. This was '86, '87—after I'd written *Goddess*. We were working on *One Saliva Bubble* and playing around with the idea of the Lemurians—if I have the timeline right—when we were approached by CAA about what became *Twin Peaks* and ABC's interest in working with us. We had started developing a treatment about it, and I believe that was when I went down the Ray Palmer rabbit hole.

The Palmer-Shaver story is pretty amazing. Richard Shaver claimed to have personal knowledge of a diabolical race of ancient super-semihumans who lived underground here on Earth. He wrote stories about them for Ray Palmer's pulp magazine, *Amazing Stories*. One of them is called *I Remember Lemuria*. Whole books have been written about the so-called Shaver Mystery.

Yeah, it's out there. There's some really strange things around the whole subject that are hard to comprehend, like the Jackie Gleason story, which I tell in *Secret History*—apparently one that Gleason told quite a few people about.

Have you ever heard of the Fermi Paradox—the contradiction between the lack of evidence and high-probability estimates for the existence of extraterrestrial civilizations—from Enrico Fermi? Basically, the argument is that there are billions of stars in the galaxy that are similar to the sun—many of them billions of years older than our solar system—with high probability some of these stars have Earth-like planets. And if the Earth is typical, some may have developed intelligent life and possibly interstellar travel. Yet every indication is that we have never been visited. So, hence, the paradox. So Fermi's question is, "Where is everybody?"—which turned out to be the title of the first episode of *The Twilight Zone*.

Maybe we have been visited. I was a fan of the work of Erich von Däniken in the seventies—the ancient astronaut theories that the Earth may have been monitored from the get-go, that something about this planet attracted the interest or attention of intelligent life somewhere else, so it has been scrutinized. That seems fairly plausible. If we take the leap that such things are real, then yeah, that makes complete sense to me.

That's also what happens in *2001*, which I know you admire greatly.

2001 was the awakening of all that for me. I was so transmogrified by it I went home and wrote Kubrick a twenty-page letter. The last time I saw it in a theater was in the midseventies at the Cinerama Dome. I looked at it again recently and was really struck by how slyly funny it is, particularly the first half. A lot of social commentary and satire in those early scenes.

In the space station?

Yeah, the mordant humor was something that maybe you don't appreciate until you're older.

Just before we leave this subject: you were talking about the trip to Spielberg's. Legend has it that he was interested in directing the season two premiere of *Twin Peaks* and then when you and Harley went back and mentioned that to David, Lynch said he wanted to direct the premiere of season two. Is that an accurate recounting of what happened?

That's pretty accurate. Then Steven just got too busy. He was about to make *Jurassic Park* and *Schindler's List* back to back, so *Twin Peaks* came off the table. We might have done an episode later in the year with him if that hadn't intervened.

Do you think David didn't want Spielberg to direct it?

I think he was protecting his turf a little bit, yeah. There were three other projects I want to mention. The first movie I ever got hired to write was for Lorimar, called *Blind Voices*, when I was working on *Hill Street*.

What was that one about?

A young-adult book—a variation of *Something Wicked This Way Comes*, a book I adored as a kid. A producer named Jay Julien, a New York lawyer who represented Robert De Niro, had optioned the book and set it up at Lorimar. A friend of mine who was an executive there thought I was right for it. Really solid script. I don't recall exactly why that movie didn't get made. This was around the time Lorimar's film division was falling apart, so that may have been the reason. The other two were script-doctor work, which is interesting as a screenwriting subject. The first was a Dick Wolf script called *No Man's Land* with Charlie Sheen [released in 1987]. The producer, a friend of mine named Tony Ganz, asked me to do a rewrite on that uncredited. Peter Werner directed.

Did you work with Dick Wolf at *Hill Street* or did you not overlap?

Our time didn't overlap, but I'd met him socially, and we had a few meetings about the film. This was pre-*Law & Order*.

What was the other project?

A movie called *Nightbreed* [1990], based on a novel Clive Barker had written called *Cabal*. Clive had become a friend through our agents at CAA. He was upfront about this and said, "Look, I'm going to take credit for the script, but I haven't actually written it yet"—if I remember this correctly. So I did a draft, and he directed—the first time he directed, I believe. Craig Sheffer was the star. David Cronenberg played the bad guy and was effectively creepy in it. Clive had budget issues, so it wasn't the movie he was hoping to make—they cut way back on what he was able to shoot—but that was the other project I ghostwrote.

You have to explain Hollywood to me. Why would somebody come to you and say, "I'm going to take credit for the script, but would you write it"?

Because it was based on his novel, he was going to write and direct, and that's how they were going to sell it. They said it's a three-week gig, and the money was good—script-doctoring works that way. You work on a weekly rate and agree you're not going to take credit, depending on what the exigent circumstances are. It's just a job, a good-paying gig, and that's the inside business of professional screenwriting. Clive was a friend; I wanted to see what he could do with it. And my friend Charlie Haid ended up acting in the movie, so I said, "Sure, why not?" This was post-*Believers*, pre-*Twin Peaks*. That was the case for *Nightbreed*. *No Man's Land* came out in '87, and this was right after that.

❧

5

"That's Hollywood, Kid"

(Frost-Lynch, The Early Years: Goddess + One Saliva Bubble + The Lemurians)

Mark Frost and David Lynch cocreated one of the most transcendent television shows of all time with *Twin Peaks*, but it didn't happen overnight. They first collaborated—or intended to collaborate—on *Goddess*, Frost's adaptation of Anthony Summers's explosive 1985 biography of Marilyn Monroe, but the project collapsed when, as Frost explains below, United Artists balked, skittish over certain political ramifications. As Frost is wont to do, he devoted copious hours of research to the project, even traveling to Ireland to meet with Summers and dig through boxes of the author's original research, a process that culminated with an epiphany by candlelight on a "long, spooky night" in the middle of a good old-fashioned Irish thunderstorm.

Considering Frost's thematic preoccupations both on-screen and on the printed page, it's easy to see what attracted him to the project, given the intricacies of the Byzantine conspiracy allegedly spun to cover up the real facts of Monroe's death.

Here we meet colorful Hollywood producer Bernie Schwartz (*Coal Miner's Daughter*, *St. Elmo's Fire*, and *Hammer*, the 1972 Fred Williamson blaxploitation film), who, in the aftermath of *Goddess*'s implosion, shared with Frost an aphorism that he has never forgotten, and that has helped him maintain his sanity on numerous occasions ever since.

The next Frost-Lynch project didn't fare any better: *One Saliva Bubble*, a wacky body-switch comedy in which both Steve Martin and Martin Short had agreed to star. The story was based on a concept—Lynch's—"in search of a narrative and execution," as Frost articulates it. This was their first real collaboration; they worked together on the script over lunch daily, bouncing ideas back and forth. Alas, the *Bubble* burst when producer Dino De Laurentiis went bust. Although the script was never filmed, it resides on the Internet, and echoes of it can be heard and felt in later projects like *On the Air* and the Las Vegas scenes in *Twin Peaks: The Return*. It *is* fun, though, to envision Frost and Lynch cracking each other up over lunch on a daily basis.

Next, Frost and Lynch turned to television, for a project called *The Lemurians*, which, as Frost describes it, was "pretty out there; it made *Twin Peaks* look like *Peyton Place*." Lemuria is the name of a mythical lost continent located in the Indian Ocean, as postulated not just by crackpot fabulists, but also, once upon a time, by certain reputable scientists.

Lemuria was originally hypothesized as a sunken land bridge between continents, to explain the discovery that the lemur, a predecessor of the monkey, had the same traits in South Africa, Madagascar, and India, even though these regions are separated by expansive bodies of water (according to Charles Darwin's then-recently published *Origin of the Species*, the animal should have developed unique traits respective to the different environments).

In 1864, a British zoologist by the name of Philip Lutley Sclater proposed the appellation, in honor of the lemur. Later in the nineteenth entry, Ernst Haeckel, a Darwin paraclete and respected scientist in his own right, proposed that Lemurians were not just lemurs, but also humans, who had migrated to India as their continent sank, eventually evolving into the first Aryans.

Once scientists accepted the theories of plate tectonics and continental drift, Lemuria fell into general disrepute (difficult as that is to believe), but was embraced by occultists including James Churchward, who believed Lemuria to be the Edenic home to 64 million telepathic beings who had invented space travel and teleportation before its destruction in the year 10,000 BCE.

Theosophist (there's that word again) Helena Petrovna Blavatsky—a prominent character in Frost's 1993 novel, *The List of Seven*—claimed in her book *The Secret Doctrine* (1888) to have learned of Lemuria in *The Book of Dzyan*, which she said was composed in Atlantis and shown to her by survivors of that lost continent. Blavatsky described Lemurians—supposedly the third of seven "Root Races" of humankind—as seven-foot-tall, egg-laying hermaphrodites with psychic abilities and a third eye. According to Blavatsky, it was the Lemurians' wickedness that caused their continent to sink into the sea.

Somehow, NBC didn't find this concept interesting enough for a series, so the network passed. No script was ever written, according to Frost.

As unfortunate as that may seem, we may never have gotten *Twin Peaks* otherwise.

***

We finally arrive at the point where you start teaming up with David Lynch. But taking a step back, when you went to see *Blue Velvet* up in Toronto, while you were shooting *The Believers*, were you just watching it as a fan, or was it because you were particularly interested in Lynch's work? What did you know about him at that point?

We met for the first time prior to my going off to make *The Believers* in spring of '86. That meeting had to do with *Goddess*, which was the first time we worked together.

Was that before *The Believers*?

It was while I was writing *The Believers*. *Goddess* was the project I wrote after *The Believers*, before the movie came out. I saw *Blue Velvet* at the Toronto Film Festival in '86 while we were in production, and *The Believers* came out the following year, in '87.

Lynch wasn't involved with the development of *Goddess*. He'd simply agreed to attach to the project. We didn't talk about it again until I finished a first draft. That would have been while he was in post for *Blue*

Velvet, I believe.

Tony Krantz introduced you and David Lynch specifically with the idea of collaborating on *Goddess*?

It was another CAA agent for *Goddess*, and then Tony helped us put together *Twin Peaks*. I'm forgetting the name of the other agent, but they thought this might be a good movie for Lynch. A producer named Bernie Schwartz had acquired the rights to Anthony Summers's book [*Goddess: The Secret Lives of Marilyn Monroe*], which was still in galleys, for United Artists. Lynch said it was a subject he was interested in and would like to make a movie about. I don't recall if he ever read the book, but we hit it off, and I went off to write the movie. I went to Ireland to visit Anthony Summers, and we had a fascinating time. He was onto his next book and hadn't gone back to Marilyn for a while. We spent a week at his place in Ireland putting the pieces of the story together.

When you were introduced to Lynch, were you familiar with his work?

Sure. *Eraserhead* and *Elephant Man*. He'd had a dreadful time on *Dune*, so *Blue Velvet* was his way of getting back to his own material.

Did David even know what *Hill Street* was? The Paley Center did a panel once on the *Pysch* homage to *Twin Peaks*—they called it "Dual Spires"—and Catherine Coulson said she didn't think David Lynch even had a TV.

I don't think he had any awareness of what was happening in television at the time. He did watch some shows later, I know, but I can't remember any specific conversations then about television. He didn't pay attention to it. In my experience, he doesn't pay much attention to other people's work, even in movies. There were a few directors he said he liked, but for the most part, he was sitting at his own table, doing his own work.

So it was really more about the chemistry, getting the two of you

together? A lot of people might think a collaboration between Mark Frost and David Lynch is not a natural thought, but rather a counterintuitive one. Your strength, it seems to me, is narrative and character development, whereas Lynch seems much less grounded in linear storytelling. I know you had that experience in experimental theater at Carnegie and the Guthrie, but it's interesting to me that somebody had the vision to pair the two of you. Do you see that?

I can see that. Leaving personal chemistry out of it, it seems like kind of a mismatch. But in another way, it matched strengths that benefited one another. What he lacked in interest in grounded narrative he made up for in sound and image and the ability to create a psychological tone that, when wedded to a strong narrative, actually enhanced his abilities. But I would say that without knowing any of that when we first sat down, we seemed to get along really well. So it was more that we enjoyed working together than it was dividing up responsibilities and saying, "You do this, and I'll do that." It was more an intuitive process than cold-blooded calculation to begin with.

The first meeting, do you remember where it was or what you talked about? Anything about it?

I remember it being at the Old World Restaurant in Westwood. We had coffee there one morning. At the time, he was living in New York and had come out to LA. He remembers it taking place someplace else. But my memory is the Old World, which is no longer there.

So that was the first-ever meeting, not the first *Twin Peaks* meeting?

Yes, spring of '86, before I went off to shoot *The Believers*.

And you talked about Marilyn Monroe?

Yes. He was fascinated with her. She plugged into his interest in the archetype of the fallen, or wounded, woman, which has been a constant theme in his work. I'm guessing that's what initially drew him to it.

Did the script mainly focus on the second half of the book, meaning her death and her relationship with the Kennedys?

It wasn't a complete biography. It picked up the story after she'd already become famous and didn't deal with any of the previous marriages. Anthony Summers was the first to research and expose her involvement with the Kennedys, ultimately leading to their falling out and her death. It was a dark vision, and his research was groundbreaking in bringing that story to the light of day.

Did you fictionalize it and retitle it?

We didn't the first time around, and it's an interesting story. As I said, I went to Ireland to work with Anthony on structure before I began the script in earnest, and we revisited a lot of his research. He had boxes and boxes of it. As we tried to reconstruct the last night of her life and follow his timeline from all the people he'd spoken to, we actually made some breakthroughs in figuring out who might have been involved—who spoke to whom and who knew what, when, and where. It culminated one long, spooky night during a massive thunderstorm in Ireland when the power went out.

We continued working by the light of his coal fire and some candles, and by the end of that night, Anthony felt he'd resolved some questions he hadn't fully broken when writing the book. We finished solving the mystery—not the crime necessarily, but the events of the night that led to her death. On the basis of that breakthrough, I wrote the script, and the producer loved it. Bernie was an experienced hand who understood studio politics. We all had a dinner with Jessica Lange, who said she wanted to play the part, and he thought that would be the final piece we needed for a green light.

What Bernie didn't know was that Ethel Kennedy had joined the board of directors of United Artists. He came back to me after the first draft and said, "They've told me we can't do this here unless we fictionalize it." So for the second draft, Marilyn and all the political figures in the book were given other names. It still proved too much for United Artists, and they put it in turnaround over a weekend and said, "Given our involvement with the Kennedy family, we can't make this movie."

Were your conversations with Bernie Schwartz or someone at United Artists?

Strictly with Bernie. He handled the studio.

And he told you very clearly that the reason they were passing on it was because of the Kennedy connection?

According to Bernie, they liked the script but said, "We can't touch this."

You just sort of wonder, if they had any familiarity with the book at all, what could they have been expecting?

That's when I asked, "Why'd they spend all this money on a book they clearly didn't read?" Bernie said something classic: "That's Hollywood, kid."

***Venus Descending*—that was the title of the fictionalized version?**

Since we had to fictionalize the whole story, we also had to move away from the *Goddess* title. *Venus Descending* was a good title, but the story didn't have the same impact as a roman à clef. It lacked the power and authenticity of biography. So despite everything it had going for it, that's where the project floundered.

David had nothing to do with writing *Goddess*? Was his name on the script?

No.

At what point does he see this script? Had he seen it yet?

He had seen the original draft, liked it, and said, "Let's turn it in and go make the movie." And then we hit this sidetrack that moved us away from it happening. Bernie may have tried to set it up somewhere else—the details are kind of hazy at this point—but it didn't go anywhere from there.

What do you think happened to Marilyn Monroe in those last days? The book says there certainly was a serious relationship at least with Robert Kennedy.

My recollection—and again this is hazy; it was over thirty years ago—is that Marilyn had been involved with Jack, but he wanted to call it quits with her and asked Bobby to break the news. Bobby liked her, and Summers's assertion was that they then become involved; she was a bird with a broken wing, something Bobby had a weakness for. He genuinely liked her and felt sorry for her. And then Bobby told her, "We have to cut this off," and she got angry and tried to confront him a number of times. Summers had phone records showing she'd attempted to contact his office in Washington repeatedly, but he never took the call.

She then learned he was planning to come out and address the American Bar Association in San Francisco, at which point she got a message to him that said, "Look, if you don't at least have the decency to speak to me face to face, I'm going to go public with this story." I believe that's all in the book. At which point, Summers alleged, Bobby hired a private plane that flew him to Santa Monica—the small airport there. And he helicoptered over to a party at Peter Lawford's house—he was married to the Kennedys' sister—big house on the beach in Santa Monica.

As Summers reconstructed it, Marilyn was under the care of a psychiatrist and told him all this. She had taken a heavy dose of the sedative he'd been prescribing to her that night, then called Lawford's house making threats. Apparently Bobby, Peter Lawford, and the psychiatrist went to her house to calm her down, which was not far from the beach house in Brentwood. And supposedly, a terrible scene ensued. Things got out of hand. They asked the psychiatrist to inject her with a sedative because she was so distraught, without realizing that she'd already taken a heavy dose of barbiturates. This sent her into cardiac arrest, at which point they called an ambulance. Tony had spoken to the ambulance driver—that's all in the book. They started taking her to the local hospital, and halfway there, the ambulance attendant announced she was gone. At which point, Bobby—who was allegedly in the ambulance—said, "Take her back." So they put her back in the bedroom and staged the scene to make it look like a suicide. They supposedly called in a team to help make that happen—none of which has ever been fully substantiated, by the way, but this was the theory. And that was the news that broke to the world the next day—that she'd been found by her housekeeper, who allegedly knew the truth and had been bought off.

There were a lot of strange circumstances we examined that night—among them the whereabouts of her publicist, who was at a concert at the Hollywood Bowl, bringing her into it to help deal with the aftermath. She left the concert in a hurry, if I remember correctly, and was never actually interviewed by the LAPD because she was immediately afterward given a job with Radio Free America or some other government organization that moved her overseas soon after the event.

There were a lot of strange elements like that. Maybe the biggest shocker that Summers hit on was that as a result of RFK's prosecution—some would say obsession—to destroy Jimmy Hoffa, Hoffa hired his surveillance expert, Bernie Spindell, to wire Marilyn's house. These wires were discovered many years later when a new owner renovated it, running through the walls and the roofing. Spindell apparently claimed he had a tape of what happened that night at the house. These details are all in the book. The implication was that this tape existed, and it somehow got to Hoffa—or somebody on his side—and the prosecution of Hoffa was dropped. In 1969, Spindell was arrested for another offense and thrown in prison. Whatever evidence he might have had was seized, and I believe he died in prison within a couple years. Another story I heard was that Francis Coppola based the character Gene Hackman played in *The Conversation*, Harry Caul, to some degree on Spindell.

Wow, that's some story. Were you familiar with the book before Bernie asked you to adapt it?

No, I read it as a result of being offered the job and thought it was riveting.

How do you react when something like that happens? You put all that work into a project you believe in, and then it gets shot down for political reasons?

You embrace the immortal words of Bernie Schwartz [laughs] and say, "That's Hollywood, kid," because literally things like this happen all the time for all sorts of ancillary issues that have nothing to do with the intrinsic merits of the project. Alan Arkin told me the same thing years earlier: "It's a terrible way to make a terrific living." But that's how it is. No rhyme or reason. People become successful for reasons you can't discern. Others fail for reasons that seem equally impenetrable. It's a bizarre alternate universe, particularly the movie business. I had a producer friend, really successful, who used to say, "You work and work and grind away at this, and if you're really unlucky, you actually have to make a movie." So over time, you see enough evidence to support Bernie's premise: "That's Hollywood, kid."

Was it difficult for you to accept at the time?

That was my first experience of it. You have to learn that if this is the game you want to play, those are the rules. Protesting or deciding they're unfair or unreasonable or not the way things should be isn't going to change the fact that this is how the game is played. So you either make your peace with it, or you do something else.

Treacherous world out there, Hollywood.

Just make sure you get paid. That's the mantra, and it hasn't gotten better. In fact, I think it's gotten appreciably worse.

Was *One Saliva Bubble* the next thing that you worked on, you and David together?

Yes. He had a deal with Dino De Laurentiis under which he'd made *Blue Velvet*. I think that was Dino's way of apologizing for *Dune*, in a weird way. He allowed Lynch to play in his own sandbox again. So he had his deal there and an office at Dino's on Wilshire Boulevard, and that's where we wrote the script. I'm guessing this is early '88. Those other scripts I mentioned came into play before *One Saliva Bubble*.

What made you and David decide to work together again, after *Goddess*, on *One Saliva Bubble*?

This was the first time we worked together, actively writing something. He had the initial idea and the title [for *One Saliva Bubble*], but not a whole lot more than that. It was an idea in search of a narrative and execution.

Do you remember what the idea was?

Secret government facility. A saliva bubble pops out of a cretinous security guard's mouth when he laughs at a dumb joke. Floats down the corridor into a lab and wedges between two wires in a console, causing a malfunction in a satellite up in space—some sort of aimed ray weapon. This changes its aim, and a countdown begins. I think he had that much, and he had this idea that the ray from the weapon causes people to change personalities with the person they're adjacent to. So we went to work populating the world and what happens to it as a result, and it all flows from there. And it was the most fun thing to write. Over a couple of months, we went out to lunch every day and never stopped laughing. And it's a pretty freakin' funny script, really a laugh riot.

I hate when people try to interpret everything you or David do through the lens of *Twin Peaks*, but I did seem to notice some tonal

similarities between *One Saliva Bubble* and the Las Vegas scenes in *The Return*.

There may be a few similarities. We had a genius and an idiot [in *One Saliva Bubble*] played by the same actor, right?

You did.

That was going to be the Martin Short character, the professor and the idiot. And then there was the hit man and the milquetoast husband. That was Steve Martin.

There was no overt referencing of *One Saliva Bubble* when you and David were writing *The Return*?

Honestly, no, it never even came up in conversation. It had been thirty years since we'd written it, and I haven't read it since probably 1990. I remember highlights, but not the moment-to-moment beats.

Was anyone else cast?

That was as far as we got, but their deals were in place. Lynch would remember better than I, but we were within weeks of preproduction, so it was real, it was happening. And then Dino revealed he'd gone belly-up, lost his whole company. Everything shut down in one day. Another of those "That's show business, kid" moments. Out of your control.

Yeah, but that was two in a row for you, and you had not really encountered a situation like that until then, right?

Look, I knew that the vagaries of the business were extreme. I'd learned that in the seventies from Alan Arkin, and there's William Goldman's famous maxim: "Nobody knows anything." You don't know what's going to happen; they happen for the strangest reasons, often not for the best or even logical reasons. So you have to let it roll off your back. I always think of the great last line from *Chinatown*—and Bob Towne knows the insanity of the business better than anybody alive. "Forget it, Jake, it's Chinatown" might as well have been his metaphor for Hollywood.

Speaking of hard-boiled private eyes, was that Thursby character who switches personalities with Wally in *One Saliva Bubble* named after Floyd Thursby from *The Maltese Falcon*?

Yes, exactly right.

Are you a fan of hard-boiled detective fiction?

Very much so. I named a character in season one of *Twin Peaks* after Edward Robinson's investigator in *Double Indemnity*, Walter Neff. There are references to noir throughout. The character of Maddie, the double for Laura, comes from *Vertigo*, and there are others as well.

How about Laura herself? Didn't she come from the Otto Preminger movie?

Of course. My experience of those films was more complete than David's. He has a good grounding in film history, but he tends to focus on the few individual movies he's drawn to. My interest has always been more broadly applied to genres as a whole. So the movies we knew about, that we both appreciated, obviously ones like *Sunset Blvd.*, and the Gordon Cole reference—

Who named Gordon Cole—you or David?

I don't remember.

He's also in *One Saliva Bubble*. He doesn't appear, but he's mentioned on a couple of occasions.

We loved the idea that Gordon Cole was seen only momentarily in *Sunset Blvd.* They imbued this essentially off-screen character with abilities and powers you never saw demonstrated, so it became an inside joke for us. When we wrote Lynch's character, it seemed like a perfect opening.

I know that *Hill Street* had very strong comedic elements to it, but *One Saliva Bubble* seemed like something completely new for you. It's hilarious, very wacky. The professor was definitely evoking Dr. Hugo Quackenbush, the Groucho Marx character in *A Day at the Races*, for me. Was it an adjustment for you? Was it hard to switch to something like that?

That had always been a huge interest of mine. I mentioned that during my high school years in Minneapolis, I became enamored with the Marx Brothers, Buster Keaton, W. C. Fields. Lynch was a huge fan of Fields, and there's more than a little Fields in the Gordon Cole character—you definitely see some of that in his timing. The Marx Brothers were right up my alley. I was always trying to find a way to use that kind of humor.

Did you contribute a lot of humor to *Hill Street Blues* as well?

Yeah, and I wrote a couple of spec comedies back then that helped me get shots at writing movies. I wanted to make it clear that was in my wheelhouse, so I didn't get stuck writing procedurals or thrillers or horror movies.

So the *One Saliva Bubble* tone was something you were very comfortable with?

Yes. When you create an absurd universe like that, where anything can happen, you're in Marx Brothers territory. And that's great fun to play with. There hadn't been many body-switching comedies at that point, other than *All of Me*, the Steve Martin comedy. Steve really wanted to play this part and would have been fantastic in it. They both would have. Marty Short makes me laugh more than anybody I can think of. He's one of the world's funniest people.

Were you a big *SCTV* fan?

I loved *SCTV*. Like for everyone else in my generation, *SNL* was a big influence, but I thought *SCTV* took it to another level. That show was flat-out brilliant.

All of Me was 1984, so three years before *One Saliva Bubble*.

Yes, but the idea of switching bodies is as old as time. Shakespeare played with it frequently; switching bodies, or identities, has been a staple of comedy for centuries.

Is it possible to look at *One Saliva Bubble* and say, "This is a Mark Frost–type joke" or "That's a David Lynch–type joke"?

You tell me. Everything was so up for grabs. We were just making it up as we went along.

OK, so moving on to *The Lemurians*. Legend has it that when Dino went bankrupt, Tony Krantz said to you and David, "Why don't you try TV?" Is that what happened?

That's pretty close to the chronology. Dino went belly-up in 1988, and it was on the heels of that that Krantz came to us. At that point, he didn't directly represent either of us; he was a young agent with a lot of ambition who thought this would be a great thing to put together.

But he was at CAA, where you were both represented?

Right.

How did you initially react to that? You personally didn't have a deal with Dino, right? You could have gone off and done anything at that point, right?

No, I didn't have any overall deals anywhere. I've never really wanted to be anything other than a free agent. I appreciate my freedom too much and didn't like the idea of being beholden to any one shop.

You could have gone off and done anything at that point, and you had turned Steven Bochco down on *LA Law* so you could go on and write films, and yet here you are turning to TV again.

I thought it was an interesting idea. We had enjoyed working on *One Saliva Bubble* so much. It was a way to keep the fun rolling, and it came forward on a silver platter, so Arkin's Law came into play for me: "Say yes to everything." There's a corollary to it I also ascribe to called Schlesinger's Law. John believed you should always alternate projects: do one for yourself, then do one for the suits. *Bubble* had been a personal project, so it was time to do one for them. So we had a couple of preliminary conversations with ABC about what they were looking for, in which they mentioned the genre of the nighttime soap, and specifically *Peyton Place*.

Are we talking about *The Lemurians* or *Twin Peaks*? Didn't *Lemurians* come first?

Twin Peaks. *The Lemurians* was another thing we did for our own amusement.

Did you and David write anything for it?

If there's a treatment, it would be three or four pages—if it exists, and I don't remember if it does. I seem to recall we had something on paper, but it was pretty out there. It made *Twin Peaks* look like *Peyton Place*.

In *Reflections: An Oral History of Twin Peaks,* Tony Krantz tells Brad Dukes that he shopped *Lemurians* to NBC, but that Brandon Tartikoff—who was entertainment president at the time—wanted to make a movie out of it whereas David was insisting on a series. Accurate?

Sounds about right. I don't think we ever had a meeting at NBC. That may have been just Tony going to Brandon and saying, "The guys have this idea." Remember, this is prior to *Twin Peaks*, so we didn't have a track record in television at that point, and it was a weird one. I'm not surprised. To Brandon's credit, he wanted to do something with it, but I can easily see them thinking, "This doesn't feel like an NBC series to us." But that's the extent of my memories of it.

Staying on *Lemurians* for a little bit, was that your idea or David's idea?

I don't remember who mentioned it first. I knew about it from studying some gonzo New Age stuff I was looking at, and this was one of the more out-there threads of inquiry I'd encountered.

Did he know about it also?

He'd heard about it. There was a famous New Age bookstore on Melrose for about fifty years called the Bodhi Tree, and I used to go in every once in a while to hunt around for obscure and interesting stuff. But we'd both heard legends about Lemuria, which is often compared to Atlantis as a lost continent and civilization—with Lemuria supposedly predating Atlantis, if I remember my obscure prehistorical, nineteenth-century legends correctly.

When did you start to get interested in that?

College years. My best friend in high school in Minneapolis had gone to UCLA when I went to Carnegie, and he had a girlfriend who was involved with a New Age group. He started going to these meetings and told me about this alternate way of looking at spirituality, which I hadn't heard much about. I found it intriguing and started reading some things he suggested—among them were a couple of volumes of [Jiddu] Krishnamurti's. This was early to midseventies. So I started digging deeper and found a fascinating alternate theory of human history that became a pet line of inquiry for me.

There's this terrific line in *The Great Gatsby* where Nick Carraway is at a party with Tom Buchanan and Myrtle Wilson. He sees someone

down on the street looking up at the window, and he says he feels both within and without—an insider and an outsider. There he is physically inside the party, but he relates perhaps more to the man on the street. With respect to this New Age material, were you an insider or an outsider? Or were you straddling the line?

This was an inherent interest that emerged first as a teenager, realizing I wasn't encultured in any particular religious theory or body of thought, so I was left to my own perceptions. I've always felt there was more to the world and the reality we experience than what my culture was telling me. It just didn't seem convincing to me that "There's only the physical world; it's only what we can see and measure. You're born and then you die and then you rot." I mean, not only was that an unappealing scenario for all sorts of obvious reasons, it just didn't square with what my intuition was telling me—that there was more here than meets the eye. So that's what led me into this line of inquiry, and when my friend started sending me ideas to look at or books to read, I followed that line.

I became interested in a book by Aldous Huxley called *The Perennial Philosophy* in college. Huxley talks about the basic unity that lies at the heart of all spiritual pursuits, some of which make it into the actual structure of religions in human history—whether they last or become failed religions, or religions that are superseded by others. But what persists is this impulse and conviction in freethinkers that a spiritual dimension to life is available to you if you study and open your eyes to it. So that was the stance I took at that point in my life, that I was going to conduct my own open-minded inquiry and come to my own conclusions.

What happened?

The words that meant the most to me were just "Believe what you believe. Don't believe something because somebody tells you to believe it. Test it, apply rigor to it. Don't take it at face value, and then see where that leads you." Create a dialogue with reality and try to fine-tune your intuitive responses to it in order to see what feels true and what feels false. That was where I came down on it. And I found I was a skeptic regarding organized religion. I did not want to accept somebody else's word at face value, that they had the key or the answer to understanding the deeper layers of existence.

The people who really spoke to me in the books I was looking at were the ones saying, "Figure it out for yourself." And that's one of the key contributions of Krishnamurti. He was one of the first who was held up as a guru who said, "Wait a minute, no, I don't want to be anybody's guru. I want people to be their own gurus; that's the future." And that was enormously appealing to me.

This is where we start to touch on Theosophy, which I know you've spoken about with respect to the Black Lodge and your novel *The List of Seven*, which was published in 1993—your first novel. But Helena Blavatsky did speak about *Lemurians*. She called them the third root race—there were going to be seven altogether. Was Theosophy something you knew a lot about by the time of *Lemurians*, or did you discover it during your actual research for the project?

The work my friend had first led me to was a lineage, or an offshoot, of Theosophy. The group was called the Aquarian Fellowship, and they followed a line of thinking developed by a writer named Alice Bailey, who was originally a Theosophist—not a contemporary of Blavatsky, but the second wave of Theosophists, like Annie Besant. She started writing in the twenties, but when Theosophy split after Krishnamurti walked away from it, Alice Bailey picked up the mantle and wrote over twenty books, which she claimed to be receiving through direct transmission from a Tibetan master. So that's how I first learned about Theosophy, through her works on the shelves of the Bodhi Tree in LA.

Did you get pretty deep into Theosophy?

Not to the point I ever called myself a Theosophist. You grow up in 1950s/1960s WASP America, and your options were evangelical Christian, Episcopalian, Methodist, Lutheran—all established, fairly rigid institutions. Or, if you're born into it, Roman Catholicism—which seemed more like a giant global corporation to me than it did a spiritual discipline. Or there was atheism—which felt barren and intellectually dry. That's what was on the menu in the fifties and sixties, and I thought, "Well, there's got to be more to it than that," and that's why I was interested in finding people who were writing about it in a different way, presenting alternate theories about what the heck we're doing here.

But at the same time, you did tell me early on that you have always had a healthy distrust of authority, which I guess would make you skeptical of anything organized.

That was also baked into the generational movement of the time. When you're in high school during the '68 election, the protests in Chicago, everything that happened in that decade—the assassinations, civil rights, Vietnam, all the political chicanery and the rise of Richard Nixon—if you didn't have a deep distrust of authority, you were just going to sign on to whatever they put in front of you and call it a day.

Even before that, the JFK assassination.

That was the thing that woke it up for me, when the government published the Warren report and said, "Well, here it is, this is how it happened," and your response is, "Wait a minute, what if that isn't true?" That was the first spark of antiauthoritarianism taking root in my personality, and not uniquely. It was true for huge numbers of people at that time.

Interesting then that some of your most memorable characters represent authority to an extent, but ultimately refuse to follow it to the letter.

I think you can see that as a theme. Characters like Agent Cooper, for instance.

Furillo, too, did things his own way in *Hill Street*.

Responsible leadership requires you to question circumstances around you. Otherwise, you're drifting inevitably toward fascism. We're seeing that in abundance right now.

Richard Shaver and Ray Palmer, who come up many years later in your work, in *The Secret History of Twin Peaks*, are also tied to Lemuria. When did you come upon that story?

Blavatsky wrote about it, but not a lot of contemporary scholars took an interest in Lemurians, so I'm sure I must have come across Shaver and Palmer at the time. I don't remember specifically reading them then but definitely while working on *The Secret History*.

Interesting that you went back to the Lemurians all those years later.

I began to think of it as part of a unified field theory of strangeness, and you can fold into that the UFO inquiry and related phenomena, because it's part of the "uncanny valley" idea in human history. How do we explain these consistent experiences of people who recount deeply strange encounters that either religion or science haven't been able to explain?

I read a description of *The Lemurians* somewhere that said you and David had Jacques Cousteau's submarine hitting something underwater, which—

As I remember, he accidentally moves a rock somewhere deep on the seafloor, opening up either a tunnel or portal that lets the Lemurians back into the world—that they had somehow earlier been sealed off. A phrase we came up with—I think it's in the treatment—went something like, "Jacques, Jacques, you had to move that rock." Which, as I mention it, suggests more of a *One Saliva Bubble* approach to the material.

So it was wacky?

That's my recollection.

Were these Lemurians going to be giant hermaphrodites, the way Blavatsky described them?

I don't remember how detailed our descriptions of them were, but in the back of my mind, I was thinking of a 1960s series—*The Invaders*, starring Roy Thinnes—in which the aliens are already here. That was the heart of the idea.

Were there FBI agents trying to track them down?

Possibly, but at least initially, I think it was more of a local law enforcement issue.

Is Colin Wilson someone whose work interests you?

Colin Wilson was one of the first to take an omnibus view of all these things. I read a lot of his work in the seventies, starting with *The Outsider*, then a book called *The Occult: A History*. He treated the whole area as a focus for inquiry, and there were many similarities among all these disparate phenomena, overlapping like a Venn diagram. He was the first contemporary author I encountered who put those pieces of the puzzle together.

If you were reading people like Wilson in the seventies, then that means that by the time you were writing *The Believers* you were already immersed in the occult. So there was some deeper connection to the material for you, given the supernaturalism in that film.

Yes, I'd say that's true. Voodoo, Santeria—these were all part of Wilson's fascination with aboriginal belief systems surviving into the modern world.

What about H. P. Lovecraft? Are you familiar with his work?

I did read Lovecraft. He struck me as a very sad person who suffered from a family history of serious mental illness. His main theme was deeply disturbing: There were ancient malign beings who did not hold us in high regard, didn't mean well for us, and they might come back at any moment to destroy us. There may have been an echo of that in *The Lemurians* as well.

Also in the *Paladin Prophecy* trilogy—the young-adult novels you published between 2012 and 2015.

Right, I did draw on all of this research and reading I'd done over the years for the *Paladin Prophecy* books.

You know, I look at all three of these busted projects—*Goddess*, *One Saliva Bubble*, and *The Lemurians*—and I see elements of all three in *Twin Peaks*: troubled blonde, electricity going haywire, cosmic battle between good and evil.

Any project you do contains bits and pieces of things that didn't work somewhere else. That's certainly a constant in Hollywood; people have a theme or a character or a setting in a project that didn't go the distance that they resurrect in something else—that's human nature. It's probably not even a conscious process. Thematically, the good-versus-evil idea—that's something you can apply universally to almost any story. I know Lynch always had a childlike fascination and fear of electricity, so that appears in *Ronnie Rocket* [an unproduced film project Lynch wrote and hoped to direct] and other things he's done over the years. That's clearly his influence. Electricity doesn't trouble me the way it does him. I plug something in a wall socket, and it makes something else work; that's the extent of it for me. But he's always had a fear and fascination of it that frankly I don't share.

But good versus evil—that seems so Frostian.

That was the shape of the world I grew up in. The long shadow of World War II. The Cold War. Vietnam. Generational conflicts. A crooked president. Guess I came by it honestly.

Which leads very conveniently into our next subject, which I'm sure a lot of people have been waiting for: *Twin Peaks.*

❧

A promo postcard of the "Welcome to Twin Peaks" sign from Gold Box DVD Set
(photo courtesy of CBS Home Video)

David Lynch and a bearded Mark Frost back in the day, on the set of The Great Northern. *(photo courtesy of Mischa Cronin. ABC).*

Mark's dad, Warren (Doc Will Hayward), a towering figure in Twin Peaks lore, here towers over the unseen body of Laura Palmer in the pilot episode *(photo courtesy of ABC).*

The 1908 murder of twenty-year-old domestic Hazel Drew in Sand Lake, New York (still unsolved), which Frost had heard about from his grandmother, helped inspire the Laura Palmer murder arc.

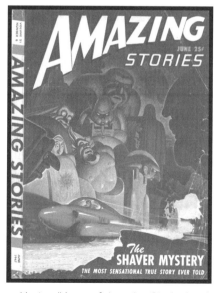

The June 1947 "Shaver Mystery" issue of *Amazing Stories* inspired *The Lemurians*, a TV show concept created by Frost and Lynch before *Twin Peaks*, and resurfaced many years later in *The Secret History of Twin Peaks*, Frost's 2016 novel. Note that the yarn is touted as "The Most Sensational True Story Ever Told."

PROPAGANDA FILMS
MEMO

PHONE # (213)   FAX #(213)

To: Mark Frost/David Latt

FROM: Tim Clawson

RE: Production Notes

DATE: 2/9/89

Here are just some production notes which I mentioned to both Eugene and Margaux that you might want to follow up.

Laura Palmer- Actress in the water? How do you keep her from freezing? How do you keep her from shivering involunarily? She's supposed to be dead. Is this a stunt? There are a lot of photos of Laura Palmer throughout the film, as wil as a home video picnic scene. Be sure to note when scheduling this actress.

Prosthetics make-up - For dead Laura Palmer, for severly beaten Sharon Pulaski, fight scene?

Stunts - Bobby backing down Shelly's driveway at 30mph, bar fight, semi truck screeching to a halt in front of Sharon Pulaski...

Music Clearance- for song the bar band will play...need track prepared ahead of time for the shoot in order to do sync playback...Rhapsody in Blue cleared? Dale Cooper whistles this throughout.

24 fps video- Needed for all video playback situations where dialogue is in same shot. Need to transfer all playback footage to 24fps video as well as playback on 24fps equipment and monitors.

Reflection of motorcycle in Donna's eye- video effect>? film optical? going to be tough if the camera that is actually shooting Donna is moving on this shot.

Talent budget- review talent deals against day out of days. Also check talent travel and living budget against schedule.

Production notes — neither requested nor paid any attention to by Frost and Lynch — from Tim Clawson at Propaganda Films, which had minimal involvement in the pilot *(courtesy of Mischa Cronin)*.

The Carnegie Tech Hollywood mafia: Frost (second from right), along with Bruce Weitz, Steven Bochco, Barbara Bosson, and Charles Haid, during 1983 homecoming at the university (now known as Carnegie Mellon) *(photo courtesy of Carnegie Mellon University Libraries).*

Tyrone Guthrie — a giant in the theater world and one of the most influential people in Frost's life — surveys his newly built theater in Minneapolis, where Frost spent hundreds of hours as an intern during his teen years *(courtesy of the Guthrie Theater).*

6

"There's a Giant in Cooper's Room"

(Twin Peaks, Seasons 1-2)

So much has been written about the first two seasons of *Twin Peaks* that it can be a challenge excavating anything previously unearthed. The ABC TV series—which aired for just two seasons (thirty episodes) between April 8, 1990, and June 10, 1991, and struggled mightily from a ratings standpoint for the bulk of that time—has spawned not just entire books, but podcasts, webcasts, websites, fan forums, fanzines, fan cuts, documentaries, specially themed issues of academic journals, symposiums, and at least two annual fan festivals devoted solely to the series.

Much attention has been paid—rightfully so—to the show's transformative impact on the television landscape, by pioneering the notion that episodic drama can be experimental, artful, oblique, challenging—and yet still impactful. Television auteurs including David Chase, Sam Esmail, Damon Lindelof, Noah Hawley, and Jane Campion all have cited *Twin Peaks* as hugely influential on their own work and, in some cases, even on their choice of career, and that alone catapults it into the pantheon of most consequential television series of all time.

Nearly 35 million viewers tuned in to the two-hour pilot of *Twin Peaks* on Sunday, April 8, 1990, accounting for one-third of all the television sets in use at the time. It was the fifth-highest-rated show of the week. Critics were orgiastic. Four nights later, the series moved to its regular time slot, Thursdays at 9 p.m., up against NBC's "Must See TV" lineup of the time, which included, also at 9 p.m., *Cheers*. Ratings dipped slightly, as expected, but *kept* dropping, *not* as expected. By the penultimate episode of the first season, *Twin Peaks* ranked fortieth among all prime-time broadcast network shows; the final episode of the season—the only episode ever directed by Frost—was moved to a Wednesday night just to avoid the NBC Thursday juggernaut. While the show garnered fourteen Emmy nominations (but won just two awards), there were serious debates within ABC's executive suites about whether or not *Twin Peaks* would return; it did, but—much to the fury of Frost and Lynch—on Saturday nights, when almost nobody, and *certainly* nobody in the show's target demographic, was likely to be watching, and of course ratings continued to plummet. This led to increasingly fractious relationships not just between the creators and the network, but also with many TV critics, who were demanding a solution to the mystery of who killed Laura Palmer. Eventually, seven episodes into the second season, they got it, triggering a whole new set of creative challenges, exacerbated by political machinations instigated by certain cast members. ABC placed the show on hiatus for almost two months before airing the two-part series finale (or so we thought at the time), which barely registered a blip ratingwise at the time, but has since come to be appreciated by anyone with any taste in television as one of the greatest series finales of all time.

Everyone who loves *Twin Peaks* loves it for his or her own reasons—the characters, the quirkiness, the mystery, the visual iconography, the music, the supernaturalness of it all—but there's something about the mythology of it—Bob, the Red Room, Owl Cave, the Dweller on the Threshold, the Man from Another Place (this could take a while)—that breeds obsessive devotion and deconstruction. Perhaps just as intriguing—both to fans and students of the show—is the history *behind* it, which has achieved mythic status of its own. Which creator is responsible for which elements? Who was around for which episodes, and who was off making movies instead? Who bears ultimate responsibility for the collapse in the middle of season two? How did Mark Frost *really* feel about Lynch discarding the original conclusion of the series finale, as scripted by Frost, Harley Peyton, and Robert Engels?

Why wasn't Frost involved in the theatrical sequel, *Fire Walk With Me?* Let's get to the bottom of it.

***

I wanted to start off talking about *Twin Peaks* by seeing if I could clear up the confusion about the famous coffee shop meeting. We've talked about how you and David remember your first meeting differently, but I always thought the story was that you and David met at a coffee shop when you were tossing around the ideas that became *Northwest Passage*, the original title for *Twin Peaks*, and I thought that was where the discrepancy in memory came from—not from your first meeting ever.

He doesn't seem to recall the very first meeting we had, which was exclusively about *Goddess*. I remember that one very particularly at the Old World Restaurant in Westwood. After *Goddess* crashed, he had his office at Dino De Laurentiis's company on Wilshire Boulevard, and there was an old coffee shop called Nibblers we used to go to that was near his office. That was a frequent location for lunch. As we started to speak more specifically about *Northwest Passage*, we may have had one or two conversations there, but once we got down to business, it was more often at Du-par's in Studio City.

Speaking of *Northwest Passage*, was the title changed to *Twin Peaks* because *Northwest Passage* was too similar to something else?

As I remember it, *Northwest Passage* was a copyrighted title held by the old MGM library—the old Spencer Tracy movie. They apparently didn't want anyone else using that title.

And was it originally set in North Dakota?

We talked about the Dakotas, which I knew from my years in Minnesota, but I can vividly remember having this lunch at Du-par's where we drew a map of the town. We were trying to think of a title, and David was writing on the back of a placemat. I was describing what I was seeing, and he was translating it into a map. "There's a mountain here" and "There's a mountain there." We were naming things, and the town was in between—a valley and a river, a waterfall and a lake. When we looked at the map after we finished it and saw these two big mountains, the title *Twin Peaks* came to mind. I can't remember which of us said it first, but as soon as one of did, it was, "Well, OK, that's it."

Was all of this before or after you had the body of the young woman coming up on the lake?

That would have been after. We'd already written the first draft.

I've read that you and David famously each came up with that idea of the young woman's body on the lake independently, at more or less the same time. You and I have spoken about how you were at least partly inspired by the 1908 murder of a woman named Hazel Drew up in Taborton, New York, where your grandmother lived—a murder that's never been solved. I've been spending a lot of time looking into that murder, as you know, and have come across some very interesting leads suggesting questionable behavior by county authorities, which Mark Givens, of *Deer Meadow Radio*, and I are still looking into. But you've also mentioned to me that Hazel was just one of two incidents that you were drawing on with respect to Laura Palmer in *Twin Peaks*, and I've never really heard you talk about the other one.

The other happened when I was in seventh or eighth grade living in Glendale [California]. My dad, for a period of time—before he went back for his master's degree at Occidental—was supporting the family by selling real estate, working for a guy in Glendale. He had a successful real estate firm, and they were friends of the family. We were close with them and did a lot of things socially.

They had two kids—a daughter, Susan, who was a year older than me, and a son, Sandy, who was a year younger. My brother and I were friends with Sandy. Susan was lovely and vivacious and friendly, and I had a twelve-year-old's crush on her. She went away to a private girls' school up north, near San Luis Obispo. In the middle of seventh grade, we got the horrible news that an escaped inmate from Atascadero, the criminal mental hospital, had kidnapped and assaulted and murdered her.

We'd never experienced anything like this. Her parents asked my parents if the brother could stay with us for the weekend, because they had to go up and retrieve Susan's body and meet with the police. We knew about it and the brother didn't, and we were instructed not to tell him. So we had to go through this weekend—I think my brother knew too—of holding this horrible reality about his sister and having to keep it a secret. It was just an awful situation. I suppose it was the right thing to do, but the family was devastated, and it charged the memory in a way that left a mark on everyone else involved.

How much longer did you live in Glendale after that?

Within a year, we were gone to Minnesota.

Do you remember what kind of impact that had on your friend, once he found out, and on his family?

I saw them later, when I moved back to California. The mother had never fully recovered—according to Sandy, who told me she'd been deeply, deeply scarred. He'd gone on to have a relatively normal life, but there was a sadness about him. I saw him a few times when I was back in Los Angeles. Something like that happens, and you're heavily affected the rest of your life. I drew on a lot of those feelings for the storytelling in the pilot.

Was Susan the only person killed by this escaped inmate?

As far as I know.

Getting back to all those changes that happened between the first draft and what we eventually see on screen—even the small things,

like Sheriff Steadman becoming Truman or Audrey getting such a large role or Bernie Hill becoming Hawk, Jacoby and the Log Lady weren't even in the *Northwest Passage* script. How do things like that happen?

There's no one way they happen. In the case of Audrey, after casting Sherilyn Fenn—I'd seen her in a movie called *Two Moon Junction*, a softcore eighties feature—directed by a purveyor of this genre named Zalman King.

Right, *Red Shoe Diaries*.

Yes, *Red Shoe Diaries* was later—the most successful example of the brand he was selling. So I saw the movie and drew David's attention to her, saying, "This could be Audrey." So her coming on board resulted in the character getting more screen time. With Steadman—what happens with any script that's going to air, you have a research company do legal clearances for you. The gold standard in television for decades was a company called de Forest Research, founded by a close college friend of my parents named Kellum de Forest. I remember going to their house frequently as a kid. Years later, I met Kellum again when I was on *Hill Street*, because they were vetting scripts for us there. So we sent the pilot script to de Forest for legal clearances, and the name Steadman came back as unavailable for some reason.

What about the additions of Jacoby and the Log Lady?

Jacoby was a character I suggested, figuring that Laura would have been under the care of a psychiatrist given her various issues. So he was a late addition to the script. And when Russ Tamblyn came in for the part, we both loved him so much as a person and his performance that the character became gradually more prominent. The Log Lady was a character that Catherine [Coulson] and David had conceived years before, and he wanted to include her in there. She was perfect as the town eccentric and made an indelible impression from her first scene, flipping the lights on and off during that town meeting. Those kinds of moments are fortuitous, often happenstance—and Lynch is really good at being alert to them during production—but can end up becoming an indelible part of the overall fabric.

Particularly interesting is the change of Bernie Hill to Hawk. The *Paladin* trilogy, the young adult books that you wrote, feature the character of Coach Jericho, and Native Americans have a significant presence in *Secret History of Twin Peaks*. That seems like more than a coincidence.

That came from me. I'd been interested in—and during my years in Minneapolis became involved with—Native American issues. I ran a theater company that produced an annual show based on writings and poetry from students at a school run by the American Indian Movement called the Little Red School House in St. Paul. I thought we should have a Native American presence in the town, and that was how Deputy Hill became Hawk. Again, really helped by a wonderful piece of casting. When Michael Horse walked in the room, we both knew he was our guy. He's a longtime friend, with a rich, soulful authenticity about him. In season one, I found myself writing more and more for Hawk, because I loved Michael and his work so much.

Much has been written about David Lynch and his style of casting, where he doesn't have people read; he just sits and talks with them. So you cast two shows with him; what's your style of casting, and how did casting work for seasons one, two, and three of *Twin Peaks*? Were you both in the room? Is your style similar to or different from his? And if it's different, how does each of you accommodate the other?

It's a little different. We were both there when we cast the pilot—sat with everybody, meeting with them, and going through the process that way. Totally in agreement about who we liked in each instance. I told him, "You're the director, you get final call on the pilot obviously, but I want to make sure I'm comfortable with people I'm going to have a working relationship with." Once the show started, he wasn't around for the day-to-day episodic casting.

If you're casting on your own, like for the second season, did you cast the same way or did you read?

I would occasionally read, but for instance, when David Duchovny came in, he didn't read. I just met with him and gave him the part. It varies. There were times I wanted to hear a line read this way or that, but just as often, I went with someone because I knew and respected their work.

On the first season, even though you don't have author credit on every episode, every script did go through you, right?

Yes. Coming from the Bochco school, the maxim was every episode passes through your hands at the beginning and at the end, but if you didn't do the first draft, you don't take credit for it. Your job is to make sure the show is on form and your stamp of approval is on every script. That often meant, depending on who it was coming from, fairly substantial rewrites. That's part of the job. That's what a showrunner does.

In terms of the staff, Harley [Peyton] had the strongest voice besides mine on writing the show after the pilot. He was the most reliable person in terms of overall narrative, who I relied on to talk things through. He was also the most experienced writer in the group.

Would the season one scripts also go through David, or was he not so involved in the writing?

He wasn't involved in the writing that much. David and I wrote the first and second episodes of season one, but beyond that, he had almost no input into the storytelling. I'd send him finished scripts, and I don't remember ever getting back substantive notes. He would talk about punctuation more than he would story, plot, and character. You know, he was off making a movie.

Wild at Heart?

Right, so he was literally not around. When you're directing a movie, you're not available. I didn't expect him there, and he wasn't planning on being there. That's the way it worked out.

You knew from the beginning that he was going off to work on a film rather than being involved in the day-to-day operation of the show?

That was always the plan.

I've seen explanations of the European ending that David Lynch had this catharsis when he was in the parking lot and he put his hand on a car. Where were you? You must have had something to do with that ending?

We had a contract with Worldvision—the Spelling distribution arm—that if the series didn't get picked up, they could release the pilot as a movie in Europe. For that to work, they needed a closed ending. We felt pretty confident the series was going to get picked up, so the idea of coming up with an ending felt obligatory, and we thought it would never be widely seen. We'd shot the pilot, showed it to ABC, and there was a buzz already building about the show, but we still owed Worldvision this ending, which felt kind of faintly ridiculous. But Lynch had this notion about Killer Bob inspired by an often-described moment where Frank Silva was hiding on set during a take, and David saw his face in a mirror in the dailies. That idea had just stayed in his head. It became a direct, if abrupt, way to weld an ending onto a story that was not designed to have one there.

He just called you up and said, "Hey, Mark, this is how I want to end it"?

I think he sent me a page he'd written—the chant had come to him about "Fire Walk With Me." Honestly, I never saw it as intrinsic to the pilot, but we obviously incorporated a lot of these ideas later more artfully into the overall story. He shot it months after we finished the pilot on some tiny little soundstage over in Hollywood. And after seeing it, I thought, "Great, that fulfills our obligation," but I was confident the series was going to be picked up, so it seemed moot at that point.

When you saw that poem, "Fire Walk With Me," did you wonder what that means or what it was about?

I didn't think anyone would ever see the ending, so it struck me as utilitarian, it did the job. It kicked up some dust and gave a sense of mystery that was a substitute for an ending, which is all it was supposed to do. It was like building a nice car and forgetting to put on a trailer hitch, so we had to hastily add one, but it didn't affect how the car was going to run. At the time, I had no idea it was going to become as important as it did to the overall mythology.

On episode two, the writing credit is you and David, and David directed. My question is—the whole thing with the dream and the Red Room, which incorporates parts of the European ending— where did that come from?

We talked about going into dream time as a way of exploring Cooper's subconscious process. We had hinted at it before, but it was a way to play with something visually arresting that also broke the fourth wall into his mind in a way that expanded the narrative into the mythic.

Right, so what's interesting about that is that in the European ending that isn't a dream—it actually happens. So David created this ending, and then you figure out how to retrofit it into the narrative in a way that made narrative sense?

Right, a way to bring that idea into useful context for the ongoing narrative. We came up with the idea of going into dream reality, and Lynch liked that idea, a way to repurpose this material most people were never going to see.

I know you've cited Carl Jung as an influence, and he had a lot to say on the subject of dreams, on duality and individuation and the shadow self, which all seems relevant here.

I'd read a lot of Jung and studied and believed in and experienced a Jungian therapeutic process, so that's pretty thoroughly woven into the whole way I view reality. I believe Jung moved much closer to the truth than Freud. He was an astronaut of the human psyche. One of the first people to walk out into that untethered area of the human mind.

Is there something in particular about his approach to psychology that resonates with you?

His willingness to work with whatever the mind produced without applying dogmatic interpretations, which is where Freud got into trouble. He tended to see through rigidly structured points of view that were a product of his upbringing and environment, putting things into boxes for ease of diagnosis. That's how it seemed to me. Jung was willing to throw away categorizations and open himself up to the powerful experience of "I have no control about where this is going so I'm going to let it lead me to what I want to know"—not through prescribed procedure, but through open-ended exploration.

When did you guys actually sit down and start to create some concept of who Bob and Mike were? Because by episode two, you're incorporating elements of the European ending, so they're emerging as fairly significant figures already.

That's where the European ending had a lasting effect on the overall shape of the show, because it introduced us to this idea of stepping outside a strict reality of space and time.

Did you have a handle on who these characters were yet by episode two, or did that come later—who they were, where they came from, what they represented? Was that something you already had figured out, or did that evolve?

That evolved out of discussions. When you're working intuitively, the ideas tend to come first, unencumbered by their place in your overall conception or context. Afterward, you can step back and see how everything connects. That's a pretty good way to shorthand-describe working on those aspects of the show.

OK, on the subject of Gerard and the One-Armed Man, who was *The Fugitive* fan? Was that you?

That was me. Let me expand for one second, because *The Fugitive* was a series I really loved. What it had about it that I found unique, particularly in that final season, was a sweaty, awful sense of dread that David Janssen's character, Richard Kimble, had to live with—he's Jean Valjean in *Les Misérables,* where the story comes from. But the idea of a good man being falsely accused and relentlessly pursued for something he didn't do—and still persisting in trying to do good under those circumstances—was a character I found enthralling. It put him in such a dilemma, where he constantly had to accommodate the pressures of being on the run with his desire to be good, constantly driven by his need to stay free so he could find justice for his wife. I was captivated by that conflict, and his performance was terrific. The finale, which I think was one of the most-watched episodes in television history, was the most satisfying conclusion to a series I'd seen, and it made a big impression on me at an impressionable age. So those references were a tip of the cap to one of the best things American television had done to that point.

Just before leaving season one, did you know when you shot the season finale—which you directed—that Josie was the one who shot Cooper?

Yes.

You wrote and directed that final episode of the first season—the only time you directed an episode of *Twin Peaks*. What was that experience like?

It was a tremendous amount of fun. I had identified one main task at that point, which was, "I have to get us picked up for another season, if it came down to it." The job at hand was to ensure that we got a pickup. Since there was an element to the show that was a—probably 7, 8 percent—send-up of nighttime soaps and the conventions of the genre, I thought I would do that in spades with the idea of the cliffhanger episode and just create an almost absurd chain of cliffhangers that went off like a row of firecrackers. I was affectionately having fun with it. At the same time, there were elements of it that had real emotional stakes. I thought it was a fun episode to write. The only reason I could direct it was because I didn't have to worry about prepping or working with directors on upcoming episodes, so it was the one that lined up that I could have the time to do it. It was a lot of fun, and it was a very positive experience.

When you say your objective was to get picked up, the interesting thing about that is that at the time you wrote and directed this you had no idea what the reception was going to be to the series, because none of the episodes had aired.

Right, it was eight months ahead of that. We knew ABC was provisionally happy with what they'd seen. They were puzzled by it and quizzical about it, but it was testing well, and they were trying to keep an open mind. We didn't even know when we were going to air yet. But I did know we had a pretty solid base with the first six, and I wanted to make sure we capped the season in a way that helped make our case for sticking around. So I saw it as the mother of all cliffhangers.

It's an interesting episode, visually. How was it different from directing on *Hill Street*, for instance?

Different circumstances. I wasn't an employee, as on *Hill Street*. Wasn't trying to please a studio or do it in the *Hill Street* "house style," which was set in stone. It was a chance to direct something I'd written that I felt could stretch the stylistic reaches of what we'd done before. The show had progressively moved from the pilot—which is, for the most part, almost kitchen-sink realism in its bones. David played it very straight first time out. Some of the performances were scaled big, particularly the grief from Sarah and Leland, which edged toward the top end of what audiences would accept. Both Grace [Zabriskie] and Ray [Wise] were completely committed and 100 percent on the mark. So this was a chance to be more playful and stylistic with some of the scenes. We'd moved in those directions throughout the first season after the pilot.

You say *Hill Street* had a very specific house style. What about *Twin Peaks*?

Working with directors as they came in to prep I always said, "You're here because I admire your work as a filmmaker, and I want you to feel free to express yourself." Often in episodic work, directors are wearing a straitjacket, so we talked out each episode specifically about tone and technique to identify how they could play scenes to their strengths. The show, on one level, was an anthology of good filmmakers working with themes and stories we were creating, while giving each a healthy amount of freedom. When my turn came, I wanted the same freedom for myself

Do you have any specific memories from directing that episode? Anything that stands out?

We were cross-boarding elements of seven and six, which Caleb Deschanel directed. So more than once, the two of us were on set shooting out a location for the different episodes, which was fun. We passed a baton back and forth to whoever had the next setup. Loved working with Caleb. I also thoroughly picked his brain about cinematography, because he's top ten. One of the best of our generation behind the camera.

What I always loved the most, though, was working with actors' performances, trying to help them find a moment if they had doubts and giving them plenty of rope when they knew what they were doing. Working in post was also a blast, because when you've got a fair number of effects while telling a story with so many moving parts, that first assembly is key, and it came together nicely. Really positive experience from start to finish.

When I commented on the visual images in the episode, I was talking about things like the eye transitioning to the roulette wheel or the Nadine suicide scene.

I tried to make it visually interesting, looking for transitions that tied things together. There's a little bit of Spielberg influence there visually. That was the episode I got to sit down and show him in post because, at the time, we were talking about having him direct in the next season. We discussed some of those shots, so it was cool to get feedback from somebody whose work I so admired.

Can you elaborate on that? Influenced by Spielberg how?

What I always liked about his eye is the boldness of movement, the way he uses different planes in the frame: foreground, midground, background, stacking up action, making it visually complex. I learned a lot about moving the camera from his pictures—dynamic movement, the camera sometimes functioning as a character whose point of view is changing and moving. I also switched up some of the music. What we had to work in general with was a sound bank of cues and themes that Angelo [Badalamenti] had written for the pilot. I worked with the music director and editor to mix 'em up. Like the Nadine suicide scene, instead of a synthesizer carrying the theme, I had them try it with a harp, because there's a delicacy about the moment—the instrument reflecting Nadine's fragile internal state.

Do you have a favorite Spielberg movie?

A.I. is, to my mind, criminally underappreciated. It started as a Kubrick script that Steven took over, which makes for a fascinating hybrid. Kubrick had that penetrating, God's-eye view, looking down at life on Earth; it's fair to say he often lacked a compelling level of empathy or feeling for the human condition. So much of his work is darkly, morbidly funny, but I sometimes feel he's examining specimens under a microscope. There are times, in black comedy, when that's perfectly appropriate, but in *A.I.*, what Steven made heartbreaking was the Pinocchio/Haley Joel Osment character's yearning for humanity. Whether it was simply programmed that way or somehow transcended its limits, I don't think Kubrick would have mined the same extraordinary feelings from the material. He might not have gotten that incredible performance from Jude Law either. So that's a film that's really stuck with me.

Schindler's List. Overwhelming in its power and simplicity. *Private Ryan* still holds up today. There's something a little pat about the story, but the action is so powerful and convincing you stop caring about plot after a while, and you're caught up in the horrors of war. For sheer fun, it's hard to beat *Jaws* or the *Indiana Jones* pictures. The third [*Indiana Jones and the Last Crusade*] is my favorite. The father/son Sean Connery/Harrison Ford pairing is so perfect and funny; I thought that elevated it above the others. Howard Hawks is the only other American director with that much range.

One of the other things that's interesting to me about episode seven is that you start to drop some hints about what happened to Laura on the night of her murder, or the night before the early morning of her murder. Those details basically form the basis of the narrative as depicted in *Fire Walk With Me*, which you were not involved in directly. I'm talking the whole story that Jacques tells in episode seven, about the cabin in the woods that night with Laura and Leo. How far in advance of writing that episode did you know those details?

We wrote the six additional scripts in sequence. The pilot had been written and shot a year and a half before, so it was a matter of building out the various arcs one brick at a time. After working with the other writers throughout, I wrote seven alone when we got to the end of the line. And that established the course for everything that followed, certainly up to and including Leland's confession and death. It turned out to include a lot of revelations and expanded the basic DNA of the show.

***

Let's move on to season two of *Twin Peaks*. This was a hugely different experience, right? Whereas every episode of season one was written and shot before even the pilot had aired, on season two, you had to start churning scripts out on a weekly basis. How difficult was it to assemble a writing and directing staff for the second season?

It was done over time. I'd had Harley on season one. Bob Engels wrote a script for season one. My brother, Scott, came on board for season two; he'd been around for season one, so he got the drill. There was a freelance writer I liked a lot named Barry Pullman, who came in and did a couple of good scripts. Beyond that, we didn't really need many others. Tricia Brock, Harley's then wife, did a nice job on one. She's since gone on to have a successful career as a television director. And we got to work with a lot of interesting filmmakers. Tim Hunter was one of our mainstays. I was really fond of Lesli Glatter, who had done a great job on episode five the first year, so she came back and did a couple more. Real pros like James Foley and Uli Edel and Diane Keaton. Steve Gyllenhaal came in to work with us. Top-notch filmmakers, so there was no fall-off in talent level from one season to the next.

It sounded to me, when we were talking about *Hill Street Blues*, that the writers' room there was actually something you enjoyed. Was the writers' room at *Twin Peaks* different?

To an extent, because it was a much smaller group. When I hear about the size of writers' rooms today, and the sheer number of people who then have to weigh in from studios and networks, I'm not sure I'd be able to function in that kind of environment.

Who was typically in the writers' room on *Twin Peaks*, besides you and Harley and Bob? Would Scott be in there?

We were the only three on staff, and we'd bring in whatever freelance writer was working with us, so there'd be typically no more than four.

And was there anywhere near the craziness that existed in the writers' room at *Hill Street*?

No.

Years ago, at The Museum of Television & Radio [now The Paley Center for Media] in New York, Steven Bochco and David Kelley were both on a panel, and Kelley said, "If Steven has a problem with a script, he's liable to call all the writers together into the room to solve it." Whereas Kelley said his own approach would be to "throw everyone out of the room and fix it myself." Which one are you?

In Kelley's camp. I figured after working my way up to showrunner, that was my job. There were times—particularly at the beginning of a year—when you wanted whoever was in the room to be involved in conceptualizing and talking about overall arcs and where characters and stories might be going. But I always felt the job included doing the last pass on every script myself, which is the way I always operated.

Even with everything going on in season two, you were still reading every script?

Until the late-middle of the second season—when we were taken off the air and our future suddenly looked uncertain, and I had this other project looming. There are four or five scripts in there that I wasn't as involved with. Aside from the one he directed, Lynch wasn't around during season one, and he wasn't around that much in season two either, except to play Gordon Cole and for the four episodes he directed. He didn't take a strong interest in reading scripts and seldom had something he wanted to change—until the last script, when he had a profound influence on that last episode and did something truly amazing with it.

We talked about David not being involved in the scripts, but was

he involved at all in the selection of the directors. Did he even see their cuts?

He suggested Duwayne Dunham as a director. After the pilot, Duwayne came in and directed episode one, did a good job and did more for us in season two. Tina Rathborne was another suggestion of David's, and she was a joy to work with. As far as I can recall, the rest came through me.

But David was looking at cuts?

I know we sent them to him, but I don't recall many notes from him. Like with the scripts, they were fairly brief if he had anything at all.

Just to be really clear about season two: You left to work on *Storyville* after all the scripts had been written but while they were still filming. Is that an accurate statement?

Near the end of season two, I started prepping. I didn't start shooting until late April of that year [1991], but it still took me away from the show at a time when I shouldn't have left. I have regrets about that. In season two, we got constant pressure to wrap up the murder mystery from the network, and they also—and I thought this was a disastrous decision—moved the show to Saturday night. We had had this great success on Thursday. I knew the time slot intimately; that's where *Hill Street* had flourished for years. In pre-internet days, that allowed viewing to extend into the day after, where people talked about it at work. The watercooler effect. So to take their prize bell cow of the moment and put it on a graveyard night was lunacy. I was furious about it, but there was nothing we could do. Those are the rules of the game.

The show held up well through the conclusion of the murder mystery that they twisted our arms to end. They wanted it disclosed in the first episode of season two, and we had to fight like hell to hold them off as long as we did. I have no qualms with anything in either the first season or the episodes leading to the resolution of that storyline. I'm proud of all of that work; it's strong stuff. The problem came afterward. Once they'd compelled us to answer that question, the question then became, "OK, now what are you going to do?" We didn't have a proper amount of time to work that out. We shouldn't have acquiesced to begin with, but we weren't given an option—which leads to curious kinds of thinking about what exactly did ABC want from us. They never truly understood the nature of the show. They loved and benefited from the tsunami of attention that it garnered, but they continued to treat it like an exotic animal that needed to be kept in a separate kennel. To that extent, they saw it accurately. It was never going to be normal network fare, and that made them perpetually uneasy. It was the sort of storytelling we became used to ten or fifteen years later, when premium cable came into its own. So the second half of season two became problematic.

You mentioned that you were extremely proud of the series up until Leland's death. I know that a lot of fans have issues with the episodes that immediately followed that, but the fans I know think the Windom Earle arc is extremely strong and compelling and profound. Are you not proud of the second half of the second season?

I am, very much so. Ken Welsh was an actor I knew from the Guthrie and wanted him for that part, and he was wonderful. So I felt that was a worthy successor. The transition to his story could have been done more artfully, but I've always felt the way the network handled the second half of that season had as much to do with the audience degrading over time. Moving the series to Saturday was blatantly self-destructive, and I think betrayed an unspoken animus for the show at higher levels of ownership. Cap[ital] Cities was an extremely conservative organization, and I was given to understand the show made them crawl inside their skin.

But you were happy creatively with the second half of season two?

There were a few elements that were goofier in terms of tone, and that upset the balance of the show. There had always been an absurd strain of comedy in it from the beginning, but the mix fell out of tune.

You mean like Nadine and her superpowers?

I'm thinking of that and the love triangle with Andy and Lucy and Dick Tremayne and certainly the Miss Twin Peaks story. That got too broad.

You said you have not read *Room to Dream*, which David wrote with Kristine McKenna?

No. I believe I'm quoted in it. I know I talked to Kristine McKenna.

You're quoted pretty extensively. I wanted to read you this quote from Kimmy Robertson, who of course played Lucy on all three seasons of the show: "David's got a connection to God, the universe, and the creative highway, and there are all these on-ramps and off-ramps in his head leading to files and rooms and libraries, and he can go to all of them at once. Mark is the librarian. He's up there checking all these things in and out and saying, 'No, you can't take those all out at once, but we can do it in a certain sequence.' It had to be the two of them together for the show to work, and they weren't there as a team for the second season." What do you think of that?

It sounds like Kimmy [laughs]. I mean it's a neat metaphor, but the fact is Lynch wasn't around for season one either. So how do you explain that?

It's weird because people keep saying that the reason season two didn't work was because Lynch wasn't around, and then the same people talk about how he was off editing *Wild at Heart* during season one, so it doesn't make any sense.

The truth is he was doing *Wild at Heart* during season one, and he was around for season two. He just didn't contribute much aside from the Gordon Cole scenes and the episodes he directed. The actors who were down on the set didn't know what was going on upstairs. They weren't privy to it, so I don't blame anyone for having their version of it. David loves actors. He's very tender and kind to them, and they're intensely loyal to him. I understand why—but their view of things was down on the floor, not upstairs where the scripts were written.

The problem, as you know—as someone with an intense interest in history—is that it gets recorded as history, and then passed down.

Well I'll only say this much: Lynch is a table for one.

He says in *Room to Dream* that the pilot and the last twenty minutes of season two are what *Twin Peaks* is, which does seem a little self-serving.

They're the ones he's most directly responsible for, so I'm not surprised to hear that. In my experience, he's not often that complimentary about other people's work. That's okay, that's who he is. He'll talk about his actors sometimes, but a lot of brilliant people work with him, and his work wouldn't be possible without them. Comes with the territory, I guess. Directing features is a little like the presidency—the endless pressure, the surreal demands on your time and energy. Lynch is singular in the way he takes all that responsibility on. After working with a lot of feature directors—and having done it once myself—it's my observation you almost have to be half-mad to want that job.

OK, so let's dig a little deeper into the second half of season two. Harley was the one who came up with the idea of Windom Earle?

Harley was the first to mention it as an idea, and we developed it over many conversations. Harley, in particular, never gets the credit he deserves for his contributions to the show.

Were there other ideas floating around about how to follow up the Laura Palmer arc?

We discussed a lot of options, but Windom Earle emerged as the strongest contender. We decided to use an intermediate three-episode arc as a bridge to take us to the Earle story, but because of circumstances had to advance it. Although there are things I really like in those episodes—I loved the Duchovny arc and that also brought Michael Parks into my life, a guy I got to know and work with again. It was fun to bring Clarence [Williams III] back for his scenes as an FBI agent with Peggy [Lipton, his costar in *The Mod Squad*]. Those shows weren't without their virtues. So, sure, the second season is uneven, but I've never felt it deserves the lower end of its reputation as a betrayal of the show.

OK, so before Harley came up with Windom Earle, did you have any idea what you were going to do when Leland died?

One of the major stories was going to be a romance between Cooper and Audrey Horne. I tread carefully around this, because it may have had to do with personal relationships, which are complicated. I was told that Kyle felt uncomfortable with that story, and the suspicion was that his girlfriend at the time, Lara Flynn Boyle, was a factor in that decision. The objection Kyle mentioned to me was that Audrey had just turned eighteen and an upright straight arrow like Cooper shouldn't take advantage of her crush on him. I accepted that as a legitimate reason and moved on. I've never asked Kyle about the other scenario, and I respect him too much to give it credence. But this happened after the scripts had already been written, and it contributed to a lot of scrambling to come up with another story quickly.

But even if they had had that relationship, weren't you still planning on some sort of mystery or conflict between good and evil?

Their relationship was going to figure into it—honestly, I don't even remember how at this point. But the upshot of it was that we had to advance the Windom Earle story faster than we'd planned, and come up with the Michael Parks storyline as the dominant narrative of that arc over the next three episodes, which also brought Duchovny's character into the show.

Whatever happened to Annie—Windom Earle kidnapping her and taking her to the Black Lodge—if the Audrey-Cooper romance had happened that would have been Audrey? Did you have it mapped out that far?

That's most likely true. I don't know that we'd gone far enough down the line of blocking those stories out, but that sounds right.

There was another element that influenced the fate of the show that's seldom talked about: the war in Iraq. My memory is that we were preempted repeatedly so some correspondent could stand in front of a wide shot of Baghdad as the bombs came down. This was the kind of show that did not benefit from people not being able to see it on a regular basis. I may have this wrong, but I believe we were preempted something like six out of eight weeks in a row for coverage of the war. That made it doubly difficult to build a new narrative thread from scratch, especially in the aftermath of the resolution of Laura's death. The show was only sporadically being aired.

I found this old quote from you where you say, "The whole mythological side of _Twin Peaks_ was down to me, and I've always known about the Theosophical writers and that whole group around the Order of the Golden Dawn in the late nineteenth and early twentieth centuries." So here you are talking primarily about the second season, with the White Lodge and the Black Lodge and the Dweller on the Threshold, right?

There was some of that in the first season as well, and I should be clear that Lynch made many contributions in this area as well. His tended to be visual and intuitive more than concrete and incorporated into the narrative, like the ending we needed for the closed version of the pilot. He just sat down and visualized some scenes. He's an intensely visual artist; he'd tell you that himself. His training was as a painter before he ever got into film. So he's deeply interested in what these visuals tell him, even if he doesn't immediately know how they fit the narrative.

He was making his contributions on set as he was directing?

He would do that, absolutely. Like the white horse that appeared. That's a good example of an image Lynch came up with. He didn't know what it meant, but it was powerful. Then it fell to me to ask, "How do we incorporate this—in a larger, Jungian sense—into what it means in the narrative without becoming too literal?" I wanted things to have a grounding in logic that made sense, even if it's dream logic. When I talk about finding connective tissue within the mythology, that's what I'm referring to.

Can we just talk about that white horse for a second? I have a theory about how he came up with that. There's a documentary titled *Lynch*, from 2007, in which he talks about seeing a French ultrarealist documentary called *Le Sang* des bêtes, or *Blood of the Beasts*, where the director, Georges Franju, intersperses idyllic scenes of bucolic life in a Paris suburb with scenes of a slaughterhouse where a white horse is being slaughtered.

He did tell me about that same movie years ago. I never saw it. This to him was an indelible, powerful image. Pale horseman, pale rider; the idea of death astride a horse is not a new metaphor. It has its roots in medieval Europe, how death roamed the land in the plague years like a thundering horse. It made perfect sense in that context. He had the impulse to include it, and I had the background to understand and integrate it. Intuitively it was right, so I tried to find a way to help it become meaningful to the overall narrative.

On this subject, I think when people talk about the Lynchian nature of *Twin Peaks*, I see all these things—dreams, duality. These are all things that figure very prominently in your own influences as well—Carl Jung's process of individuation, for example, or his preoccupation with the symbolism of dreams. I mean, people credit you with the Arthurian legend and Theosophy, but some of the more outré things, I feel like you don't get enough credit when people describe those as Lynchian. To me, they're Lynch-Frostian.

He once said, "Mark deserves at least half the credit for the show," and that covers it as far as I'm concerned. This seemed to be a function of the fact that he had a reputation with critics coming into the show, so they tended to ascribe things to him that they perceived as his. A lot of that is fair. It doesn't really matter to me. The show is the show, and we own it equally and our names are on it equally as creators. If people want to see it as somehow more his than mine, so be it.

Can I throw some questions at you about the meaning of events in *Twin Peaks*? I've been wanting to ask you this question for a really long time. There's a scene after Laura's murder is resolved where Cooper and Briggs are in the woods, and when Briggs disappears, we see a hooded guy in the forest—we only see a shadow, and there's a white flash. If you don't remember, I can show you a screen grab—

I do. I wrote the scene.

Who is that guy?

It's the concept we talked about earlier in the show. The Dweller on the Threshold. As I think back to that moment, I *believe* that's what we were trying to convey. Major Briggs was about to be confronted by the sum total of all his fears and doubts and self-doubts. I go into this more in *The Secret History*, about what led up to that moment and the work that he's been engaged in. There's more context for understanding this moment in the book, but my memory is that's what this meant.

Where did Briggs go when he disappeared?

It's his first exposure to the place he's taken to, or escapes to, in *The Return*. That may or may not involve what we might more conventionally call a UFO abduction. That's a prosaic way of describing something a lot more mysterious.

On the subject of the Dweller on the Threshold, Martha Nochimson, in *The Passion of David Lynch*, references the "Frostian conception of

Bob as the indomitable Dweller on the Threshold." I never saw Bob as the Dweller on the Threshold, did you?

No.

But what was your perception of the Dweller on the Threshold? I know that's a Theosophical term, but how do you see his role?

As I understand the idea, the Dweller on the Threshold is something anyone on the spiritual path eventually has to confront: the accumulation of all the person's wants, dreams, desires, and negativity. Somewhere along the path to enlightenment, those qualities have to be confronted and transcended. It's apparently a step on the path to enlightenment that requires this sort of ordeal or test. I see it as metaphorical in some ways, but also as a useful psychological model for how a psyche, or a soul, develops over time. At some point, you have to confront that which you're most afraid of.

So pretty much how Hawk describes it in season two?

Yes, that's the scene introducing the concept.

I came across that term years ago in a book called *Zanoni*. Have you ever heard of that one?

I don't know that one.

It's by Edward Bulwer-Lytton, who's actually more famous for having written the opening sentence of a book, "It was a dark and stormy night." OK, next: Did you ever have any strong sense of who the Tremonds and Chalfonts were?

No. I have to say they seemed a little obscure to me.

I'm sure you've seen these photographs that Richard Beymer took of Josie's body double in the Red Room, that supposedly Bob had taken her to the Red Room and you can see her body in the Red Room but not the head. Have you ever seen those?

I've seen some of them. But I don't think I've seen the particular one you're describing. Was that taken during season two?

Yes.

I don't remember Josie ever being in the Red Room.

Well, that's the question. I think people started to believe that she had made it to the Red Room, that the footage had been shot but never made it onto the air. Another question: Have we ever seen the White Lodge? Let me read you something from this description I read of Theosophy: "The masters are believed to preserve the world's ancient spiritual knowledge and to represent a great white brotherhood or white lodge, which watches over humanity and guides its evolution," which automatically makes me think of the Giant or the Fireman and his screens watching over humanity.

That's probably the closest approximation of it you'll find.

Here's another one: The relationship between the Red Room and the Black Lodge. You said earlier that there were instances where you were given things that David had created on set that you then had to integrate into a narrative and come up with some sort of narrative purpose for. Throwing out the European ending, the Red Room that American viewers first saw was, to me, not particularly threatening. It was weird and discombobulating, but I don't know that it was evil. Laura whispers the name of the killer, the Man from Another Place is giving Cooper these oblique clues. But I think the distinction between the Red Room and the Black Lodge—it became progressively difficult to distinguish between them. Do you have any sense of what the relationship was in your mind and in David's mind?

I can't speak to his mind, but to me the Red Room was clearly a chamber or antechamber connected in some meaningful way to the Black Lodge, a purgatorial place before you moved on to whatever that next stage was. It's the only place we got to see—so if you want to use Dante's model of different circles of evil or hell or whatever you want to call the place, the Red Room seems to be an outer circle. When you see Windom Earle spontaneously combust and disappear, he's presumably going to some darker and more dire place, a deeper level. It's best to not get overly specific about these things and to suggest rather than insist.

Do you think the Red Room could also lead to the White Lodge, depending on how—

No, no.

You said you can't speak for David, but did the two of you ever have conversations about what the Red Room meant or what the Black Lodge meant or why Josie wound up in a doorknob or who the Giant was?

He would every once in a while call me and say something like: "There's a giant in Cooper's room," or that he wanted Josie to end up in a doorknob. When you're in the middle of—you know what production's like; deadlines are chasing you down from every direction—there wasn't time to stop everything and say, "What does that mean, and what are the implications?" There weren't many opportune moments to have those conversations. We actually had many more of them while talking about season three. That was the first time we really had a chance to chew over a lot of that stuff. And because he's first and foremost a visual artist, he worked in visual ideas, like a giant or Josie in a doorknob. I don't think he worried about what they meant intrinsically. So I tried to take these arresting images, ones that were rich with mythic overtones, and incorporate them into the narrative. That's one way in which our different natures and interests manifested.

Those clues that the Giant gives Cooper in the first episode of the

second season, which go on to be so important, did you know at the time that you were writing them that what they would mean? Or was it just a matter of creating these oblique clues? Did they have meaning when you wrote them, or did you have to go back and retrofit?

It was more the latter. Again, Lynch would get an image or a line of dialogue in his head. They were usually intriguing and cool, and they ultimately worked, but they weren't necessarily premeditated in terms of how they fit whatever else we were doing.

And you took responsibility for going back and finding a way to make them work narratively?

Often, yes, that was the case. Thematically there was usually a way to make them work, so I'm not trying to portray it as a hardship or a fault. That was just his method, and this was mine.

Am I right that when you wrote the pilot you knew that Leland had killed Laura but not that Leland had been possessed by Bob. Is that a fair statement?

That's probably a fair statement. We wanted to keep the process of discovery open between us to finding out who did it—which allowed us to go down a lot more interesting alleyways along the way, until we finally got to the point where it was clear we had to name the person, and we had to tell the actor. Even then, we kept it secret. We told three different actors they might have been the killer, and we wrote a couple of scenes that were never going to be in the episode—misdirection—to try not to tip anyone off.

One thing I never quite understood about the chronology is this: Supposedly more than one killer was filmed, to disguise the reveal, even to the point where most of the cast members didn't know who the killer was. But if you were filming episode eighteen, which is Leland's wake, before episode fourteen aired—which is where he's

revealed as the killer—doesn't that mean everyone on set knew by then?

This is my memory of it. We told three different actors they were the killer, and we were probably going to shoot it three different ways and swore everybody to secrecy. So that was our way to minimize the possibility that somebody might leak it. We told Ray [Wise, who portrayed Leland Palmer]. I think Richard Beymer [Ben Horne] was one of the three. And honestly, I can't think of who the third one was off the top of my head, but that was just a way for us to create enough plausible deniability that if word were to leak out—which it didn't—we'd have an alternate way to deal with it.

But did they not know who the killer was until the episode aired—the rest of the cast?

No, we eventually let Ray know it was him. I just don't remember when that happened.

No, I mean the rest of the cast.

I don't know. I wasn't privy to the conversations they might have been having with each other. We had instilled in everybody the importance of secrecy here, and as far as I know, everybody honored that. We didn't have any internal leaks.

OK, so let's move on to the philosophy of *Twin Peaks*. Who do you think killed Laura and Maddie? Do you think it was Bob, or do you think it was Leland?

I think it was Leland. And whether or not he was—in the end, it doesn't matter. It was physically Leland, and whether he was mad or not is a separate issue, whether he was possessed.

But not an uninteresting one.

No, it's a fascinating one that you can entertain forever.

Do you have an opinion? Does David? Are your opinions necessarily the same?

No. I don't know what his opinion would be.

Do you think Leland was mad and Bob was just a figment of his imagination?

Let me step back a second. My point of view is usually that of a novelist—an omniscient point of view, where everybody's point of view matters. Leland's experience—as we've learned from fifty years of psychological profiling—may be pathological, but there's a 2 percent chance it's something else. So because I believe in psychology as a fundamental human tool for self-understanding, that was probably the case with Leland. But the omniscient point of view says you also have to bear in mind that we don't know anything for sure. Perhaps this other idea is valid—that some other being or entity was driving his actions. So the case in my mind is not absolute one way or the other, but I lean more toward the notion of pathology driving the individual to do terrible things.

Did your thinking evolve at all as a result of what happened in season three?

No, we just gave more screen time to the alternate point of view.

I always thought that Bob was some sort of evil, otherworldly entity inside of Leland in the first two seasons, so that it was Bob who killed Laura and Maddie. But in *Fire Walk With Me* it seemed different—that it was Leland who killed Teresa Banks. When he's killing Teresa, he never assumes Bob's physical appearance.

It's kind of a dance. It's easier to more definitively say, "These are the actions of a being who's lost his senses," but it's also intriguing to entertain the notion that "there's more in heaven and earth than is dreamt of in our philosophy."

Ah, *Hamlet* by way of Major Briggs. So I was going to ask if there was a character in *Twin Peaks* through whom we hear Mark Frost's voice? Is that Albert? Or Major Briggs?

Albert's was a voice I love. I loved writing for Hawk, obviously. I remember thinking that because Major Briggs in the pilot was a perfunctory character, I had the instinct to make him the most spiritually advanced person in town. Lynch really liked that idea, and we went with it. And we found Don Davis, who was just wonderful in the role.

Let's stay on Major Briggs for a minute. I've heard you talk about the "vision in my sleep" conversation between him and Bobby in the diner. Is that your favorite scene?

It's one of my favorites. I'd had this vision of Briggs as a surprisingly enlightened figure, and this was the first time to give full voice to those possibilities. And when you see where I went with him all the way through *The Secret History*, that was a chance to open up that idea.

I think it really speaks to your gifts as a writer, and it's really the beginning of Bobby evolving into something more than just a jerk.

He was a character who got a second chance at life, and that was one of the best ideas to work with in season three: the reveal of Bobby now as a deputy and a good, decent man, which also spoke to the influence his father had on him.

In writing all those scenes between Bobby and the Major, did you draw at all on your own relationship with your father?

No, that was imagination. I was not a troubled or rebellious kid in that way. I was trying to create an idealized dynamic of a concerned and seemingly straightlaced father whom you'd expect to be authoritarian and disapproving, but who instead takes a more generous view of his son and imparts to him a belief that his future will be bright. As we find out twenty-five years later, that was a key moment for both of them.

You know, Angelo Badalamenti's music is so crucial to *Twin Peaks*. I was reading an interview with you when you were writing book two of the *Paladin* trilogy, and you said you were playing soundtracks for inspiration. We know a lot about David Lynch's taste in music, but I've never really heard you talk about yours. I mean, I know you like the Beatles, but beyond that.

I like all sorts of different music and all kinds of different artists. Obviously, the Beatles. That whole generation of singer/songwriters we grew up with. Paul Simon to Carly Simon, Joni Mitchell, James Taylor. That sort of troubadour, storytelling class. Crosby, Stills & Nash. The Band was my favorite "American" group, even though four-fifths were Canadian. They had an extraordinary feel for "Americana," nineteenth-century history, and musical chops that few others could match—true originals and hugely underappreciated to this day. I loved jazz—Miles Davis, John Coltrane, Oscar Peterson, Stan Getz. Classical music. David Bowie, early Springsteen. *Pet Sounds*, Brian Wilson's masterpiece.

I joined the Columbia Record Club when I was twelve, so I could get an album every month for pennies—amassed a massive record collection by the time I went off to college, which my brother promptly appropriated. As they say in *The Godfather Part II*, that's between the brothers.

Do you remember what you were listening to for inspiration during seasons one, two, or three of *Twin Peaks*?

I don't actually listen to music when I'm writing. I'll listen when I'm not. I find it distracting, particularly if there are lyrics. But at that time, I was listening to Sting, the Gypsy Kings—who had a really original sound. World music was coming on stage at that point with Paul Simon and *Graceland*, King Sunny Ade, reggae. I listened to just about everything.

OK, let's move on to something completely different. Did you watch *The Sopranos*?

I loved *The Sopranos*.

What did you think of the ending?

I thought it was absolutely perfect.

Do you in your own mind go over the possibility of whether Tony died, or does it not matter to you one way or the other?

Doesn't matter one way or the other. To me, if he's not dead in that moment, he's going to live the rest of his life *in* that moment, in that purgatory of not knowing when or where the bullet was going to end his life. That's what was brilliant about what David [Chase] did there. Tony had made his life a living hell, and by ending it when he [Chase] did, he made it clear that that hell was gonna continue until he died. In a hundred years, you couldn't come up with a more perfect way of framing the right fate for this charismatic sociopath.

So you would never be one of those people who plays that ending over and over and over again looking for clues as to whether Tony lived or died?

It didn't matter. Even if he was still alive, he was dead.

But do you understand that mind-set? Because *Twin Peaks* fans have spent over twenty-five years trying to deconstruct the ending of season two. And now they're gonna do the same thing with *The Return*. So let's talk about that season two finale—which some people hate, and some people think is one of the greatest episodes of episodic television ever, even today. Conventional wisdom among the *Twin Peaks* fan community is that the challenge in that episode was to reconcile two somewhat conflicting mythologies—whatever David had in his head versus whatever you, Bob Engels, and Harley

146

Peyton had conceived—and that accounts for some of the difficulty in trying to deconstruct the events once Cooper descends into the Red Room or Black Lodge or whatever it is. Is that a fair statement? Were you guys on different pages?

I was in New Orleans when that was shot—doing prep on *Storyville*; I may have even started shooting. At that point, it seemed clear—given the way the network had been treating us—the show was going down. The original script had a more conventional ending, in case we got picked up for another season. Lynch had been scheduled to direct that one from the start. I wasn't in meetings with him, but by the time he started shooting, the writing was on the wall: the show was ending. So he redid the last third of the script and came up with a powerful, visceral ending that is one of the most memorable sequences in the series. It's indelible.

You and Harley and Bob also had Cooper trapped in the Black Lodge, right?

That idea was in place: Cooper's doppelgänger escapes, and Cooper is trapped. That was the destination. Lynch just changed up the journey to get there.

This is one question that's always bothered me: Why did Cooper end up in the Black Lodge? To me, he was willing to sacrifice his life for Annie, the woman he loved. I didn't really see any failure of courage there. I'm just wondering why it was important to you and to David that he wind up there.

We were trying to extend the narrative and thought for season three we could take this into the dual realms we'd been dealing with narratively, take even more chances with the storytelling. I pitched this to [ABC Entertainment president] Bob Iger over the phone. A way of doubling down against ABC's need for the show to be conventional and fit into their schematics. We weren't going down that road. So in a way, it was a defiant middle finger to their idea of what the show should be.

It had nothing to do with Cooper's failure in any way?

Cooper had had an earlier failure, a moment of weakness: the affair with Windom Earle's wife that led to her death and Earle's madness. So if there was a karmic component to Cooper being trapped, it had more to do with that than it did anything he'd done in the present.

I know Joseph Campbell is someone you greatly admire. He said that the "ultimate aim of the hero's quest is neither release nor ecstasy for oneself, but rather the wisdom and power to serve others." Do you think that Cooper's journey as a hero was in any way influenced by Campbell, consciously or subconsciously?

Consciously. We tried to build into Cooper this idea of the shadow self he was chasing—that on the surface he's a squeaky-clean, by-the-book agent of the law, but I wanted to build in the flaw of a past indiscretion, the affair with Earle's wife, though there were extenuating circumstances that made it less egregious. Earle at that point had already been exposed as a madman, and it wasn't a long-term affair—it was short-lived—but it still resulted in her death and Cooper's near death. That was one of the better things that came out of the Windom Earle story: we learn that Cooper wasn't only just a paragon of virtue, but had a more complex history.

Do you think Cooper's primary motivation during the Laura arc in seasons one and two is self-redemption?

Yes, and obviously it's compounded by what happens with Annie Blackburne.

Do you think he failed? Or succeeded? Again, I'm talking just about seasons one and two.

I think he failed. He found justice for Laura. He found who he thought was the killer, but *The Return* cast some doubt on that, and by attempting to go back—maybe I'm getting ahead of your question, but I was going to talk about where he goes in the third season, in trying to right that wrong. It's the law of unintended consequences—the butterfly effect, that every action has an equal and often unknown reaction—and in trying to do too much, he creates different and greater difficulties for himself and the person he's trying to save.

Just before we leave the subject of *Twin Peaks*—for the next twenty-five years, at least—I wanted to touch on a couple of related topics, like the tie-in books, *Fire Walk With Me*, and *Mulholland Dr.* How involved were you and David in those books—*The Secret Diary of Laura Palmer*, *The Autobiography of F. B. I. Special Agent Dale Cooper*, and *Twin Peaks: An Access Guide to the Town*?

Lynch wasn't really involved with those, aside from *The Secret Diary*, which his daughter [Jennifer Lynch] wrote. She did a great job, and that moved him to make *Fire Walk With Me*.

How did Jen Lynch come to be the author of that book?

Lynch suggested her. He thought she'd be the right person to write it, and he was right. It was her first book. It was at times a struggle for her, as her first publishing gig, but in the end, she nailed it. I created an outline for Jennifer to use, and she really made that story come to life. People really responded to it.

I interviewed her a while back for *The Blue Rose* magazine, and she told me this story about how David called her and said, "Do you remember what you told me one day when I think you were about twelve and I picked you up from school?" She had told him she wanted to find someone else's diary and run home and read it to "see if they were terrified by, curious by, aroused by, hurt by, brought to tears by, or made joyful by the same things that I was." So she told him yes, she remembered, and he said, "I want you to write Laura's diary."

That's interesting. I never heard that story.

What about the other books?

I don't think he had any input into those. The Cooper book is a different form, the transcripts of his tapes. At times, it takes Cooper into more jokey character territory than we had originally conceived, but it still provides some solid backstory.

I actually think that book is hilarious.

It's very funny. It's not as much in the tone of the show as *Diary*, but it's a lot of fun.

We've talked about your dad and his experiences in World War II. I'm just wondering—since your brother, Scott, wrote the book— where that story about the French farmer came from, the one who is killed because he was supposed to be a collaborator, but he really wasn't. Someone in the village was angry at him, and they just want to get back at him. Is there any basis in truth in that?

You'd have to ask Scott that. It wasn't a story my dad told me. He was in the Navy and never went ashore in France.

The fact that there are so many inconsistencies between the Pittsburgh events in the book and the story that was revealed in the series, does that mean that you pivoted at some point, that you were originally planning to go in a slightly different direction with Cooper's backstory with Windom and Caroline Earle?

My guess would be that that had to do with timing, that maybe Scott wrote it before we'd finished all the scripts. I honestly don't remember the sequence. That may have been him laying some things down before we had a chance to incorporate them, or we found them inconvenient to incorporate.

You didn't have other plans for Windom Earle, other than what we wound up seeing?

No, that was the intent. I thought he was a good villain. We wanted to bring in one with a direct relationship with Cooper, a reason for wanting him dead. More like Professor Moriarty with Holmes, rather than just another case. It becomes a personal journey. We thought that was the way to go for Cooper in the second half of that season.

And the access guide?

We had a contract for three books, and my literary agent knew the guy who'd created the *Access Guide* series, Richard Saul Wurman. I thought it would be fun—he'd never published one to that point—to do a fictional access guide, and that one was all hands on deck. Harley and Bob Engels worked on parts of it, I wrote some, and it was mostly for a laugh. That's the least serious of the three. But taken together, they were a unique addendum to the series, and each had its own unique way of filling in blanks for people. Fans of the show seem to appreciate them.

Can you tell me definitively why you decided not to get involved in *Fire Walk With Me*?

I was busy doing *Storyville*, and given where we ended—how we'd left the audience at the end of the series—I thought it was an opportunity to go forward and tell more of the story rather than backward and go over what felt to me like familiar ground.

It was a combination of those two things, that you were busy and you didn't like the direction of the film? Was it predominantly one over the other?

It was predominantly that I didn't have the bandwidth at that moment. I was up to my eyebrows. If it had been my choice alone, I would not have gone that way. Lynch felt strongly this was the film he wanted to make. So I said, by all means, go ahead.

It wasn't similar to these stories about Lara Flynn Boyle or Sherilyn Fenn or even Kyle MacLachlan, that they had had enough of *Twin Peaks* at that point and they wanted to move on to other projects? That was not the case for you?

As I said, it wasn't the choice I would have made if it was up to me. We had done, from start to finish, four immersive years of *Twin Peaks*. If I was going to go anywhere, it would've been forward, but it all worked out in the end. We were able to do that twenty-five years later.

Did you see *Fire Walk With Me* when it came out? Before it came out?

He showed me a rough cut.

Did you and David ever have any discussions about *Mulholland Dr.* starting out as a spinoff of *Twin Peaks*, with Audrey?

I lived on Mulholland Drive at the time. I thought it was a great title, and we had considered spinning off the Audrey character and setting her loose in Hollywood, in a modern noir. We had very preliminary talks; it drifted away, and then six years later, I hear it's going be a pilot at ABC.

Were you going to spin her off when *Twin Peaks* was still on the air or had it been canceled?

I don't recall. I know Sherilyn was eager to do it at the time. She was ambitious, and we probably could have built a show around her. I don't know exactly how it went from there to a pilot script without her—that was eventually treated at ABC even more rudely than *On the Air*.

They rejected it. Do you know why?

I don't. Maybe because *Twin Peaks* had crashed and burned, there wasn't much appetite for spinning off a series from it? I wasn't involved, and frankly, I needed a break from working with Lynch at that point. After six years, I had other things I wanted to, and so did he.

This is when Lynch/Frost Productions dissolves, about this time?

Right, somewhere in the middle or toward the end of 1992.

Do you remember anything about that conversation, or did it just sort of happen by itself?

We had signed a three-year deal with Spelling in '89 and fulfilled all our obligations. It was clear our interests were moving in separate directions, so there was no need to extend it.

Did you and David have much contact after?

No. By that point, *Fire Walk With Me* had come out and flopped, and that put a stake in the heart of *Twin Peaks* as far as I could tell. Time to move on. I'd started writing *The List of Seven* by then. *Storyville* was coming out, and I was ready for something new.

❧

7

"Fork in the Road"

(Extra-/Post-Peaks)

The early nineties was a prolific time for Mark Frost. In addition to running season two of *Twin Peaks*, he was working on two other Lynch/Frost productions, both brand-new: *American Chronicles*, a documentary series for Fox, and *On the Air*, a period sitcom that aired on ABC, the same network as *Twin Peaks*. Also during this time, Frost was prepping *Storyville*, which he both directed (in New Orleans) and wrote (very loosely adapting from the Australia-set novel *Juryman* by Frank Galbally and Robert Macklin).

The task of getting *Storyville* released (amid behind-the-scenes duplicity, financial shenanigans by the studio, and no marketing support) was painful and left Frost particularly scarred—so much so that he has never directed another feature film, despite some extremely positive reviews for his work.

Chronologically, *American Chronicles* comes first, running from September to December 1990. Frustratingly—but also not surprisingly—many contemporaneous accounts of the program contextualize it within the oeuvre of David Lynch, who had almost nothing to do with it. Some even credit Lynch and Frost as codirectors of the episode "Champions," which never aired in the United States—in fact, neither of them directed it.

An impressionist travelogue intended to redefine the traditional concept of the documentary, *American Chronicles*, with narration by Richard Dreyfuss, was a half-hour show in which filmmakers roamed the country capturing idiosyncrasies of the American landscape. Frost wrote and directed a single episode, the New Orleans–set opener, titled "Farewell to the Flesh," an evocatory exploration of Mardi Gras. According to Frost, the idea was "to create a very lyrical, visual style that lets the pictures tell the story."

American Chronicles had a terrible time slot—9:30 on Saturday nights—and Fox, by its own admission, did a lousy job promoting it. The network was baffled by the show, especially the early installments. Displaying no fondness at all for what Frost had termed "docu-poetry" (ironically, seventeen years later Noel Murray of *The New York Times* would refer to season three of *Twin Peaks* as "televisual poetry"), Fox eventually issued a series of edicts, barring the use of classical music (such as Orff's *Carmina Burana*), insisting that each program comprise two shorter segments, and encouraging celebrity appearances. (Frost found the network's behavior "troubling," according to reports at the time.) Reviews were mixed—some praised it as bold and innovative, others derided it as condescending and off-putting—but the ratings, unsurprisingly for something so experimental and relegated to the Saturday-night necropolis, were abysmal, and Fox pulled it after twelve installments.

On the Air had even less luck: though seven episodes were produced, only three aired, in June and July of 1992. Set behind the scenes at *The Lester Guy Show*, a 1950s live variety program on the fictional Zoblotnick Broadcasting Company network, the series was a broad, zany comedy (the AV Club rates it "ten out of ten for weirdness") starring three *Twin Peaks* alums, Miguel Ferrer, Ian Buchanan, and David L. Lander, plus Marla Rubinoff, Nancye Ferguson, Gary Grossman, Mel Johnson, Jr., Marvin Kaplan, Kim McGuire, and Tracey Walter. Off-camera *Peaks* creative talent included writers Robert Engels and Scott Frost (Mark's brother), directors Lesli Linka Glatter and Jonathan Sanger, cinematographer Ron Garcia, editor Mary Sweeney, and composer Angelo Badalamenti.

The pilot episode, coscripted by Frost and Lynch and directed by Lynch, was shot in March 1991, by which time *Twin Peaks* had been yanked from the ABC schedule, with the network refusing to say whether it would ever return (it did, but was officially canceled two months later). It was another year before *On the Air* finally made it, well, on the air, and even then, it—like *American Chronicles* and *Twin Peaks* before it—was relegated to Saturday nights (Miguel Ferrer told the *Los Angeles Times*: "Why don't they just put a bullet in its head?").

The final Frost project covered in depth here is *Storyville*, a moody, politically themed thriller set in New Orleans. Released on August 26, 1992—two days before *Twin Peaks: Fire Walk With Me*—Frost's film stars James Spader as Cray Fowler, the scion of a powerful, dynastic family not unlike a southern-fried version of the Kennedys. Cray, an attorney and Democratic candidate for Congress, is lured into a strange sexual encounter with a Vietnamese woman named Lee (Charlotte Lewis), whose father soon turns up dead. Lee is charged; Cray defends her.

That's the narrative, anyway. The film is really about ghosts—not the literal kind, but rather secret transgressions from the past that persist in haunting us ("The past is never where you think you left it," Katherine Anne Porter wrote in *Ship of Fools*). Sometimes compared to *Chinatown*—one of Frost's favorite flicks—*Storyville* is Frostian in its intricate plotting and social conscience (rich/powerful versus poor/marginalized), plus the Byzantine conspiracy at the core of the story. Frost got to work with top-notch actors, including not just Spader, but also Jason Robards, Jr., Joanne Whalley-Kilmer, *Twin Peaks* alumni Piper Laurie and Michael Parks, and, from *Hill Street Blues*, Michael Warren and Charles Haid.

The movie fared poorly at the box office—Frost has strong thoughts about why, as articulated below—grossing just $422,503 domestically, ranking 193rd among feature films for the year.

However, some of the nation's most esteemed critics were extremely kind; Roger Ebert, for instance, dished out 3.5 stars (out of four). Hal Hinson of *The Washington Post* was effusive, calling it a "spectacular" directorial debut. "You only have to watch a few minutes to know you are in the presence of a major new moviemaking talent," he wrote. And, in a review that must have been particularly rewarding to Frost, Vincent Canby of *The New York Times* praised Frost's "remarkable work with his actors," adding that Spader "comes of age as an actor in *Storyville*."

Interestingly, both Ebert and Hinson chose to compare Frost's directorial style with Lynch's, and not unfavorably: Hinson wrote that Frost "has learned from his partner how to create a sense of dread out of the most innocent details, and the slow, suggestive pace he sustains is a Lynchian technique as well. But Frost has a tighter narrative focus and his story follows a more conventional path." Ebert—no fan of Lynch's more outré work—also drew a comparison: "With Lynch's recent work, it's as if he wants you to know he's superior to the material. Frost doesn't mind being implicated—he likes this kind of stuff, and plunges into the dark waters of his plot with real joy."

***

The early nineties were an incredibly prolific time for you. *American Chronicles* **is airing in the last quarter of 1990. In 1990 and 1991 you're working on the second season of** *Twin Peaks. Storyville* **I believe was shot in '91.** *On the Air* **premieres in the summer of '92—and I know it was delayed for a while by ABC. And then** *The List of Seven,* **your first novel, comes out in '93. First of all, is that chronology correct? And second, how do you do all that without going insane?**

I think that chronology is pretty accurate. We were shooting *American Chronicles* concurrent with season two of *Twin Peaks*, so I had two different productions going. Their offices were a couple of miles away from each other in the Valley, so I was driving back and forth constantly. We were heavily pressured by our distributor, Spelling/Worldvision— we had a three-series commitment with them, and they wanted them "now." So it fell to me to do the work on *American Chronicles*. It was something I created, that I pitched, directed the pilot, and ran the show. Lynch had virtually nothing to do with it. To fulfill our contractual obligation to Worldvision, we then had to write *On the Air*. I remember this as an endless marathon. At the end of which I went down to New Orleans to shoot *Storyville*—already exhausted from the previous three years.

What about something called *The 72 Hour Club?* **Do you remember that one at all? Was that around this time as well?**

No, that was much earlier. A spec romantic comedy I wrote in the early eighties that never got made, but it brought me to the attention of a few producers I later went on to work with. A reworking of *The Philadelphia Story*—*Philadelphia Story* meets the Marx Brothers. A lot of fun to write.

Who were those producers?

I ended up putting it with my friend Larry Brezner, who I later wrote the sequel to *Good Morning, Vietnam* for, and many years later we did *The Greatest Game Ever Played* together. Larry became a lifelong friend, as did his partner, David Steinberg. They were Robin Williams's and Billy Crystal's managers, so I got to know all those guys. That was the most fun I had on the social side of show business, because they were so much fun to know. David was the closest guy in the world to Robin. He'd managed him since 1977.

That was *Good Morning, Chicago*, right? When did you write that?

There was a writers strike in '88, and I wrote *Good Morning, Chicago* just before or after that, after the *Twin Peaks* pilot.

And what happened to that film?

Disney liked the script a lot, and I got to know Robin during the writing because his managers were such good friends of mine. Robin Williams got an Oscar nomination for *Dead Poets Society*, and he just didn't want to do a sequel. Sequels were looked down on at that time, as hard as that is to imagine now, when eight out of every ten films is a sequel. It was considered bad form or a cash grab, particularly on a "prestige/ Oscar picture." Robin had done great work in *Poets*—that opened up a whole other world for him in terms of what he was being offered. He just didn't want to go back and repeat himself, although the two movies would have been radically different.

OK, so you're writing season two of *Twin Peaks* at the same time that you're doing *American Chronicles* and *On the Air*?

No, we wrote *On the Air* a bit later. I had directed the pilot for *Chronicles*, because at that point we didn't know if *Twin Peaks* was going to be picked up for season two and Spelling was saying, "You have to give us another show." I had a pretty good idea *Twin Peaks* was going to be picked up, so I tried to think of something really different that wouldn't be as labor-intensive as a scripted show. I had this background in documentaries, so I pitched the idea to Barry Diller—running Fox at the time—and he bought it on the spot. By the end of the year, I realized I'd bitten off more than I could chew. *On the Air* was written after I'd done the pilot for *American Chronicles*—during season two of *Peaks*, before I went down to New Orleans to shoot *Storyville*.

The internet has you and David codirecting the *American Chronicles* episode "Champions," which supposedly aired in the UK but never in the US. That is inaccurate, correct?

That's utter nonsense.

Did you direct it yourself?

I don't think I did, either. What was the subject matter?

I haven't been able to find it anywhere.

I know we did a profile of George Foreman. Could it have been that?

"We" meaning you or you and David?

Me. David had zero to do with *American Chronicles*. I don't believe he ever saw anything beyond the pilot.

If you go back and look at contemporaneous newspaper articles about *American Chronicles*, it's incredible how many of them have "Lynch" in the headlines. So beyond "Farewell to the Flesh," the first episode, which you directed, what was your specific involvement in the show?

Most of the subject matter came from ideas I developed with my team, all documentary folks. They'd go off and shoot it. Then we'd put the shows together in the editing room.

It was a pretty bold experiment—to sell half-hour "docu-poetry," as it was being referred to at the time, to viewers of American prime-time commercial television. What was your goal with that show?

I had that background in documentaries in Minneapolis, and I wanted to try something a little less driven by traditional narrative, that was more visually oriented. So this opportunity came up after getting heavy pressure from the Spelling organization, even though we had the hottest show in America, to get a second show on the air. Aaron was a volume producer, that was his MO, and I kind of stupidly said, "Well, OK, I'll try to get another one going."

I wanted to do the original pilot about Mardis Gras in order to set the tone for the series—a colorful, immersive way to look at slices of Americana, visual tone poems that were more impressionistic than information driven. Unfortunately, it got picked up [laughs], so I had to do both shows simultaneously.

Do you remember anything special about that shoot?

We shot Mardis Gras 1990 for the pilot, if I have that right. I pulled in some crews I knew from the documentary world that I'd worked with, four in all. We plotted the schedule for the entire two weeks of Mardi Gras. Then it was complete madness. Running around that crazy town at the peak of its insanity, shooting everything in sight—tons of material and interviews. What I like about documentaries is you find it in the editing room. You don't lay down the script with an iron hand and then execute it. It's more a process of discovery, an enjoyable contrast to more structured storytelling.

Was there any model film you were trying to emulate, or did you see this as a new idea?

It's a weird comp, but for Mardis Gras, the film I remember looking at was *Black Orpheus*, set during carnival in Rio. It captured the kind of pageantry I wanted, because I saw Mardis Gras as a uniquely pan-American tradition—with French, Spanish, Cuban, African-American, Creole culture. A real gumbo of influences. I felt that was woefully underappreciated when we think of Mardis Gras. That was the story I wanted to tell.

And what about Richard Dreyfuss, who narrates? Where did he come from?

There was a guy who used to do radio dramas for KCRW in LA named Joe Frank, and he had a deadpan, stream-of-consciousness way of speaking that was really effective in telling stories for that medium. They weren't documentaries. He did this sort of free-form magical-realism storytelling; his delivery was really effective, so I tried him as the narrator initially. He'd never done anything for anybody other than himself. It turned out he worked fantastically well with his own material, but when we played him against the visuals here, it didn't enhance them—it tended to flatten them out. I realized I needed a more expressive voice, and I'd always loved Richard's work. So we asked if he'd be interested in doing something like this. We met, got along well, and he did become the voice of the show.

OK, so let's move over to *On the Air*. Where did that idea come from?

ABC wanted us to do another show, and as I said, we were obligated to deliver three shows within a certain time frame for Spelling, so we owed them one more. My dad, as you know, had worked in live television—he was the stage manager for *Philco Playhouse*—and I'd heard stories for years about the wacky stuff that would go on during live broadcasts. I told David about this, and we started talking about it and came up with the idea of trying a half-hour comedy about it. I drew on some of my dad's stories for them. Obviously, it took a more surreal tone by the time it was finished. After the pilot, I stepped away from it. I was too busy with *Twin Peaks* to get hugely involved in the series. So I cowrote the pilot and one other script and supervised some of the writing, but I wasn't involved with the production much.

Right, the first episode is credited to you and David.

We definitely wrote that pilot together.

For this and for the original *Twin Peaks* pilot, and later on season three, you and David were in the weeds together writing all those?

For those, we were on Skype for a year. Not every day, but close to it.

And who would you say was the showrunner for *On the Air*?

I don't recall. It might have been Bob Engels.

You're credited with two and a half episodes. Bob Engels has two and half, Scott has one, David has one and a half.

It was probably Bob. I wrote the one my friend Chuck McCann was in. I don't remember what the other one was.

The second episode. It's a funny episode. Betty [Marla Rubinoff] is invited to dinner by the owner of the network, and Lester [Ian Buchanan] and Miguel's character are very jealous. It's really funny.

That's good. Unfortunately, your memories of these things get colored by the reaction, and the reaction was honestly calamitous. Really, ABC treated it like we'd brought in a leprous corpse and laid it at their doorstep. They were really rude about it.

Is this something like what *One Saliva Bubble* would have been?

I think there's a little overlap there. It certainly felt that way while writing it, a callback to that deadpan, absurd tone of *Bubble*. I just know the pilot ended up a lot broader than I thought it was going to be. I mean it's way out there, and it's really funny, but I thought it was going to be a hard thing to sustain.

One of the funniest things is Bozeman's Simplex, that sight condition that afflicts Blinky, the FX guy. Do you remember where that came from?

Bozeman, Montana. Lynch had lived in Montana, so I guess that's where it came from. I don't know what Simplex is supposed to mean. I was a big fan of *SCTV*—I thought it was more daring and original than *Saturday Night Live*—so *On the Air* was probably a little ahead of its time for network in terms of broadness of tone. Honestly, I haven't looked at it since, and I don't remember much about it. ABC wanted it off the air so fast they just dug a shallow grave and kicked dirt on top of it. Not the sort of thing you look back on fondly. I know the show has its fans. We're trying to get it out on DVD at some point, and I hope we do. I'd probably look at it again now and find it funny.

Next came *Storyville*, which was your first theatrical film since *The Believers* and also the first—and only—feature film you ever directed. The film has an interesting history to it: based on an Australian book, optioned in 1983, originally announced in 1985, and then you began writing the script in 1986—so even before *Goddess*. Plus you are co-credited as writer with someone named Lee Reynolds.

Lee Reynolds wrote the first draft before I ever came on the scene, which I think was in '88.

How did the final script differ from what you inherited?

I don't recall much about it. The novel was set in Australia. His draft had moved it to New Orleans, but it felt like window dressing more than culturally the feel of New Orleans. Having been down there a lot, experiencing the Mardis Gras trip for *American Chronicles*, scouting a lot of locations—I felt like I got to know the city pretty well. Most of the films set there just use it as an exotic backdrop instead of digging into the fabric of the place. So that was my intent—create something redolent of the real town, the real feel of the place. I drew heavily on the past of New Orleans. In the way that *Chinatown* is about water in LA, this story was about oil in New Orleans, mineral rights, and how that shaped the dominant political culture. So I told the producers, "I'm gonna start over." I kept some of the basics of the plot but not a lot else. He did get a credit on it, as often happens, because he was the first writer in.

You shot in '91, down in New Orleans, but the studio held up the release, to time it to the presidential conventions?

It was a little more pragmatic than that. They had some independent Australian money to make the movie, but they didn't have enough to release it. They made a deal with a producer at Fox who had a put picture deal—which means you basically rent the studio's distribution system—and $5 million of print and advertising money that he promised to the movie so it got a proper release.

What happened was when the picture was finished, time to write the check, he claimed he didn't have the money. We still had the release slot, but it was a picture that Fox had no vested interest in whatsoever. If it had been the biggest hit of all time, they wouldn't have made a nickel. So they basically dumped it. It was horribly demoralizing. The producers couldn't believe it, but they had no recourse. The producer who'd screwed them, in essence said, "Well, if you want to come after me, just sue me." He undoubtedly had the money; he just didn't want to part with it, and meanwhile, he walked away with a hefty producer's fee. So it was a very bitter lesson. Have you found a copy of it? Have you been able to see it?

Of course, yes. I really like it, especially the atmosphere. It's unsettling.

I really liked it too. It was an incredibly bitter experience to work so hard on something and get screwed like this by a producer's bad faith. A real eye-opener in terms of how the movie business works, and it soured me on directing, frankly. It drove me to go write my first book. I said, "I don't want to be at the mercy of an unscrupulous producer—particularly for a job as hard as directing a picture—ever again." It was a pivotal life moment for me, because it made me realize I didn't want to do this for a living if I'm surrounded by a bunch of pirates I can't trust. And that's what put me firmly on the path of a dedicated publishing career.

You had a screening in Sundance, right? How did that go?

It went well. It just didn't help us at all. It was the same year *Reservoir Dogs* set the world on fire, and *Storyville* was much quieter and more old-fashioned than that. I realized I'd made something closer to a Sidney Lumet movie at a time when the taste of the audience was moving in a decidedly different direction.

Did you run into Oliver Stone down there at all while he was shooting *JFK*?

We actually ended up shooting in the same courtroom. We got in there first, and I brushed up against him once. The climax of our movie is set in the same courtroom that Kevin Costner is in as Jim Garrison.

Ironic, given your interest in the Kennedys. Plus there have been comparisons made between the Fowlers—the political dynasty in *Storyville*—and the Kennedys.

That was an intentional connection. James Spader was right for it, the right look and the right feel. I thought it was one of James's best performances, actually. *Storyville* was a dynastic drama about the hidden secrets behind the New Orleans happy, fun time facade. It's a truly sinister place in some ways.

I tried to ground it as a family story, generations of rivalry and greed—the usual things that drive people to act in their own self-interest, against those of the people they love and those around them. And it's a story frankly of post-Reconstruction racism in the South, which warped how the South developed. I thought, "Wouldn't it be interesting to see a guy who's this kind of louche, go-along get-along good-time Charlie suddenly be thrust into a situation where he's got to stand up against not only his own family but generations of malfeasance on the backs of poor and indigent people?" That felt to me like a worthy subject.

When you look at some of these reviews *Storyville* got at the time, it's hard to believe you never directed again. I'm reading here where *The New York Times* is commenting on "the director's remarkable way with his actors," and *The Washington Post* says, "You only have to watch a few minutes to know you're in the presence of a major new moviemaking talent." Do you read reviews, by the way?

I'll read reviews from people whose point of view I respect, because I think it's worth knowing how people react. My dad taught me a long time ago you have to the skin of a rhinoceros in this business. Bad reviews always make you angry, but I've learned to shake it off. Maybe you're mad for three minutes, but there's no reason to think about it beyond that. It's my favorite line from *The Big Lebowski*, right? "Well, that's just, like, your opinion, man." That's all any review is. None of it really matters.

What about fan comments on the internet. Do you read them?

Fans have been pretty great, for the most part, especially for *Twin Peaks*. They're smart, engaged, inquisitive, and to a large extent, it was their keeping the thing alive that created the opening to come back. So I've always felt a strong connection to that community. I've tried to show my appreciation for them, and I don't mind doing that at all. I just let them know "I'm not going to give any definitive answers to your questions." I'll encourage the questions, and I'm happy to engage with them, but I also tell them it doesn't matter what I think. What matters is what you think; you're the one who watched it. When you make the sausage, you don't want to have it for breakfast every day.

At some point along the way, I'm going to disagree with you about that. You and David Lynch both say it doesn't matter what you think, but I think it does. It doesn't necessarily mean it has to be the definitive determination—and I can see that you don't want to influence people—but I do think it matters what a creator thinks his work is saying.

And I agree with you. The difficulty there is that's always been Lynch's MO to resolutely refuse to talk about his work. And my suspicion is, knowing him as I do, that he may not have done the spadework that would allow him to be articulate about it, because he works so often out of his subconscious. I don't mind having those conversations; it's just that when he's involved, I try to avoid definitive statements because I know it only pisses him off.

Anyway, I'm digressing, because what I started off meaning to say was that that's pretty high praise, from the *Times* and the *Post*, which are not inconsequential publications.

It was cold comfort, but some comfort, when the film opened and closed without a trace because it didn't have any marketing support. What I learned about myself was that the reason I enjoyed directing was—coming from the theater—I loved directing actors. I got to work with Jason Robards, Woody Strode, legends in our business. Piper Laurie was marvelous as always, and Spader was just a champ to work with. That was the fun for me. The rest of it—the politicking, the studio stuff—all felt corrosive, and nothing I really wanted to do for a living. I regret that I haven't directed another movie, and I've thought about it. But the overall experience was so negative it pushed me back into fiction and prose, and that's been the most fulfilling work I've done since.

So much of what you have to do as a filmmaker is all that currying of talent, showing the studio you're willing to work for them before you work for yourself. And it's only gotten worse. I look at most of the films being made today—and I'm a fan of a great number of them—but there aren't many I look at and say, "Gee, I really wish I had directed that."

Watch a *Star Wars* movie, and you think it may have once been the vision of one creative person, but now it's a corporate work of commerce, albeit entertaining, that minimizes all risk at the altar of profit. I just realized this wasn't the lifestyle I wanted for myself. I wanted something more contemplative, and I thought my best work would probably lie elsewhere. So that became a fork in the road for me.

Was it worse than working for network TV back in the day?

Yes, at least that had a system to it, one that was reliable. There weren't a lot of crazy people. You'd run into unreasonable dimwits occasionally, but not many who were truly malevolent. There's more than a few in the modern motion picture business who fit that description.

You mentioned that when you got the opportunity to direct *Hill Street*, Gregory Hoblit was an influence on you. Did you learn anything about directing from David?

The thing you learn from Lynch is he has a wonderful way—I'd noticed this even before, in John Schlesinger—this way they had in common of being open and available to the moment. You're working with roughly a hundred other people around you, and although everything's planned down to the studs, you need to allow ideas to occur to you in the moment. They may occur to anybody on set, from the lead to the prop master's assistant. So be open to all sorts of different ideas and make use of them. I compare the job to being a conductor of an orchestra.

I'm not a huge fan of the auteur theory to begin with. Film is—except in very few instances—in my experience much more collaborative than the auteur theory wants to let you believe. But there are a few singular voices. I would include Lynch in that group, because he's also a writer, and his take on things is inimitable. You'd never mistake a Lynch film for anybody else's, so he deserves his reputation. He's like a painter working in a room surrounded by a lot of other people, and for better or worse, that's what you're gonna get. Most directors are there to get everybody else to do their best work on time and budget and give the studio a product they can successfully promote. So I don't have a romantic view of the film industry; that can't survive working in it as long as I have.

Just following up on that for a moment: Do you believe in the auteur theory as it applies to TV? Can you identify a Steven Bochco series or a Mark Frost series or a David Chase series?

I think it's more possible now, because there are more distinctive voices working than ever before. Television, for the most part, has been of the moment and, with rare exceptions, had very little on its mind other than entertaining. Certainly in broadcast television, network television, you can argue the programming is there primarily to lull the audience into a state of drowsy receptiveness for the advertising that props up the whole enterprise.

You can even take that further. The research shows us that television advertising doesn't have much of a firm basis in science. It doesn't really work. That's the astonishing myth at the center of broadcast TV: this idea we're doing all this work because advertisers are reaching their consumers and shows provide the vehicle for their message to be conveyed. But the research tells us it isn't terribly effective. It's a hard mathematical path to take you directly from "Well, this is how much I've spent on advertising for television and this is how much return I see on my dollar." It's largely illusory.

8

"I Much Prefer Working Alone"

(An Author's Life)

Following a run of unpleasant experiences in his television and film work, Mark Frost made a momentous decision: to focus on authoring books instead, convinced it would empower him as a writer. As he himself puts it below, "I wanted to be more in control of my own destiny."

His first two novels, *The List of Seven* (1993) and the sequel, *The Six Messiahs* (1995), are supernatural-themed steampunk thrillers pairing a real-world historical figure, Arthur Conan Doyle, with a creature of Frost's imagination, a Sherlock Holmes-like secret agent by the name of Jack Sparks. There's plenty here to evoke *Twin Peaks*: a cosmic battle between good and evil, a doppelgänger of sorts, and Theosophy (Madame Helena Blavatsky, a Russian occultist who became the leading theoretician of Theosophy in the late-nineteenth century, even appears as a character in *The List of Seven*).

Frost's next novel, *Before I Wake*, a police procedural, was published in 1998 under a pseudonym, Eric Bowman, at the counsel of his agent, to avoid confusing his authorial brand (the surname lifted from a lake by his grandmother's house in upstate New York); it too is a meditation on the nature of evil, focusing on a New York homicide cop (Jimmy Montone) who, like Agent Dale Cooper in *Twin Peaks*, becomes romantically entangled with a subject in his investigation, and confronts an adversary (Terence Keyes) who is, in some ways, a mirror image of himself.

Between 2002 and 2009, Frost published four nonfiction sports books. Three of those—*The Greatest Game Ever Played: Harry Vardon, Francis Ouimet, and the Birth of Modern Golf* (2002), *The Grand Slam: Bobby Jones, America, and the Story of Golf* (2004), and *The Match: The Day the Game of Golf Changed Forever* (2007)—were on golf, a sport he has played since youth. His fourth sports book—*Game Six: Cincinnati, Boston, and the 1975 World Series: The Triumph of America's Pastime* (2009)—was on baseball, a game that he himself played when younger and that his sister's son Lucas Giolito (a pitcher) plays professionally (for the Chicago White Sox as of this writing).

His fourth novel, *The Second Objective,* published in 2007, marked a change of pace: set during World War II (Battle of the Bulge), the trifurcated narrative shifts among three main characters: a ruthless SS officer (Erich Von Leinsdorf), a conflicted German private (Bernard Oster, who was raised in Brooklyn before returning to his homeland with his German parents), and a no-nonsense American MP (Earl Grannit) who was a New York City cop before enlisting.

Next, Frost turned his attention to the young-adult market, publishing a trilogy of *Harry Potter*–esque books collectively known as *The Paladin Prophecy Trilogy: The Paladin Prophecy* (2012), *Alliance* (2013), and *Rogue* (2015). The tomes follow a supernaturally gifted boy by the name of Will West who finds himself at the epicenter of—you guessed it—a struggle between titanic forces of good and evil.

Finally, as we talked in 2018 and 2019, Frost was deeply immersed in a new book, on the life and times of Jiddu Krishnamurti (1895–1986), one of the greatest philosophical and spiritual figures of the twentieth century, and a man for whom Frost has long had enormous respect and admiration. At the age of fourteen, Krishnamurti was discovered by the Theosophist Charles Webster Leadbeater, who proclaimed him to be the "vehicle" of a messianic entity known as the World Teacher, whose imminent arrival Leadbeater and other members of the Theosophy Society had anticipated.

Krishnamurti was adopted by Dr. Annie Besant, then president of the society, but had a falling out with Leadbeater, who was booted from the society in 1906 after a sex scandal involving adolescent boys. Krishnamurti eventually renounced his role as the World Teacher and cut all ties to any religious or spiritual organization. His core message resonates deeply with Frost and has inspired him in his own spiritual journey over the decades: "Truth is a pathless land. Man cannot come to it through any organization, through any creed, through any dogma, priest or ritual, not through any philosophic knowledge or psychological technique. He has to find it through the mirror of relationship, through the understanding of the contents of his own mind, through observation and not through intellectual analysis or introspective dissection."

***

Your first book, *The List of Seven*, came out in 1993, so two years after the demise of *Twin Peaks*. When did you start writing that book and thinking of becoming a novelist? Was that during *Twin Peaks* or after the show had ended?

Twin Peaks had ended at that point, and as I said, I was determined to try something new. I had met the man who became my literary agent—a very important and wonderful figure in my life, one of the great literary agents of the last seventy-five years—a man named Ed Victor, who we lost in 2017. We first met when Ed handled—and I worked closely with him—putting together deals for *The Secret Diary of Laura Palmer*, the Agent Cooper book [*The Autobiography of F. B. I. Special Agent Dale Cooper: My Life, My Tapes*], and the [*Twin Peaks*] access guide. He was a tremendous help navigating the publishing business, and we were becoming fast friends when I told him I wanted to take on writing a novel and asked if he'd represent me. So that was the start of my second career. I owe a tremendous amount to Ed for his guidance and just his savviness about how that business worked, and through it I was able to start this whole new way of expressing myself.

Was that an adjustment for you, working in a room by yourself instead of in a writers' room?

No, not at all. I'd be writing since I was nine, so the things that were actually more of an aberration in my life had been collaborative writing. And I literally just did it for those years with *Twin Peaks* and Lynch. I much prefer working alone.

172

How long did it take you to write *The List of Seven*?

I wrote the first 125 pages, and we sold it on that basis. We had an auction, and William Morrow bought the rights. That took about three months. The rest of it took another ten dedicated months.

Hemingway once said, "Writing is easy; you just open a vein and bleed." Is writing hard for you?

It's always been a way of life for me, so to say it comes easy is doing it a disservice. There were twenty years of apprenticeship and growing pains before I really felt, "OK, I understand the instrument now." I hear stories, horror stories, of people who have been blocked, can't get unstuck, and have trouble producing. I've never had that trouble. I just sit down and do it.

At one point, you were thinking of calling the book *The Left Handed Path*, but you went with *The List of Seven* instead. Do you remember why?

In Theosophy, the Left Handed Path is associated with evil, with black magic. That was the path Alexander [the villain in the book] had followed. But I once asked Ed Victor what constitutes a good book title, and he made it a simple axiom: "A good title is a title of a book that sells well. Those are the ones people remember."

Not that much help, though.

Well, it only helped in retrospect. What he was saying is, it doesn't matter what it is. If it connects and the book works, then it's a good title. There's no surefire formula. Titles are funny things. Sometimes you have it right away, sometimes it's the first thing you have, and sometimes it's unbelievably difficult to find exactly the right one. Titles are fungible.

When you sit down with a book idea—here we're talking about fiction, novels—how much of the plot do you know in advance? How

much of it comes to you as you're writing?

I do a lot of collecting and thinking about ideas for a certain amount of time that's not the same from project to project. Just until I feel I've got enough tools in the toolbox to start writing, so it will vary a lot from book to book, project to project. And I think as I've gotten older, I spend less time outlining and more time collecting my thoughts. Then I just let it rip once I'm ready.

Do you find yourself going in unexpected directions?

Constantly.

Even on major points? Did you know before you sat down to write *The List of Seven*, for example, that the villain of the piece would be Jack's brother?

No.

Do you rewrite a lot?

Always. Writing is ninety-five percent rewriting. It's also a good way to prime the pump when you're starting the day. Get the gears working. But I would say that in the last ten to fifteen years writing has become—I don't want to say easy, that's not what I'm trying to describe. You get to a point where you have a sense of mastery, where a lot of the work takes place at an intuitive level. After these many years, that's where I've ended up.

So here are you talking about writing novels or any kind of writing?

Writing in general.

Did you have somebody whom you were showing pages to as you were writing it?

On *List*? Only to Ed.

Two-part question: how and when did the structure or theme come to you, and how much research was involved? Did you have to go back and read every Sherlock Holmes story ever written, to say nothing of Doyle himself and all that research?

I did a tremendous amount of research into Doyle. I read—or reread, since I'd devoured Holmes as a teenager—I read all the stories, loved them. I'd written that first 125-page section, the part that sold the book, then went to London to do some research. I was on my way to the British Museum—there's a big sequence in the museum in the book—turned a corner in that neighborhood and came face to face with a Theosophy bookstore. In the window was a gigantic photograph of Madame Blavatsky. I'd already written the scenes with her, so I took that as a good omen.

If you remember, there's a scene in the museum basement with the mummies. So I went in, hired a tour guide to show me around, and he tells me there is a massive subbasement—à la the last shot in *Indiana Jones*—of an unimaginably vast collection of things that aren't on display. So those sort of intuitive, synchronistic moments tell you,"OK, I'm on to something."

I traveled up to Whitby, in Yorkshire, the area where they go near the end of the book—and where Bram Stoker had set part of *Dracula*—to visit the ruined abbey, the inspiration for [Stoker's] scene of Dracula's arrival in Britain. I love doing that kind of research. There's lots of facts in research that are useful and important, and you have to pay attention to them, but what I value more is the sensory exercise of going to a place, feeling what it's like, and then writing from that. The book benefited, I think, a great deal from that attention to detail, and it set the pattern for everything I've done subsequently.

Were you surprised to discover that the creator of Sherlock Holmes had so avidly embraced spiritualism? Is that something you already

knew or you discovered it in the course of researching the book?

A little of both. I knew some of it, but the spiritualism angle, which is on page one of any biography of him, really gave me the key to the story I wanted to tell.

But Doyle really ventured deep into spiritualism. A lot of people thought he was a crackpot. Is that the sense that you got, that he went over the edge?

I think that happened to him later in life. He lost a son in World War I. Until that point, he'd been a rigorous, scientifically trained observer of the laws of science, and that's how I characterized him in the book. He didn't go over the edge until well into middle age, when he'd become somewhat deranged by grief and, like a lot of people then, was suckered by frauds selling access to lost loved ones through phony séances.

Following the route of the story, he did begin as a skeptic and helped debunk some of these spiritualist quacks, but later in life fell prey to it—most famously the investigation into photographs of alleged fairies two young women had claimed to have taken. You write about somebody that intimately and you get a feel for them. The poor man was taken advantage of and exploited, and then the whole thing turned out to be a fraud. I have a lot of sympathy for him.

There was also that really famous split between Doyle and Harry Houdini over the 1922 séance in Atlantic City, where Doyle's wife—a self-proclaimed medium—claimed to have contacted Houdini's mother, and then Houdini essentially denounced her as a fraud.

Had I done a third book, I would have brought Houdini into it. I still think about that every once and awhile.

I either read or heard that you had a séance experience once yourself, in Minnesota.

I did. It's when I was a student intern at the Guthrie Theater. We got to know the stage crew who ran the theater and started hearing stories that the place was haunted. Most theaters have stories like this. There had been a kid in his late teenage years, early adulthood, who'd been an usher in the midsixties, and this poor soul had apparently taken his own life a few years earlier. The one place he felt comfortable in life was supposedly working as an usher at the Guthrie, to the extent he was buried in his usher's uniform. So they told us his spirit allegedly was in the theater, and there were some kids in the theater intern group who were monkeying around with ouija boards. So somehow this turned into a conversation about, "Well, if it's a real ghost, we should try to contact him." The idea did not come from me; I was just along for the ride.

Long story short, it ended up with a group—six or seven of us and one stagehand with the keys to the backdoor—going in there late one night. After midnight, when the show had let out, and everybody had left the theater. As you may know, there's an old tradition in the theater: you never turn off all the lights. You always leave one light burning on stage, known colloquially as the ghost light. I think every theater on Broadway does it, and it's an English tradition as well: you leave a ghost light burning in case there are spirits in the theater that need comforting.

So under the light of the ghost light, we went out onto the mainstage at the Guthrie, and we set up a ouija board on a table. I can't remember if I was actively on the little plastic gizmo that shoots around—the planchette, I think they call it. I think I may have been, with someone else in the group. Suddenly, I started to feel something tugging at this thing.

I've never used a ouija board.

I wouldn't advise it. It's probably a really bad idea. This was the first time I ever used one. The ouija board was a staple of nineteenth-century spiritualists.

Sure enough, all of a sudden this planchette starts zooming around the board as we're asking questions, and it's spelling out letters faster than we can even keep track of what they're spelling. Someone was writing down the letters, and afterward would figure out what they said.

Long story short, it appeared that the spirit, or whatever this was that was responding to the questions, identified itself as the poor late, lamented usher. And somebody asked, "Where are you?" and it spelled out TOP. Well, at that time, the Guthrie had a second stage—it was an old downtown mansion on the other side of Loring Park that was known as The Other Place, The Other Place theater; TOP was the acronym. Everybody called it TOP. And I think it may have even been me who asked the question "You mean The Other Place?" It shot immediately to "no." Someone else looked up and asked: "Do you mean up in the catwalks?" And at that point, we heard footsteps in the catwalks above us. The next thing I remember, I was standing outside the theater. We ran so fast.

That would pretty much make me a believer. Not you?

It certainly made me a questioner. Although it's possible the stagehands were playing an elaborate prank on us—scare the crap out of a bunch of teenagers—but nothing like that ever surfaced. So I don't think that's what—I mean, I don't know what it was. I know I never laid my hands on a ouija board again.

That was Doyle, right? He was convinced people could talk to you from beyond?

Right. And I was curious about this, as I tend to be. So after it happened, I did a bunch of research. I'm sure all that was in the back of my mind whenever it was—twenty-some years later—when I wrote *The List of Seven.*

I know you had another brush with death—only this time your own—one time on the golf course, and I'm wondering what sort of

impact that had on you.

I was vacationing in Palm Springs. Before *Twin Peaks*, 1988 or so. In the spring, but it was really hot, crazy hot, and also really humid, which was unusual. What had happened was Palm Springs had changed since I'd gone there as a kid. They'd added so many golf courses with so much irrigation that the humidity had gotten extremely high there. So I was dehydrated, and I was taking some kind of cold medication, maybe for allergies. I came off the course, back to the room, and started having a rapid, irregular heartbeat. So I said, "I gotta go get this checked out." It was frightening. I was in the ambulance—the first time I'd ever been in an ambulance—on the way to the hospital, and it seemed to me that at one point, I was floating above my body and hearing voices. I don't remember what they said, but it was either hallucinatory or something like what I've often heard mentioned in near-death experiences. So I got to the hospital, and they gave me something that calmed my heart down, checked me out, and said I was fine and let me go within a few hours.

Did that experience change you in any fundamental way?

I think it made me a little less fearful of dying, a little less anxious about it. And it probably led me to look at some of the spiritual, nondenominational stuff I started to investigate.

I don't know if you read Martha Nochimson's book *The Passion of David Lynch*, but she says that you look at the irrational warily and that you try to find a rational explanation for things, and she's drawing this dichotomous relationship between you and David. When something like that happens to you, are you prone to believe the supernatural explanation, or are you naturally inclined to look for the rational possibility behind it? In other words, do you think you were hallucinating, or do you think it's more likely that you were undergoing some sort of otherworldly experience?

In that instance, I keep an open mind and say it could be either—

or it could be both. I don't know; I try not to get too dependent on definitions. If it's not a straightforward objective experience, I don't necessarily expect a concrete, rational explanation. Nor do I dismiss out of hand the possibility it could be something else.

So, in your mind, there could be an otherworldly explanation for it? You don't have to find a rational reason?

Right.

That was one of the problems I had with that book: her characterization of you seems off target, at least to me.

I remember speaking to her once, but she didn't know much about me and didn't seem interested. She's an academic who had worked up all these pet theories about Lynch and was just looking to have them confirmed.

Just before we leave the subject of research, did you also read earlier detective stories by people like Wilkie Collins and August Derleth?

Yes, in high school.

But not specifically for *The List of Seven* and *The Six Messiahs*?

No, but I reread some Poe, and I read *The Moonstone* by Wilkie Collins.

Not to digress, but I can't leave this subject without asking if your *Twin Peaks* character, Cyril Pons, is named after Solar Pons—the Derleth detective created as a pastiche of Holmes?

You're the only person who's ever picked up on that, but yes, that was a conscious choice.

All your novels—*Before I Wake*, the Jack Sparks books, *The Second Objective*—they all touch on this subject of duality and the shadow

self, the psychology of it. That really seems like a recurring theme in your work. We had already seen a lot of that in season two of *Twin Peaks*—season one, really, if you consider Maddy and Laura. This is particularly prominent in the Doyle books with Jack and his brother, Alexander, who are mirror images of each other. I know that Carl Jung has influenced your work. Is this Mark Frost riffing on Jung's shadow self?

This was my theory of Holmes, having read all the stories and lived with them. I had a frustration with Holmes's limitation as a logic calculator. Doyle never delved deeply into his psychology. He was presented prima facie as a human supercomputer; the darkness was only hinted at. The recent iteration of Holmes with Benedict Cumberbatch does a brilliant job of opening that up; on the surface, they make it clear he's a sociopath. Everybody accounts themselves brilliantly in that work. I don't know that anybody else got there—aside from Nick Meyer [author of *The Seven-Per-Cent Solution*]—before *The List of Seven*. My thought was that Sparks was the model for Holmes, who's then obviously sanitized in Doyle's stories. My thought was: how crazy, how tormented, how troubled, what kind of twisted genius would he have been to inspire the man Doyle wrote about?

But the doppelgänger, or shadow self, how did they become such a preoccupation of yours? Because you see it not just in the *Twin Peaks* and the Doyle books, but also variations of it in *Before I Wake* and *The Second Objective*. Did that come from Jung? Have you ever read Poe's "William Wilson"? Was David equally preoccupied with this idea?

In *Twin Peaks*, it evolved in bits and pieces and coalesced as a theme. I don't think we ever sat down and talked about it. There was no time, and Lynch wasn't around.

It's also a part of primal mythology in countless forms throughout history. Joseph Campbell touches on it a lot as something present in both the individual and the collective psyche: the shadow self, Jung's idea of the unincorporated darkness that lies within the psyche. Although Lynch is resolutely antipsychological, I think that is something he's also tapped into. It's a universal phenomenon, and he's dealt with it in almost everything he's done.

"Darkness within the psyche." I look at your whole body of work—novels, TV, film—and I see this as another Mark Frost preoccupation. What is evil? Why does it exist? Why do some people turn out evil and others good? I mean, there's that whole conversation in the woods in season two of *Twin Peaks* where they debate what Bob is, what evil is. This is also a hugely prominent theme in the *Paladin Prophecy* trilogy—the young-adult books you wrote between 2012 and 2015.

Yes.

You deal with it very broadly on two levels: a human level and a cosmic level. Let's talk first about the psychological approach. In *Before I Wake*—which is a police procedural you wrote pseudonymously in 1997 as Eric Bowman—you write about a psychotic killer and the policeman who chases after him, establishing that the two have a lot in common. So why did one turn out one way and the other another? The psychologist in that book promotes the theory that evil is something that people choose, rather than something that is thrust upon them by whatever influencing factors are at play. They have a choice. Was that you talking?

I think it's both. Obviously, there's an evil-doing aspect of human consciousness residing in a neural network that evolved from animalistic origins, so there is a pull in the limbic system and the brain stem toward violence, self-preservation, savagery, and survival of the fittest. That's brain-stem reality, the reptilian part of the brain. So it's a challenge for humans to rise above that, and always has been. Add to that a particular toxic mix of social/familial experiences—usually involving abuse, deprivation, isolation—that can give a turbocharge to the underlying animalistic aggressions that everyone struggles with. So in that sense, I see it as nature and nurture. For the most part, you don't find a sociopath or a psychopath from a happy, well-adjusted home. That much we think we know at this point. Our president is living proof. So if I was going to parse it in terms of nature/nurture, I would put it about fifty-fifty.

I once interviewed a very successful TV showrunner who said he was something of an anomaly in Hollywood because he feels—and I'm quoting him here—that humans are "stupid, evil, and uncivilized, children must be civilized, and we must all do the exact opposite of what we feel and would like to do constantly every day. You have a good wolf and a bad wolf, and whichever wolf you feed will be supreme." He said, "That's anathema to many of my brethren," a reference to other writers and producers in Hollywood. Do you agree with that?

Well, Hollywood is a particularly Darwinian system, and when the ends justify the means, sociopaths are often inordinately rewarded. But I wouldn't entirely agree with that. Plenty of people emerge from poverty or ignorance or deprivation to become extraordinary without either the church or some authoritarian institution casting dark shadows over them out of fear. That may have been more true in previous eras than it is now. If you read somebody like Steven Pinker, who looks at the history of the human race from an Olympian point of view, all evidence seemingly to the contrary, we're nowhere near as ignorant and evil and malfeasant as we have been in centuries past.

I'll fall back on Lebowski again: "Yeah well, that's just, ya know, like, your opinion, man." I'm not going to dispute your personal truth, but that doesn't mean it's true for everybody.

Let's stay on this nature-versus-nurture theme a bit. So in your mind, when you were writing *The List of Seven* and *The Six Messiahs*, why do Jack and Alexander Sparks turn out to be on different ends of the good-versus-evil spectrum—two brothers from the same biological parents? Is there an answer to that?

Sure, and it's a simple one. It's free will.

You're saying Alexander chooses to be a psychopath?

Let's say he chooses not to be a person who ignores those impulses. Jack has them as well; you see it in his behavior. He knows what he's capable of. Where do you draw the line? Let's take an obvious example: behavior during wartime. I'm rereading Audie Murphy's autobiography, *To Hell and Back*. It's a famous war memoir. He was the most decorated United States soldier in World War II. He went on to become a movie star and world-famous eventually. He was a poor Texas farm boy, unprepossessing, not very big, not very strong. Yet when he joined the infantry, and they sent him into Italy, where he saw his first action, he turned into a killing machine. Because he was doing it in the service of a good cause, he became a hero. So it then becomes a question of, "What does your society value?" Most of the people who had those kinds of experiences never recovered from them psychologically. Some of them were able to brush it off and move on, but what does that say about them? Some of them ended up in Hollywood. Lee Marvin saw a lot of heavy action in World War II, in the Pacific. He drank a lot, had a lot of darkness in him. Neville Brand—you may remember from the old TV western *Laredo*—was a decorated soldier in Europe in World War II. Fred Rogers, decorated, World War II. Jimmy Stewart went off to war a gangly juvenile lead in the movies, came back a haunted, tormented bomber pilot, and an even greater actor—

Haunted like in *It's a Wonderful Life*.

That's his first movie back from the war. Watch how haunted he is in the George Bailey nightmare scenes. War does something to you. I always felt within that generation was a vast population of men dealing with PTSD—before we knew what is was or what to call it—and many of them drank heavily. You see it in the excesses of the fifties and sixties, the classic cocktail-hour rituals. I know from my own father that that's what he was doing—medicating himself. So what's the difference between Audie Murphy, who killed over a hundred Germans, and a modern serial killer? Audie Murphy was killing because he was told to, told he was doing it in service of a good cause. He would never have chosen to do that on his own and would have been treated like a mad-dog criminal if he had. What I'm trying to establish is how slippery the line is here.

The Second Objective, **your World War II novel, has a really interesting take on this. Germans basically legalized genocide—mass murder, but legalized mass murder.**

There's talk about the banality of evil and how could these people have succumbed to this. How could ordinary people have been drawn into such madness? I would argue that was a self-protective response to an untenable psychological situation. They're being ordered to commit mass murder. Most people aren't going to roll up their sleeves and howl at the moon while they drink blood at midnight. Most are going to treat it like they're punching the time clock, normalize it so they can reduce the impact on their nervous system and psyche. That makes perfect sense to me. That's an adaptive mechanism. That's why they appeared to be automatons. They couldn't begin to fathom the horror of what they were participating in. They'd go mad.

On this subject of Germany under Hitler, let's delve a little deeper into the themes of *Second Objective*. There's this very dynamic character, Von Liensdorf, who is what I would call pretty evil. His father was one-quarter Jewish, on his mother's side. One character says of him that he seems determined to eradicate his father's heritage. So he seems to be somewhat driven by some degree of self-hatred.

That's what I saw. That's where the thorn got twisted and grew into something that pierced his soul. Then you throw him into that system, where the nurture part of it comes into play. He's thrown into the Hitler Youth and forced to deny that part of his identity in order to survive. Of course he came to hate it, because it was the one vulnerability that he knew, if exposed, would probably end his life.

In creating the character, I was trying to look for what was at the heart of the Nazi phenomenon, the ones who became the true believers. How did they cast aside all these civilizing influences so completely to turn, in such a routine and mundane way, to utter depravity? It's astonishing. So that's what I was looking for: what was going on here?

There's a scene in the book where Bernie—who grew up in America but had moved to Germany with his German-born parents, and who chooses the opposite path from Von Liensdorf—asks, "Are people just born bad? Is that what makes them do it?" And Grannit, the American, tells him, "It's a choice. Everybody's always got a choice." There's that theme popping up again.

I do think that ultimately that's the case. You can make a choice to try to return to a balance of sanity and health, or not. You may like flaunting norms too much, so that the rewards are overwhelming to your senses and you want them to continue. That's how I look at Trump. He's someone who was utterly denied any maternal or paternal warmth, love, comfort, acceptance, unconditional affection—I'm sure he was denied all those things. But instead of seeking it elsewhere, finding a mentor who could course-correct that for him, he went full tilt into materialism, hedonism, and self-aggrandizement. In this way, he's a comprehensive vehicle for understanding the shadow of American culture. He personifies it.

My favorite scene in *Second Objective* is when Von Liensdorf hears the music from the church and, for a brief moment, sees a path of light, but it's just too much for him to accept, to accept all the evil that he had committed and admit he had been wrong all along. That was powerful.

It's too late for him at that point. I thought what was interesting about that character, to follow him to the extent that we do, was that he had done extremely evil things, predominantly in response to the way he'd grown up and been treated and the things that were done to him. As his time is running out, I thought, instead of just seeing somebody maniacally driven to do even more violent things, what if he caught a glimpse of what might have been? What would that be like? That's a more humane way of looking at a villain. You know, if you're writing strict genre your villain is all bad/all the time, and you can't wait to see him meet his end. Here I was trying to delve a little deeper into the heart of what made him tick.

OK, so let's switch gears and talk about this concept of a "supernatural evil"—the way some people interpreted Bob in _Twin Peaks_, for instance, at least during seasons one and two—or the Devil.

That's the starkest, black-and-white look at goodness and evil, and it's more typical of Old Testament thinking; that was the way reality was drawn when this was a less global world. With communities, city-states, and entire nations that were kingdoms cut off from each other, it was a lot easier to maintain this idea of the Other, with a capital O, as the adversary or antithesis of whatever your group valued.

That's useful as a metaphor, and I think writing and speaking about the presence of evil in people and groups—and even in national behaviors—is something we don't spend enough time studying. As to whether you can point to some external entity as the sole source of evil, I personally think that's a bridge too far. So entertain the question, engage with it, live with it, and then decide for yourself what degree this is metaphorical and what degree you treat it as factual—that's up to the individual. In the past, we relied on institutions—churches, governments—to provide that authority for us. We bowed to them, and in an earlier stage of human development, that may have been necessary.

One of the things that drew me to the Theosophists and then ultimately to Krishnamurti, whom I'm writing about now, was his feeling that we had reached an age where people needed to sort this out for themselves, that it would become essential for individuals to do the hard work necessary for self-examination and ownership of one's own beliefs. Look at the world we're in now. You see an entire class of people who identify as evangelical Christians standing behind Donald Trump as their champion—willing to ignore, all evidence to the contrary, one of the most profoundly unsound human beings this country has ever produced—because he amplifies their deepest, darkest fears. And in return, they welcome authoritarianism. That's no accident; it's the system they were raised in.

I don't feel we can move forward as a species and survive unless we get to the point where authoritarian rule and authoritarian decision-making recede from human history. We may be a ways away from that, but the idea of this country as an experiment—to try a different way of living by giving our citizens an unprecedented amount of participation—still holds the most promise for where we need to go globally. Whether we're up to the challenge in front of us right now will tell us everything about how the future unfolds, and I'm hopeful that we're gonna do the right thing.

Regarding Krishnamurti, what was it that drew you to the material?

They had decided he was the next Messiah, and he was going to be the world teacher. He was raised to become that person and in the end, walked away from that—because he felt it was a straitjacket, and that it was essentially misleading people. He didn't in his heart of hearts believe the same mythology the Theosophists did. He'd been steeped in it and reared to believe it, but then his own experience—his own enlightenment or whatever you want to call it—revealed everything that they taught him as just a construct that he didn't fully engage with or believe. So he rejected it and walked away.

And he really believed that people had to find their own way.

Yes, that was his message. That's what made him unique. He was at the forefront of what we now think of as New Age thinking. There weren't many people talking about these things in the 1920s, certainly not with the kind of audience he had. What Krishnamurti did was reject the whole idea of gurus and say, "People are capable of getting to this on their own. I'm happy to discuss with you how you might bring that about, but there is no one or easy way to do it. And anybody who tells you differently is selling you a bill of goods." That was his message. So he was encouraging the freedom of the individual and the responsibility of the individual to work out their own answers about why they thought they were here, what they thought the true nature of reality was. There was nobody else coming close to that as a message at that point. He talks about it with Joseph Campbell in the book. Campbell reminds him, "Look, Jesus and the Buddha didn't set out to start a religion. They just started talking about the truth they felt they'd discovered, and it was the people who came after them who turned it into something else." I think that's the most solid truth he hit on: that the moment you try to concretize a revelation or an inspiration, it stops being fresh and alive and organic and becomes something other people are supposed to follow. That asks them to turn off their own critical faculties and accept the revelation as gospel, which deprives the person of reaching that point of view independently and finding their own version of that truth. That's what he was trying to encourage.

And you actually have that great anecdote, which I think is in one of the Campbell chapters. I forget the exact anecdote, but it's exactly what you were just talking about.

The Devil says he's left a piece of truth by the roadside, and a friend of the Devil says, "But that's awfully dangerous." And then he says, "Oh, no, it's perfect. They're going make a religion out of it."

One of the things that's really interesting to me, as a *Twin Peaks* fan, is trying to understand exactly what your perception of Theosophy is. In the Krishnamurti book, Annie Besant represents that because to me, as a reader, you appear to have this ambivalence toward her, whereas I'm reading it and getting angry at her for the things that she's doing. *Twin Peaks* fans, because they're acutely aware of how you integrated your interest in Theosophy into the mythology of the show in such a huge way—I mean, look at the significance of the Black Lodge—this is something we find really interesting. But I don't think we really know how you feel about it.

By the end of writing this book, I felt very much the way Krishnamurti did, which was that Theosophy largely sprang from the books that Blavatsky had written, and because he was reared in it, and trained and conditioned to become their Messiah, when he got to the place where he was able to articulate his own feelings about what enlightenment could or would or should be, he exposed the essential hollowness of their assertions—that Theosophy was basically a cult that borrowed from a bunch of different disciplines and passed itself off as revelation. That was what he came to resent about it. It impacted him like a straitjacket he was forced to wear. I think he was grateful it turned people's attention to the spiritual side of life and asked them to engage with some of those questions, but the answers that it provided were altogether too pat and simply asked you, the believer, to follow as you would any other religion, without individual choice about what you accept or reject.

Why do you think he was so forgiving of Annie, who was such a devoted Theosophist, to the very end? Who even defended his nemesis, Leadbeater, who was clearly a pederast?

She defended him to a point, but then she also removed him from Krishna's life for the most part, when she realized he was in fact a pederast. She couldn't quite go all the way to rejecting him personally, but he was banished, sent down to Australia, and started his own weird religion down there. Annie actually did throw him out to protect Krishna, so her choice was clearly made. He was in effect her surrogate son; she was his surrogate mother. And I think that love always held them together, even as she couldn't quite completely follow him when he chose to go his own way. She never condemned him for it. But her conditioning just ran so deep. She was, at that point, not as sharp mentally as she had been. It was just too much for her to turn against what she'd believed all her adult life, but neither did she turn against him. So that conflicted response was interesting to me. And his compassionate reaction to it—he never rejected her, and never stopped loving and being grateful to her—I think that was evidence of his true and deepest wisdom.

I'm reading this book, a novel called *The Devil Aspect* by Craig Russell,

and he actually reminds me a lot of you. It's about a psychiatrist in 1930s Czechoslovakia who goes to work at an asylum for people who are psychotic. There are six patients there who all claim to have been visited by the Devil. And this is all happening as the whole specter of Naziism is hovering. But this psychiatrist says something that made me think of you: "I believe the Devil is responsible for all the darkness and evil in society, all the madness and violence in individual people. But the Devil, I believe, is no supernatural being. He's a natural force, alive in all of us, and most alive in the violently insane. And because the Devil hides in the shadow aspect, his presence is often denied. That's why so many psychotic patients can't remember their violent actions." He also references the shadow self. And he says, "We all have parts of ourselves that we seek to deny, which is where all our dreams and nightmares come from, where our instincts and all human creativity live." Do you do you think that's a pretty close approximation of what you think?

Yes. I've articulated that in the work I've done as well. I'm not familiar with the title.

There's a Hebrew term, *yetzer hara*—a congenital inclination to do evil by violating the will of God. The underlying principle in Jewish thought states that every human is born with both a good and an evil inclination. Which seems a little different to me than the Christian idea or even the Islamic idea, that Satan is some external force, some external tempter, as opposed to some internal darkness within you. Does that sound reasonable to you?

I don't think you could separate one from the other. There's no objective scientific evidence to suggest that it's purely an external force, unless it's a principle in nature— if you take the creative principle and the destructive principle and posit that those two are the polar opposites that govern life. In Hindu mythology, deities personify these things— Kali and Krishna, Kali being the destructive force. It may be that it's a natural principle, that it's just a fact of life. But until the next Einstein comes along and writes the theorem that proves it, I don't know how we can say it with certainty.

You told me once that Albert Rosenfield in *Twin Peaks* was a pretty effective surrogate for your voice. In that scene in the woods that I was just talking about, he says that maybe Bob is just "the evil that men do. Maybe it doesn't matter what we call it." So, a metaphor.

These externalized representations of evil are all, at some level, archetypes more than metaphors. Archetypes are fundamental building blocks of the human psyche; they run deeper than a literary trope. It's embedded in human consciousness.

If you look at mythology, and comparative religions, almost all of them at some level suggest there are evil forces at play attempting to influence human behavior. That's true from ancient societies in Babylon and China and India and Africa, up to and including Christian nations, with the idea of the fallen angel. This is a consistent theme. Joseph Campbell would ask, "Why is this such a persistent part of humans trying to understand their own nature?"

So maybe it's just a useful metaphor, but it's been a part of human experience since we started telling each other stories. That's what I was trying to get at in that scene in the woods. There's no way to definitely know one way or the other where evil comes from or why it exists. These archetypes are all just a way of trying to untangle this maze we're in, leading to the nature of what it is to be human. That's what artists are after. We're trying to hold up a light to gain wisdom and insight into ourselves and our behavior. Because it's now risen to the level where these aren't just skirmishes or local conflicts anymore. Technology's made it possible to destroy the world in twenty minutes, so there's an urgency in talking about these themes, driven by the knowledge of what truly evil people can do with the available technology.

I think people expect you and David to have the answer—well, not *the* answer, but an answer—to know who or what Bob is, and maybe the events of season three reinforced that belief.

People who want to embrace the idea that an externalized notion of evil is real may want to sit with the question of self-responsibility, ask if this is just a handy way of talking about the way these behaviors creep into human expression. Take a rigorous inventory of the contents of your own soul and you may stop blaming something you can't see, the equivalent of the bogeyman, to explain away things that are actually the actions of human malfeasance.

In the novels I've done—*The List of Seven, The Six Messiahs, Before I Wake,* and *The Second Objective*—that's pretty clearly a through line. All of that tried to get at the evil that men do. What is this about? Why does this happen? Before *The Second Objective,* I'd never written about World War II, which is a great vehicle for examining how these things happen. What corrupts the heart and soul of entire countries to the extent that they'll engage in this genocidal madness? I'm far from the first person to work that particular patch of ground, but it's of interest to me.

I read a description of you in a newspaper story that said, "It's clear that his fascination for this odd stuff"—meaning supernaturalism—"is tempered by skepticism," and that you're "more tickled than obsessed by it." Would you say that's fair?

I don't know if "tickled" is the right word—intrigued, maybe—but I wouldn't say I'm obsessed. What I'm trying to do is home in on what we've just been talking about: what's the purpose of the "evil" metaphor, about this persistent part of human nature? And if I'm correct in saying we use it as an occasional excuse to absolve ourselves from personal responsibility, if it keeps us from contending with the true horror of what humans are capable of doing to each other, then it may be standing in our way.

Some of these themes that keep coming up in your work—they do seem tailor-made for a straight-out horror novel. Weren't you at one time working on one, called *Stoneheart*?

Yes, I wanted to try. I'd never written a flat-out horror novel, and I had the whole thing worked out. I started to write, and honestly, it started to creep me out so much I decided not to pursue it.

What was it about?

I don't want to say because I don't want somebody else to steal it, but I thought it was a really good idea, and wrote almost a hundred pages. It's one of the only things I've ever set aside and didn't go back to.

Essentially we've been talking about the very Frostian notion of using genre as a narrative form, but also transcending it to explore deep, existential questions. For instance, *Six Messiahs*, I think, raises the question of whether there's even a point to life. Do you think life is absurd? Do you think it's all random? Do you think there's a larger design? And if I'm not getting too personal, how do you raise your son in that regard?

I do think there's a point to life, but it's up to the individual to perceive it, to apprehend it, and to develop your consciousness to the level wherein those things can become apparent to you. That's one of the few demands I think life makes of us. I don't see life as random; I see it as purposeful. I believe the ultimate purpose of life for us, in our current stage of development, may be unknowable, but I believe—and have a certain amount of faith—that this is the journey we're on toward finding peace with yourself, making peace with the world around you, and learning to respect and be kind to all forms of life that are here with us.

So I do think there's a purpose, and there are spiritual practices that people pursue—some are experiences I've had myself—where you feel you're able to see beyond the surface of things toward a deeper sense of reality.

But how do you communicate that to our children, for instance? You can't find a lot of that in conventional religion. The dilemma for conventional religion seems to be that most of them originally coalesced around the idea of "Here's something luminous and eternal, so let's dedicate ourselves to it, some part of our lives to being the best that we can be to honor that feeling," and then inevitably it becomes about forming an institution around that idea. And then, as all institutions tend to do, the institution becomes more concerned with the perpetuation of its own existence than the idea that they were created to honor. That's my beef with organized religion.

You even see that happening in Theosophy—there was a lot of infighting and retrenchment to the point where it seems like they're becoming more preoccupied with their own power and status than they are about any philosophy or core values.

That's the book I'm writing now about Krishnamurti. Those are precisely the themes I'm working with. How do you retain something authentically spiritual within the context of an institution built in essence to entrap it, hold it like a holy relic and worship it? When what you really need to do is go find whatever that thing is for yourself, not worship someone else's version of it That's what Krishnamurti was, at his center, trying to communicate, and I think it was his greatest gift as a spiritual being.

Did you ever meet him?

I never did. He died in 1986. I have friends who met him, friends who came up to Ojai to hear him speak. The thing that grabbed me—I was reading him as far back as the seventies—is the phrase he's probably best known for: "The truth is a pathless land." Which implies that in a perfect world we have to discover these things for ourselves. We can rely on others for a sense of community, a sense of shared experience, but ultimately you have to verify those feelings and experiences through the lens of how you perceive reality. That, I thought, was his greatest message, one that will become increasingly important to people going forward: that it's up to you. You can't rely on someone else to do the scut work for you to advance in any spiritual way. It's not enough to show up, sit in a pew, sing along with the hymns, and do what you're told. It's an active, participatory experience, and at some point to follow it, you have to be willing to undertake that journey.

OK, switching gears, but still on the subject of writing books: We talked a lot about sports, which obviously has played an important role in your life. And we talked about Joseph Campbell and the role that sports played in his life, being a competitive runner. All of your nonfiction books to date, with the exception of the one you're working on now, have been sports themed. I'm wondering what you find so fascinating about sports generally, and golf specifically.

I put it into words in *The Match*. I tried to articulate the appeal of watching sports, watching excellence, watching people who are in the zone, so in the moment that they're playing or performing at their highest level of effectiveness. There's something immensely satisfying and inspiring about that; this is the attraction sports offers, because you get to see it fairly frequently when you become a real fan of a sport—and golf in particular, because it's so difficult, and because every action is self-initiated. So there's nothing you're reacting to. You're simply making it happen. Golf is particularly satisfying in that sense. People like Tiger Woods and Jack Nicklaus show us how to transcend the difficulty of the moment and still perform under pressure.

[Here is the passage Frost was referring to from *The Match*, about a legendary 1956 best-ball competition pitting amateurs Harvie Ward and Ken Venturi against Ben Hogan and Byron Nelson, considered the greatest professional golfers of the time:

"No four men will ever play such a match again. No four men like these. The genuine way they lived their lives makes most of today's fast and frenzied sports and entertainment culture seem like so much packaged goods, a self-conscious, inauthentic hustle. In their best and worst hours alike each one of these four stood his ground, put all he had on the line, and for better or worse lived with the consequences of his actions and moved on. Some green, untested souls might be tempted to wonder why one should still care, but none of us are here forever, we're not even here for long; and if it's true that our collective past exists inside all of us, unless we take time to bear witness to the best of those who strived before us, our chance to learn from their lives will be lost forever, and we will be the poorer for it."]

The Greatest Game Ever Played was the first of these four books, published in 2002. You once told me that your experiences summering at your grandmother's home as a kid in upstate New York played an important role in making you aware of class friction. The Greatest Game Ever Played may be a golf book, but there's a lot more going on than that, and a lot of it is exactly addressing that theme.

As you go through life, you become more aware of things. In the fifties and sixties, when I was a kid, there was less emphasis on class status and a much broader sense of being in the middle class, which is where we landed. My parents weren't making a lot of money, but we didn't want for much. There was nowhere near the focus then on conspicuous consumption and keeping up with the Joneses. It didn't feel that way to us. As you grow older and learn more about history, you realize that social injustices are baked into any society, but in particular, a society that runs on a capitalist economy.

The Greatest Game Ever Played was, for me, thematically almost entirely about class. There's no villain in the story other than the class system itself. And you realize that these very different characters—Francis Ouimet, the young American kid, and Harry Vardon and Ted Ray, the great English champions—are all fighting the same system. They didn't come from money or advantage, and they had to use their skills—and in Vardon's case, his innate genius—to play this game and fight for a place in that system. It's one of the compelling stories of the history of golf as a sport, and it's still relevant today. Class is germane to the history of the American experience—one we're still struggling to resolve. It's at the heart of the calamity we find ourselves in as a society right now.

How did your experiences in Sand Lake awaken you to that?

My mother's grandfather, the man who took the family up there, was an accomplished engineering professor and a skilled engineer in his own right who supervised a lot of infrastructure projects in upstate New York. He was a faculty member at Rensselaer Polytechnic Institute, one of the first-rate engineering schools on the East Coast. So pretty well-to-do people by that era's standards. They were Victorians, by nature and temperament. Their move to the country was prompted by the influenza epidemic in 1917–1918, the Spanish flu. He had two young daughters and wanted to get them out of the city. Millions of people were dying around the world. So he bought most of the land around this lake at that time. As I grew up, I became aware we were living in the big house at the end of the lake, and there were a lot of these folks who worked for him who lived up on the "mountain," as they called it. They weren't from anything like the same advantaged background. Most were subsistence-level folks with no education. That was my first experience of a divide among people, economically and socially.

What age was that, when you started to develop that social consciousness?

Around seven or eight. There was a handyman my grandparents used, a real hill country guy who would have been right at home in Appalachia. The rumors were some of the old families up on that mountain were descendants of Hessian mercenaries who had deserted during the Revolutionary War. I don't know whether it's ever been substantiated, but a lot of mercenaries the Brits brought over allegedly deserted, and a fair number of them settled on this mountainous plateau between New York and Massachusetts, because it reminded them of the Black Forest. It has similar topography to Germany, the *Schwarzwald*, lakes and streams and old-growth forests. This was the story I was told, what brought all those people there, and they're still there to this day.

So we had this handyman, his name was Chris, and he had a son named Joe who was mentally challenged. He was like Boo Radley in *To Kill a Mockingbird*. He could work like a horse—they made charcoal for a living, among other things—and they would have been right at home on the pages of *The Grapes of Wrath*. Simple folks who did simple jobs. So I became aware of this divide between folks who lived in the big houses and the people who worked for them. Later I started studying writers who wrote about this. One of the great themes of [Theodore Dreiser's] *An American Tragedy* is this yearning for upward mobility by the poor relative in a wealthy family. Based on a real murder in 1906 that had happened in upstate New York. Chekhov was another writer I came to appreciate in high school, at the Guthrie. When he wrote plays like *The Cherry Orchard*, he wrote about everybody: the servants, the wealthy landowners, and their aristocratic friends. You saw the ways in which these symbiotic relationships across social class developed over time, the dependencies that became an inevitable part of the inequality. That just drew my attention. I just said, "This is something I want to know more about."

I do love that character of Harry Vardon in *The Greatest Game*. He's such an elegant character. You just sense this soulfulness to him.

I found Harry a really compelling character. He did aspire to climbing out of his class, which was a battle he fought not just for himself, but for all golf pros, who in those years were second-class citizens who weren't even allowed to step foot in clubhouses. They could be hired and fired at the whim of a member. Many were Scottish immigrants who had mastered the game but had no financial status to speak of. To me, the most interesting thing about those books—*The Greatest Game Ever Played*, the Bobby Jones book *The Grand Slam*, and *The Match*, the last in this trilogy about the history of golf in America—is that it's a story of class, how this particular set of athletes gained social status and recognition over the course of a few generations. Walter Hagen, an American golfer, played a huge part in this as well. That's the central theme of the books. It's social commentary masquerading as sports books.

Where did you first hear that story about the three-way playoff involving Ouimet, Vardon, and Ray at the 1913 British Open?

I first heard about it from my maternal grandfather, Doug Calhoun, my mom's father, the obstetrician. His father was a Scottish immigrant, and he loved golf and inherited it almost genetically from his family. When I was young, he belonged to a lovely little country club in Troy, New York—not far from Taborton, where we spent summers—called the Country Club of Troy. We'd go to visit, and I'd play one or two rounds of golf with him and his wife each summer. She was a superb golfer, a perennial club champion. One day out of the blue, he told me the story of Francis Ouimet, the caddy who won the US Open. It stuck with me all those years, and eventually, it was a story I wanted to tell.

OK, let's switch over to your one baseball book—*Game Six*, published in 2009—which covers the historic twelve-inning game of the 1975 World Series between the Red Sox and the Reds. I know you're a longtime Dodger fan, and your nephew, Lucas Giolito, was drafted by the Washington Nationals and pitches now for the Chicago White Sox. So why pick a game between Boston and Cincinnati?

I watched that game on a twelve-inch black-and-white television in 1975, and I've never been more electrified in my life. The most exciting I ever saw. So I had this idea and wanted to challenge myself: a baseball book about one game, what could I do with that? And when I narrowed it down to that as a narrative challenge, that was the one game that came to mind, one that had the most inherent drama and one of the greatest cast of characters in major league history. The number of Hall of Famers who participated in or broadcast the game was in the high teens—you'd be hard-pressed to come up with a higher number in a single game. And I was lucky enough to have a good in with the Reds, so I got to meet nearly every guy. Then I was able to meet about ninety percent of the Red Sox roster as well. So it was fun to tell their stories. And I dedicated the book to [longtime Dodgers announcer] Vin Scully, because he was my model for "How do you spin a comprehensive narrative out of a single ballgame?" because no one was ever better at it than he was.

Do you see any analogy procedurally between making documentaries and writing nonfiction books?

Yes. Documentaries taught me a lot about how to work in nonfiction. When you go into the cutting room for a documentary, you need to give yourself as many options as possible: shoot everything, hose everything down, get as many interviews as you can. So that was my approach on the golf books and even more so on the baseball book. I talked to as many people as I could, read as much as I could about the teams, the era, the players, the managers—so I could work with a full spectrum of information.

Just out of curiosity, do you have a favorite all-time baseball player, other than Lucas of course?

I have favorite players that I associate with different periods in my life. When I was a kid, it was Sandy Koufax, because I saw him pitch. We lived near Chavez Ravine [site of Dodger Stadium in Los Angeles]. And because my dad—although we lived in Brooklyn—grew up a Giants fan, my brother and I worshipped at the altar of Willie Mays growing up. When we moved to Minnesota, during those years, my favorite player was Rod Carew. I don't think I've ever seen a better hitter. Then I went to college in Pittsburgh and got to see Roberto Clemente, who was just unbelievable. So I've been lucky. When I came back to LA in '81, it was the summer of Fernandomania [fan reaction to Dodger pitcher Fernando Valenzuela]. I got to see a couple of games in the World Series in '88 and became a big Orel Hershiser fan. So I've been lucky with the baseball I've been around, to see some truly great players.

Looking back at your overall body of work as an author—both

fiction and nonfiction—one thing that sticks out is that you've really jumped around all over the place—sports books, Victorian steampunk, almost a western, a police procedural, a World War II story. Do you believe you have a writing style, or do you like to be fluid in that regard?

My style is probably consistent from book to book, but I never wanted to write the same book twice. It's the same issue I faced with television—I grew quickly bored with anything formulaic. It's a good way to make money, but I didn't stay engaged beyond a certain point. So that may have something to do with why I'm drawn to all sorts of different genres and stories. Although, as you've pointed out, you've identified some constant themes I keep coming back to. But I never wanted to write—and these are some of my favorite books as a reader—I didn't want to write twenty-one Travis McGee books. I didn't want to write Patrick O'Brian's naval stories, the *Master and Commander* books. I inhaled that whole series, loved it, but I was never drawn to the idea of making a career out of one story or set of characters, which O'Brian did with that incredible series. It's a reflection of the individual and what you're drawn to. I'm a bit more of a restless and curious mind. I remember early on in my career meeting authors—I don't want to name names—who had written successful mystery series, and I quickly realized that wasn't for me, that wasn't something I wanted to do. It would be like making ten years in a row of *Law & Order*.

9

"I'm Living in *A Thousand Clowns*"

(The Late Nineties + Beyond)

Though focused now on book writing, Frost was determined to continue penning film scripts (particularly adaptations of his own books), but he had no interest in committing the time and energy needed to work on another episodic program. However, things didn't work out quite that way. A number of projects—including a film adaptation of his first novel, *The List of Seven*—collapsed, so by the end of the nineties he was once again producing episodic television (though still writing books).

The two TV shows that figure most prominently during this time—neither a commercial success by any stretch of the imagination—are *Buddy Faro* (1998) and *All Souls* (2001). Both reunited Frost with über-producer Aaron Spelling, whose Worldvision company had distributed *Twin Peaks*, *American Chronicles*, and *On the Air*.

Buddy, a Frost creation, was a lighthearted crime drama starring Dennis Farina in the title role, as a legendary, ring-a-ding-ding private eye who had disappeared twenty years earlier during an investigation into the murder of a woman with whom he had fallen in love, but is tracked down by neophyte PI Bob Jones (Frank Whaley), and together the two set up shop in Hollywood.

The series was eagerly anticipated, and critically embraced—reviewing the pilot, *Variety* praised Frost's "stylishly engaging script, inventive direction from 'Hill Street Blues' alum Charles Haid, Joel McNeely's jazzy soundtrack and a self-deprecating performance from

Farina that paints him on arrival as the coolest man in primetime"—but ratings were definitely *not* cool, and CBS pulled the plug after just eight episodes, leaving five unaired.

All Souls, a paranormal hospital drama in the vein of Lars von Trier's *The Kingdom*, fared worse, running for just three episodes in the spring of 1998 before being yanked by UPN. It returned three months later, for three final episodes. The series was created by Stuart Gillard and Stephen Tolkin; Frost was brought in subsequently to oversee production and wound up writing two of the six episodes. Grayson McCouch starred as a medical intern who uncovers nefarious goings-on in a haunted hospital, rooted in behavior dating back to the Civil War (for *Twin Peaks* fans, an evocation of the mid-second-season arc involving a delusional Benjamin Horne). Ill fate notwithstanding, *All Souls* had its boosters, including Howard Rosenberg of the *Los Angeles Times*, who called it "paranormal fun."

Later in the decade, Frost, a Marvel fan since childhood, wrote the first *Fantastic Four* movie (2005), and has story and screenplay credits on the second, *Rise of the Silver Surfer* (2007), though he disowns it. He also penned the theatrical film adaptation of the first of his three golf books, *The Greatest Game Ever Played* (2005), starring Shia LaBeouf and directed by Bill Paxton. The film grossed $15.3 million domestically—ranking 139th at the box office for the year—and earning generally positive reviews.

***

I know your career as a novelist took off in the early nineties, but was the intent to give up on film and TV completely at this point, at least for a while?

No, but I shifted my axis. My point of view from that day forward was: "I want to be a novelist first. I'd like to see my books sell to a studio. I can adapt them; I can produce the movie and make a living that way." I wanted to be more in control of my own destiny.

I knew I didn't want to get tied down in series TV, but I did write a few scripts during that time. One of those projects was to adapt *The List of Seven*, which had been optioned by Universal, and I was going to write and produce that movie. We didn't sign a director right away, and Universal ended up putting it in turnaround. But at that point, Guillermo del Toro came into my life. He had made his first feature, *Cronos*, in Mexico. He was a huge fan of the book and really wanted to do *The List of Seven* as his first American film, and I just loved the guy. James Cameron was Guillermo's mentor at that point, and Jim was going to step in and executive produce the movie. We set it up at Fox and started trying to cast it. Then another Bernie Schwartz moment happened: Hollywood bad luck. We needed one actor to sign on. And the movie was gonna go. Jim had a breakfast arranged to meet with Hugh Grant to discuss playing Arthur Conan Doyle, and the night before the meeting, Hugh got busted on Sunset Boulevard.

That thing with Divine Brown, the prostitute?

Yeah. So he didn't show up for breakfast.

And that killed the whole movie?

Soon afterward, Jim got the go-ahead to make *Titanic*, which utterly consumed him for a good three years, and Guillermo got an offer to make *Mimic* for Harvey Weinstein. We tried a couple of times. Again in about 2007—the year before *Iron Man* came out—Guillermo came back into the project, wanted to do it again, and we all felt Robert Downey was the right guy. We were setting it up at Lionsgate and could not get Lionsgate to say Robert Downey was somebody they wanted to make a movie around. I was finishing up the *Fantastic Four* movies with the guys at Marvel, and they had shown me some early scenes of Downey as Tony Stark, the role that brought him back to life. I told Lionsgate, "Guys, he's gonna be the star of a huge franchise here, and he's perfect," and they wouldn't go for it.

Did you ever have anybody in mind for Jack Sparks?

No, we wanted to cast Doyle first.

Have you lost any hope that it will become a movie one day?

My fear is that the Guy Ritchie Sherlock Holmes movies put an end to it. It'd been done at that point. *The Mummy* cribbed a lot of material from it as well, including a scene in the British Museum—which was a pretty direct lift. But if it had come out when it was supposed to, it would have been groundbreaking and would have taken us back to Victorian steampunk before it became cool, but we just missed it.

Did you work on other films during this time as well?

I was mostly writing the sequel to *The List of Seven*—*The Six Messiahs*—and that was about a year and a half of work. But I did a couple of other projects for hire, just to keep my hand in.

TV or film or both?

Mostly film.

Did any of those other projects get produced?

I did a couple of rewrites of things that got made.

Anyone who knows much of anything about David Lynch knows *Lost Highway* emerged from his thoughts about the O. J. Simpson trial. I was surprised to discover that you too were working on a film at one point in response to that trial.

It was actually developed at TriStar. We had Robert De Niro attached, and then it fell apart when we couldn't find a director he wanted to work with on it. It was called *Affirmative Action*—an LA detective story about a racist cop who finds his way back to redemption by going undercover with a group of white supremacists. A little ahead of its time, I guess.

What was your reaction to the O. J. trial?

I knew him. He played golf at the same club I did, and I'd played golf with him. I'd actually been hit by a golf ball he hit.

What were you thinking during the trial?

From a purely evidentiary, procedural sense, it was pretty clear he did it, but what it exposed socially was incendiary. The first national case that pointed us toward issues that are front and center now: Michael Brown in Ferguson, the Trayvon Martin case, all these innocent people of color being gunned down. There's a strong racist component in our criminal justice system. I'd worked in theater in tough neighborhoods in Minneapolis and Pittsburgh during high school and college and saw inequities that were built into society, but my education really started when I taught in the Minnesota state prison and saw it in action. These felt like issues that had to come to a head at some point in our social evolution, and I think we're there. We're there now.

Let me ask you about a couple of other projects that turn up during this time. One is *Moby Dick*.

I wrote a screenplay for Columbia that Roland Joffé was going to direct, but the studio decided we just know the story too well now. There was no pressing need to make the movie. They've made a couple of versions of it since, and nobody's showed up to them. At this point, it's better as a monolithic piece of American literature—and a metaphor—than it is something that needs to be seen on screen.

Is that a story that particularly appeals to you?

The idea of it appealed to me. Once I dug into the book, I realized it's almost impossible to dramatize, because nobody ever changes in the story. It has a kind of biblical narrative power leading to a pretty grim ending, but you can't say that anybody in it fundamentally changes throughout the experience.

How about *Flight of the Passage*? **Do you remember that one at all?**

That was a screenplay I did for Disney based on a book by Rinker Buck. A literary memoir about when he and his brother were the first kids— they were fifteen and seventeen—to fly cross-country by themselves. It was a lovely book. Don't think I licked the screenplay in that one. I wanted to stay true to the book, but by the end, the studio was saying, "We need to make this more exciting. Just make stuff up." I found I had a hard time doing that.

Writing screenplays was a good way to make a living, and it offered me constant employment for a long time. It's always been devilishly difficult to get a movie made, but at least back then, they were still making movies about relatively smaller-scale subjects, and it wasn't all about comic books yet.

Spoken by the man who did two *Fantastic Four* films.

Once a philosopher, twice a burglar.

You've also mentioned to me how much you loved *The Prisoner*, the 1960s TV series with Patrick McGoohan. Didn't you try to negotiate the rights to that, to adapt it into a feature film?

I did in the nineties, and I forget what the issue was. The rights were tied up. McGoohan was still alive at that time, and no one wanted to give them up. Sadly, they were eventually, resulting in an utterly pallid adaptation with Ian McKellen and Jim Caviezel, that was hugely disappointing. That was something I was keen on doing, as it was such a formative experience for me, but in retrospect, it's just as well I wasn't involved.

You were also talking to Turner TV about the *Crazy Horse* biopic around this time, right?

The original plan was for me to write and produce, and then I got too busy when *The List of Seven* got picked up as a feature. So I had to set it aside, but it was a story I found fascinating

And then *The List of Seven* never got made. Were you getting frustrated by the film business by this time?

You know, I was making an adjustment. I was trying to move away from the grind of TV toward publishing, so writing screenplays felt like a good bridge to carry me over that divide from one career to the other. I looked at it pragmatically. Studios were developing so many screenplays and making relatively so few movies; there was never any guarantee anything you wrote was going to get made, but it was a good way to keep working. I was also trying to move away from doing work for hire, and it was less of a time commitment to write screenplays than it was to create and run a television show.

Plus, I had my own writing. Schlesinger's Law in action, "That's one for them, and this is for me." But sure, I would get frustrated from time to time. Some of these folks were very frustrating to work with.

Did you ever read Peter Biskind's book *Easy Riders, Raging Bulls: How the Sex-Drugs-and-Rock 'n' Roll Generation Saved Hollywood*?

I really liked that book.

Do you think there's any way to build an analogy to television, if we're talking about American film being reinvented in the seventies by people like Steven Spielberg and Martin Scorsese and George Lucas and Francis Ford Coppola? Do you think American television ever went through something like that?

Yes. When the industry expanded into premium cable and the networks lost their hegemony, something very similar happened.

Would you say that was around the time of the first *Twin Peaks*?

I'd say *Twin Peaks* heralded that happening. That's what a lot of people seem to believe now, that it foreshadowed what was coming. The end of network television was at hand, initially more through how the business would be monetized in the future than it was about storytelling style, which is similar to what happened in the seventies cinematic revolution. In a way, it's all interconnected, because television cut the legs out from under the movie business starting in the fifties, and by the late sixties movie studios were on life support. They were willing and ready to take chances on younger talent who wanted to tell stories in a different way, mostly out of desperation. That's what Peter identified in his book.

Did you find a difference in the television environment between *Six Million Dollar Man* and *Hill Street*? Did this transformation start as early as the eighties?

No, that was still the world I'd basically grown up in. It hadn't yet changed appreciably. I'd had that experience of the factory environment at Universal, and MTM was like the boutique version of that. It was a great place to work, and it had a particular kind of house style—the cool kids' version of Universal, more about quality than volume. I mean, Lew Wasserman [chairman and chief executive of the Music Corporation of America, the parent company of Universal] just wanted to make money. [MTM cofounder] Grant Tinker was genuinely interested in making quality product as well as making money. So they were different in that regard. But I recognized it as something that I knew; it wasn't that radically different.

Did you ever feel part of some movement to improve TV, even in the nineties, or does TV just not function that way?

It's really hard to identify that when you're in the middle of it.

How about if you look back?

If I look back now, I know lots of people point at *Twin Peaks* and say this was the start of a movement that carried us into premium cable.

These filmmakers whom Biskind writes about—they all knew each other, they hung out. Was there ever a genuine camaraderie among

the people who changed television in the nineties?

Not in TV. On *Hill Street*, we all felt like we were doing something different, and it was a group effort. Bruce Paltrow was making *St. Elsewhere* downstairs, also different from what had come before, but I don't think it extended industrywide. It was and is an extremely competitive business. People were interested in what they were doing. Television is so dependent on pumping out multiple episodes. It wasn't as adventurous or artistic an atmosphere as it is now, in an era of twenty networks and limited series.

Maybe the first television-series project of yours that I came across during this period was something called *The Repair Shop*, a pilot with Jane Rosenthal and Tribeca, Robert De Niro's company. That was 1998. What do you remember about that experience?

That was a pilot for CBS. When I decided I wanted to do some TV in 1999, I did two pilots that year, both for CBS. One was *The Repair Shop*, an espionage piece, and the other was *Buddy Faro*, which I ended up doing for them that year.

I wrote *The Repair Shop* on spec and sold it to Les Moonves. I'd known Les since his days at Lorimar in the eighties. He called me out of the blue in 1998 and said, "I'd love to try to develop something with you." I sold *Buddy Faro* to him over the phone.

But *The Repair Shop* was something that Rosenthal and Tribeca got involved with, right?

They did after it was written, yeah.

Phillip Noyce directed, right? He had done a couple of those Tom Clancy films with Harrison Ford.

Yeah, he directed it. I was the executive producer, and we ran it through Tribeca.

What was that about?

It was about a former spy who's nearly killed when they try to take out his section. He then identifies a hundred people who are—this is eerily prescient for today's world—who are part of a vast criminal network, not unlike SPECTRE, and who have infiltrated the United States, are in positions of power, and are about to take over the country. So he starts taking them down one by one, with a couple of former associates in *Mission: Impossible*-style stings.

It was pretty straightforward drama?

It was pretty dark. And we had a strange experience with it, because I'd written the pilot, which everyone liked. But it was an origin story, and Les said he didn't want us to make that as the pilot. He said, "I want you to write the second episode and make that as a pilot," which was a hard thing to pull off, because you haven't gone on the shakedown cruise where you figure it out. So making the second episode first was difficult, and that contributed to why they didn't pick it up.

CBS passed on *The Repair Show*, but picked up *Buddy Faro* instead?

They picked up *Buddy Faro* instead. I shot them almost simultaneously. I left New York on the last day of production on *The Repair Shop* and got to LA during the last days of preproduction on *Buddy Faro*.

When did you write *Buddy Faro*, though?

That same year, '98. I sold Les the idea and wrote them back to back is my memory. Very different in tone.

Uncle Monkey Productions, was that a new company that you formed?

Yeah, that was my little vanity company to run the production through.

Where did "Uncle Monkey" come from?

It's funny, that's what Lucas [Giolito, his nephew] used to call me when he was a kid. He had trouble pronouncing Mark, so he just called me Uncle Monkey.

Looking back at the work that you'd done, if you throw out *On the Air* and *One Saliva Bubble*, *Buddy Faro* seems like a real change of pace for you—lighthearted, episodic. What was the story behind where this idea came from? What interested you about it?

The tone I wanted was a cross between the Hope-Crosby *Road* movies and the Rat Pack ring-a-ding-ding comedies of the sixties. Take a character like Buddy, who had been part of that Rat Pack scene, throw him forward in time like Rip Van Winkle, and see what happens. I really liked it. Dennis [Farina] was perfect for the part. Charlie Haid directed the pilot and did a great job. Then I realized pretty quickly we were at the wrong network for it. It was a little too stylish and smart. They ended up putting it on Friday nights after a really average Don Johnson detective show. *Nash Bridges*?

Yup, *Nash Bridges*.

So there we were at 10 o'clock on Friday night—when not one young or hip person in the universe was watching CBS—and that just murdered the show. It was really badly programmed.

A lot of people would look at *Buddy Faro* and see similarities to the Las Vegas material in season three of *Twin Peaks*. Did that Las Vegas stuff come from you?

A lot of that storyline came from me.

Do you see the similarities between *Buddy* and that material?

I do, yeah. And as I told Lynch, the Vegas scenes had a little bit of everything, but there was definitely a callback to *One Saliva Bubble*, and it was a little more lighthearted than the rest, which I thought we needed. The Dougie story line and the comedy of errors that follows him around definitely had that kind of feel.

We've talked a little about this, but can you go deeper into your comedic influences and whose comedic work you particularly admire?

As a kid, the Three Stooges were on wall to wall every Saturday morning, and Laurel and Hardy—all their stuff was in that King-syndicated library they sold cheap to independent stations across the country, so I grew up laughing at the Stooges and Laurel and Hardy. And as I've told you, in high school, I got into 16mm prints of the Marx Brothers and Buster Keaton and W. C. Fields, screwball comedy in general. To laugh like that at movies thirty, forty, fifty years after they'd been made became a big influence on my sense of what comedy should be. *Philadelphia Story*, *The Awful Truth*, and that great Jack Benny World War II movie, *To Be or Not To Be*.

Ernst Lubitsch.

I learned all about Lubitsch, all those great comedic directors. That's one of the signal achievements of the American motion picture—there'd never been anything like it. I mean, *Bringing Up Baby*, what other culture could have made a movie like that?

Did you ever get into S. J. Perelman and Dorothy Parker and that whole *New Yorker*—

Sure. When I was at the Guthrie, they produced a play of Perelman's on their main stage—*The Beauty Part*. That same wiseacre, George S. Kaufman, Broadway wit is where all of those great Hollywood pictures came from. They were all playwrights who came out to the Coast to write those sorts of things. I just adored them and said that if I ever did comedy, that's what I'd shoot for—high-style, often lowbrow physical stuff mixed with witty dialogue. I seldom had a better time at the movies than I did at those sorts of pictures.

And then on TV, I guess you might have been too young for this, but were you watching Jack Benny or Ernie Kovacs or Jackie Gleason, who turns up in one of your books later on, *The Secret History of Twin Peaks*? Phil Silvers?

I didn't see Kovacs live but came to appreciate him later. There were kinescopes of all those shows. When I was living in LA during the eighties, one of my next-door neighbors was Edie Adams [Kovacs's widow]. So we became friendly, and I learned all about Ernie from her. She was terrific.

The ones I remember the most from that period were Benny and Sid Caesar, who is still hysterically funny. *The George Burns and Gracie Allen Show* really made an impression, because they kept breaking the fourth wall. George talked to the camera and would step out of the play or the show, and talk directly to you, which I thought was mind-blowing. I used to watch Gleason every single week, thought he was tremendous.

Garry Shandling would do the same thing Burns and Allen did many years later, breaking the fourth wall, in *It's Garry Shandling's Show*.

I just watched *The Zen Diaries of Garry Shandling* by Judd Apatow. It's extraordinary. I knew Garry. We worked out at the same gym in the early 2000s, used to see him all the time. He'd be doing his boxing, working with the same trainer I was. Such an interesting, soulful, deeply funny guy. You know, my dad played his dad on *Larry Sanders*.

I didn't!

I think it was only one episode, but he called me his TV brother. Once you know the story of his relationship with his own brother and how that loss played such a profoundly fundamental role in shaping his life, his mother's inability to cope with it, how he was able to finally resolve his wounds about that—it's an amazing testament to his character and the journey he went through. I thought both his shows were as good as television got in the eighties and nineties. I don't think *Larry Sanders* has been surpassed as TV comedy, and may never be. It was an amazing body of work. We lost Garry too soon, and it was really moving to see Judd do such a wonderful job of conveying the entirety of who he was.

He certainly was a challenging subject, given how complex he was.

I can testify to that just from the degree to which I knew him. His need to be truthful and authentic at every moment is a challenging stance to take in life and doesn't make it easy for yourself, but he stuck to it. As a result, every interaction with him felt very real. You came away feeling reinforced that authenticity and honesty aren't just the most important things in life; they're the only things, particularly when you're trying to do creative work. He was a great inspiration to me, and I liked him a lot. The piece gave me a chance to understand the depth and complexity of him in ways that were truly satisfying.

Did the two of you ever come close to working together?

No, he was already in that period of his life after *Larry Sanders*, where he'd kind of hung 'em up. I asked him about it, and he just said he was more interested in living right now than in working. Some of that had to do with the Brad Grey lawsuit, I think, and what he was going through on that side of his life. All his nerve endings were on the outside. That's a challenging way to live, but it can also lead you to, in his case, something close to enlightenment.

Getting back to *Buddy Faro*: If I'm right about this, this was the first time you really dealt with a private eye, instead of a cop or an FBI agent or some crime-fighting organizational employee. But Buddy's his own free spirit, and I think I've seen articles where you've referenced *77 Sunset Strip*, the old, fifties TV show created by Roy Huggins. Was that an influence at all?

That and there were others, like *Peter Gunn* and *Adventures in Paradise*. I loved the snappy tone of those shows. There were similar ones a bit off to the side of them, like *T.H.E. Cat* with Robert Loggia, *To Catch a Thief* had a little of that with Robert Wagner. So that was a favorite genre. Even *The Man from U.N.C.L.E.* leaned on that tone. They had that Bond, tongue-in-cheek attitude toward danger, which made them fun and breezy to watch.

Another title I've seen referenced with respect to *Buddy Faro* is *The Thin Man*. Were you a Dashiell Hammett fan at all?

I was, although I was more a fan of William Powell and Myrna Loy's version, which is much funnier than Hammett was on the page—that screwball sense of fun and wonderful, assured performances.

You told me once before that you've read a lot of private-eye fiction over the years.

Yes, all the standards—Raymond Chandler and Ross Macdonald. My favorite is John D. MacDonald's Travis McGee series.

What made those stand out for you?

They're actually extremely well written and often transcend the genre. Kurt Vonnegut said the twenty-one books MacDonald wrote about Travis McGee should be put in a museum and studied as the most vivid picture in literature of midcentury America.

TV in the late eighties and nineties, this whole law-and-order, criminal-justice thing—I'm thinking about shows like *Moonlighting*, which was a little like *Buddy Faro*, but also shows like *Homicide: Life on the Street* and *NYPD Blue* and *Law & Order*, which were much darker and grittier. Were you impressed by any of those?

I didn't watch them much. I knew everybody involved and thought it was good work. *NYPD Blue* just felt like an iteration of what we'd already done on *Hill Street*, similar in a lot of ways. High quality, extremely well written and produced, but I wasn't watching a lot of TV during that period. *Law & Order* I saw; Dick Wolf found a wonderful device to cross genres and show you how the criminal justice system worked, and he's turned it into a kingdom and a vast fortune. *Homicide*, I thought, was the most interesting of the bunch. They offered me *Homicide*, the David Simon book [*Homicide: A Year on the Killing Streets*], and I was just enough removed from television and cops that I turned it down. Tom Fontana I'd known from *St. Elsewhere*, and he did a great job with that set of characters. I just wanted to do my own work at that point.

When you say "they" had offered you the book—

The studio, through CAA. I don't remember who at the agency, probably Tony Krantz.

I've heard some horror stories about what happened to *Homicide* after the network became a production partner, which leads me to my next question: From interviews I've read with you after *Buddy Faro* ended, it sounded like that was not a great experience with CBS.

More in terms of how they positioned and sold the show. They basically used it as ratings cannon fodder, putting it at 10 o'clock on Friday when the show was designed and geared to a younger, hipper audience. But that just wasn't their demographic. I put that question to Les, and he said, "Well, this will be our chance to try to get that segment." Then they went ahead and programmed it on Friday at 10, so that was kind of a moot point. We were doomed right out of the box because of that.

How about *Forbidden Island*? That was a year later, so I'm assuming you wrote that after you wrote *Buddy Faro* and *The Repair Shop*?

As part of selling *Buddy Faro* to Spelling, I signed a two-year overall deal. So when *Buddy* got canceled, they said, "We've got a pilot coming up." I didn't write it, but they wanted me to produce it. We had a good time, shooting in New Zealand. And if you could find a tape, you'd be astonished to see how closely it resembles *Lost*, a show that debuted a couple of years later. The same idea. I thought the story worked and it had a chance to go, but instead, they picked up *All Souls*. They were both for UPN.

Do you have it?

I don't. It was the same story: an airliner mysteriously crashes on a tropical island in the middle of nowhere. It's a hodgepodge of people ethnically, racially, socioeconomically, a couple of military. They were escaping an embassy that was under siege, and those who survive the crash find themselves cut off. They don't know how they got there; they don't know how to get away. The radio doesn't work; they can't contact anyone; there's all sorts of odd coincidences; they encounter strange animals that shouldn't be there. I mean, it's literally the same story. What I'd heard, although UPN didn't pick it up, the pilot—which was well directed by a friend of mine, Stuart Gillard—made the rounds, and within two years, Spelling was trying to repackage it and get in on *Lost* when that script came along. You'd be shocked to see how similar it was.

Another project that turns up around this time is something called *The Deadly Look of Love*, a 2000 TV movie with Vincent Spano and Jordan Ladd, who's the daughter of onetime *Charlie's Angel* Cheryl Ladd. We talked about this earlier because it was the screenplay CAA had sent to John Schlesinger before he hired you for *The Believers*.

I had written a spec screenplay in 1980, just before moving back to LA to work with Bochco, thinking it would be useful to have a screenplay in hand. Based on a true crime story in Minneapolis in 1977; a disturbed young woman named June Mikulanec was accused of stabbing Susan Rosenthal ninety-seven times. She was in love with Rosenthal's husband, delusionally believed he was in love with her and that the wife was keeping them apart. I followed the case, and sought out and got to know the defense attorney, a man named Doug Thomson. He was well known in the area, and very forthcoming. It was an unusual and striking crime, set in the bland Twin Cities suburbs—*Fargo*-like, in a way—and Mikulanec was actually found not guilty by reason of insanity.

So you fictionalized it?

I wrote a fictional version originally called *True Romance*. A friend of mine named Sollace Mitchell, who was a writer I'd worked with, wanted to direct it, and so, twenty years on, he produced it for Lifetime.

OK, so let's switch over to *All Souls*, which premiered in 2001. I read a quote by your brother, Scott, and I think he was comparing the *All Souls* experience to *Twin Peaks* here, because he said, "Whatever the executives at ABC might have been like, they were geniuses compared to most of the people at UPN at the time."

That's accurate. It was the last thing I did as part of the Spelling deal. I'd had a good experience working with Stuart Gillard on *Forbidden Island*. He had cowritten the pilot for *All Souls* with Stephen Tolkin. UPN picked that up as a pilot, so we went to Montreal to shoot it. Six months later, they picked it up with an order for six episodes, and once again, they just completely messed it up.

How did they mess it up?

They just didn't know how to sell a show. Their marketing department was geared toward wrestling; that was their big tentpole. I'll never forget being in a meeting with—I don't want to name names, these weren't the sharpest knives in the drawer—with their head of programming. He was elated because they'd just come up with a marketing slug for their Christmas wrestling special: "Season's Beatings." And I thought, "I'm living in *A Thousand Clowns* here." Who pats themselves on the back for that?

I watched every episode of *All Souls* I could find, and I have to say I think it's a really interesting show. I mean, it's a supernatural show, but you work in this whole concept of the privileged versus the

marginalized, which we've seen is a theme you keep coming back to. Here the hospital is choosing poor people to conduct these tests on. Was that you?

That was there, but I leaned on it thematically going forward as something we could hang our hat on. The idea of a haunted hospital is fine, but you can't just do "ghost of the week," you need something deeper going on. So we'll play an underdog story and emphasize that moving forward. It was a show that had a chance. It was well done. But again, UPN didn't know how to sell a cup of coffee. They were hopeless.

The whole Civil War plotline had me thinking about season two of *Twin Peaks*.

That was in the pilot, something Stuart and Stephen came up with. To establish the evil that had been going on for a long time.

Was the show influenced at all by *The X-Files*?

Not for me, but you'd have to ask Stuart and Stephen. I didn't see it that way. I thought this was more horror than sci-fi.

Did you watch *The X-Files*?

Occasionally, because I had friends working on it. I didn't watch it regularly, but the chemistry David [Duchovny] had with Gillian Anderson was really good.

I once interviewed David Greenwalt, who was an exec producer on *Buffy the Vampire Slayer* and *Angel*, and he told me he had really wanted to work on *The X-Files*. So they told him that if he helped Joss Whedon out with *Buffy*, they would put him on *The X-Files*. But then when he got to *The X-Files*, he found out he had no idea how to write it, because, for him, the show had no heart, no soul to it. So he went back to Whedon.

Every show eventually runs out of gas, but their chemistry carried it for a long time.

The X-Files is one of those shows that people talk about as being influenced by *Twin Peaks*, but I read an interview with David Lynch once where he said it had absolutely nothing to do with *Twin Peaks*, at all. First of all, I can't even imagine him watching *The X-Files*, but do you agree?

I do. *X-Files* dealt exclusively with the supernatural and, occasionally, UFOs. That was one of a hundred threads in *Twin Peaks*. And the casting of Duchovny, who came right out of our show and into that one. Other than that, they couldn't have less in common.

I don't know if you remember this, but back in 1993 you went on *Charlie Rose*. Do you remember being on that show?

Oh that, yeah. Can I just tell a quick story? I've met a lot of people in media, been interviewed dozens of times over the years, and I never had a worse impression about anyone than I did Charlie Rose. And at the time, he was Mr. PBS, but he was cold and just seemed off to me. He would ask a question—and this isn't uncommon: as you're answering a question, if you're on Camera A and he's on Camera B and there's no wide shot, the questioner will often be looking at notes to find the next question. I don't remember Charlie Rose looking up once when we were talking.

It was off-putting, but you have to act like it wasn't happening. I'm not saying people shouldn't look at their notes and get oriented, but they usually give you some kind of human contact, like you're having a dialogue, and that just wasn't the case at all.

Yeah, the stories about him are kind of scary. But when you were on, in 1993, you talked about a multipart series for PBS about trying to find out what happens to the human soul after people die. Do you remember that?

Yes, it was a proposal for a series that just never came together. They couldn't get the funding. It was gonna cost more than they could afford. But it was an idea far enough out there that I didn't think it would find much interest at the networks. This was prior to premium cable being a force, so I didn't feel there was another market for it.

That didn't eventually mutate into *All Souls*?

No, not at all. I came in later—and I didn't create All Souls.

By the way, what *do* you think happens to the human soul after you die? Were you going to take a position on that?

I have to think back. I imagine I was.

I don't wanna put you on the spot.

I don't want to answer hastily, because I don't honestly remember. It was just a proposal, so it didn't get that far.

This was about seven years after *The Kingdom*, the Lars von Trier series for Danish TV, which Stephen King adapted for American television in 2004 as *Kingdom Hospital*, which are similarly themed and also set in a haunted hospital. Are you very familiar with King's work? Does that speak to you at all?

He can still come up with stuff I really like. He's written so many things. The one about the Kennedy assassination—

11/22/63.

When Stephen's good, when he's on—like in *The Stand* or *The Shining*—there's nobody more compulsively readable, and he's helped keep the entire publishing industry alive for forty years. But almost nobody in the Hall of Fame hit over .350 for their career, so I'm not sure you can expect that from writers either.

The Stand **is rather famously on your bookshelf in** *The Secret History of Twin Peaks*. **Is there any particular reason for that? Your dad is in that TV movie. So is Miguel Ferrer.**

I still think that might be his best book.

Does it play any fundamental role in your philosophical outlook or your creative output, or is it just another book that you really liked?

It's a book I really like, but I don't think it was hugely fundamental. Whose favorite book was it in the Bookhouse?

Lucy's.

It was mostly for comedic value, as a contrast to who Lucy is.

How about the *Dark Tower* **books? Have you read those?**

I didn't find those particularly compelling. I think he's often better than his genre, and often he transcends the genre. *Dolores Claiborne* is a really good book, and Taylor Hackford made a good movie out of it. Like anyone else, when he taps into stuff that really matters to him—*Misery* is another obvious example—his books go up a notch.

You mentioned that you did *All Souls* **for Aaron Spelling. One of the stories I read about the show referred to you and Spelling as Beauty and the Beast, because he was always casting his series with these incredible-looking young people and you were always excavating the darkness underneath. How did that partnership work? It does seem like a strange partnership.**

It was. His company had been the foreign distributor—a company called Worldvision—for *Twin Peaks*, and that's how I got to know Aaron. I liked him, and he was a great friend of the show [*Twin Peaks*]. He had nothing to say or do with it creatively, but he enjoyed having—well, let's just say critical esteem had not been a big part of his experience up to that point. He was a guy who made vanilla, chocolate, and strawberry, that was it. So it was a novelty for him, and we just liked each other.

In the late nineties, after I sold *Buddy Faro* to CBS, I got a call from my then agent at CAA: "Aaron would like to know if you're interested in making this show part of an overall deal," which I'd never done, but I was in midtransition to my publishing career and saw it as a way to pay the bills for a while.

So *Buddy Faro* became part of that deal and so did *All Souls* and the *Forbidden Island* pilot. I had a great relationship with him and his staff, and they were pleasant experiences. It also bought me the time I needed to write *The Greatest Game Ever Played*. So it was pragmatic on my part. I knew what I was getting into, what to expect and what not to expect. Aaron was a man of his word, he lived up to his end of it, and I did the same. And when the two years were over, I was ready to move on.

Aaron was an interesting guy to know, because his life was so unusual. To visit his infamous mansion, where he was doing a lot of his work by that point, and to see this *Sunset Blvd.*/Gloria Swanson existence he was living, it was a glimpse into a way of life you don't usually see, and it's telling you something about human nature. So it ended up being a fruitful experience on a couple of levels.

What was it telling you about human nature?

To put it simply, money isn't everything. Aaron was trapped in his existence and his addiction to fame. He barely left the West Side of LA and had a terrible fear of flying, so he never went anywhere. He'd been to Europe once when they arranged a train to take him across the country, took the Queen Mary to England, and had an audience with the queen. That was the way he traveled. He had no interest in seeing the world from street level. His life was utterly bizarre to me, but I liked him personally.

I don't know if you know his story, but he was the son of a struggling tailor in Dallas, Texas, and to be poor and Jewish in Dallas, Texas, in the thirties was no picnic. He grew up in a shack with dirt floors. He'd been a struggling actor, and when he finally struck it rich as a writer/producer, he was pushing forty and never looked back. I realized everything about him, all the excesses were driven, Rosebud-like, by the extreme deprivation of his childhood. A fascinating American character study.

So UPN placed *All Souls* on hiatus after just three episodes. Then it came back three months later for three more.

They just didn't give it a chance. Nobody was watching the network anyway, so what difference did it make? They were always chasing numbers and had no cohesive vision for what the network was going to be or who they were appealing to. It was really silly and not a compelling argument for the continued health of network television.

There's a quote from you in a newspaper article calling this "the worst experience I've ever had with a network."

I wouldn't back off that at all.

You mentioned to me once in passing that you had David Tennant— who went on to great fame in *Doctor Who*—in mind for a pilot you had written.

This was after *All Souls*. A sci-fi idea with an artificial-intelligence theme that I sold to TBS, but it didn't go anywhere. I think that was the last time I ever walked into a meeting at a network, until we brought *Twin Peaks* back. There were too many faces in there for me now.

I remember, once on the podcast *Twin Peaks Unwrapped*, Harley Peyton compared you to Dick Diver in *Tender Is the Night*, the F. Scott Fitzgerald novel, in that you give off this vibe of calmness and confidence. Does that surprise you, that you're perceived that way?

Is that really what's going on inside you, or are you putting up a front?

I think it was something I developed as a response to stress in the business. The people I've respected were people who projected that attitude, and eventually, it became more authentically who I am. The more experience you have, the more you're able to handle whatever comes your way. So it was probably an adaptation that I grew into. That's part of leadership. That's what good leaders need to exude.

Whom have you watched and admired for their calmness?

It started when I was at the Guthrie, watching Tyrone Guthrie direct a production of *Uncle Vanya*. I was sixteen, a production assistant running for coffee, and he was a living legend in the theater. So I just sat and watched him work—calm, patient, prepared, unflappable. But he also had the ability—and this was something he pointed out to me—to get strategically angry when you need to spur what you're doing. Over time, you absorb these lessons.

On *Hill Street*, I used to go down and watch people direct on the stage. David Anspaugh had that quality, Randa Haines and Greg Hoblit all had that ability to be in the moment but stay unflappable. That's a pretty good reflection of my personality anyway. But I also retained that ability to know when to get strategically angry when you need something.

Can you think of an example where you had to do that?

Yes, directing *Storyville*. We were on a tight budget, around ten million, and if the movie was gonna work—there were no special effects, it was a mood piece, a thriller, and completely dependent on performances. You needed good actors to elevate it beyond the genre, so I used lots of takes sometimes to get that. And we had a line producer, whom I had not chosen, who was there to babysit the budget. I was in the middle of a complicated scene performance-wise, with Piper Laurie and James

Spader. This guy came in and started griping that I was using too much film, because I'd done like eight takes of this very complex setup and a big performance piece for Piper. So I took him outside and reamed him in front of the crew, because the crew didn't like the guy, and I wanted them on my side. I strategically got mad and said, "We're here making a movie, and film is the cheapest resource we've got. And you're telling me you want us to go to war without any bullets." I made sure everybody heard me. He backed down, and that bought me enough space to get the couple of takes I needed to nail the scene.

It seems to me as we've talked over time that you would have been perfectly justified in losing it with network executives on occasion as well. Is that something you can't afford to do?

It's not smart to do as a rule. You do get a reputation very quickly in the business if you're a screamer. That's the term we use to describe it, and I don't respect that in anyone. If you can't control yourself, how can you control a set or control the work you're doing? I've never liked working with screamers and was damn sure I wasn't going to be perceived as one myself. I always felt it better to just politely say no and hold a very firm line, and that's what I'd end up doing.

I've told this story before: we still had to deal with standards and practices on *Twin Peaks*, which—the thought of that now, in today's world. I mean, I'm watching the show *Big Mouth* with my kid on Netflix, and it's hilarious. But it's absolutely filthy; it's scabrous. It would make Lenny Bruce blush. So there was a scene with Richard Beymer and Piper, who've just had a roll in the hay in a no-tell motel, and Richard gets out of bed and says, 'I'm going to give little Elvis a bath." Funny line, but I got a note from ABC after reading the script that said, "Oh, heavens, we think he could be referring to his sexual organ." I think that was even the phrase they used; it's like talking to the Church Lady.

They said, "We don't want people to get the wrong idea." And I said, "They're in a motel, they're having an affair, and you're afraid people are gonna get the wrong idea?" So when it came time to film it, I didn't change the line, but I had the prop master make up a small little rag doll of Elvis à la Las Vegas—glittering jumpsuit, pompadour. We gave it to Richard to have in the pocket of his robe, and I said, "When you're getting up, take this out of your pocket and say, 'I'm gonna give little Elvis a bath.'" He played it perfectly, and people remember that moment. Off the wall, but a way of saying, "Come on, grow up. We're all grown-ups here, allegedly." The world is completely different now. I haven't done network television in years, but I can't imagine they have anything close to those sorts of ridiculous conversations anymore.

Speaking of which, I was actually surprised to learn that *The Return* wasn't your first work for premium cable. At one point, you were working on a pilot at HBO with the people from *Band of Brothers*. A post-9/11 story set in London.

That was 2004. A great producer I'd known for a while, Tony To, who'd line-produced *Band of Brothers* and *The Pacific* and later became the head of physical production for all of Disney. Really smart guy. He came to me with an idea for a CIA show. *Real Politik*, set in the CIA's Berlin Station. Excellent pilot script. That was the only experience I've had at HBO, and their development process was pretty torturous. I thought that was a show that should have happened.

But never shot?

No, never shot.

On the subject of the CIA, do you know this book *The Death of Truth* by Michiko Kakutani?

I know about it, haven't read it.

Is the death of truth really something new? Even in your own work, you go back to the Kennedy assassination. I mean, this is a topic that you've been pretty obsessed with over the years. What makes it worse in the Trump era? It seems like this has been the case throughout

our history.

What's worse is the permission Trump's given to say the worst things you can think of out loud. No shame, no filter, just proudly declaring your unfitness as a human being. All the ignorance, arrogance, racism, misogyny, corruption—the elements that comprise the shadow side of American history and have held back social development are now just flopped out in front of us by a cohort of venal, immoral, stupid people saying, "Yeah, suck it," as if that's a governing principle. They think that's a way to run a country. It's astonishing. This is a coup by an ugly, vicious, insecure minority, and until we get to the bottom of how much foreign actors influenced it, we're never gonna get to the truth. It's the greatest crisis in our lifetime.

This isn't really a fair question to ask you, because you could write a thesis paper about it, but—to paraphrase David Byrne—how did we get here?

It's a really big question, and there are so many different components to the answer. Number one, you go back and you examine fault lines that were established by the way the country came together. Have we talked about the book *American Nations* by Colin Woodard?

You've mentioned it.

He outlines brilliantly how everyone talks about the United States as one people, but there's no other country in the world anywhere near as diverse as this one. We are literally a nation of eleven, twelve different cultures, and in times of stress, groups tend to revert to tribal identities, particularly now. We have a declining white minority, the roots of which go back all the way to the first immigrations that brought this subset of people into Appalachia, the Deep South, and the Far West. How they struggled, how they kept migrating, and how their social development in most cases lagged behind other sections of the country, for a variety of reasons—economic indifference, indolence, and lack of opportunity—all compounded by the evils of slavery. In some ways, it feels like we're paying the price for the sins of our history now. The genocide of Native Americans. The internment of Japanese Americans during World War II. The oppression of Chinese immigrants coming into San Francisco for the Gold Rush. Even to the great Irish migration in the nineteenth century, when we were keelhauling them straight off the boats, throwing them into the Army, and sending them down to fight in Mexico. Two months earlier, these poor bastards had been sitting in a pub in Cork; now they're pointing a rifle at fellow Catholics in some poor Mexican village.

I don't want to sound reductivist, but people refer to Donald Trump as the first reality TV president and compare the Republican primaries to *Survivor*. Do you think—

That's a huge part of it. I remember this moment acutely, summer of 1999, my wife and I were in upstate New York, and we watched the first episode of *Survivor*. That was the first prime-time reality show of this era, the granddaddy of 'em all. I turned to Lynn when it was over and said, "This could be the end of American society, right here." An artificial way of turning the cooperative business of living as social animals into a dog-eat-dog, reductive, nasty, brutish battle. The only value is winning. Morality and compassion are out the window, and it's a zero-sum game. Losers get eliminated. I had the strong feeling right then that if this catches on—because it's compelling to watch naked aggression and scheming, it feeds the lizard brain of "us against them"—this is going to have a disastrous effect on television and a calamitous effect on American life.

I wish I'd had a tape recorder that night because we said all of that, word for word. Lynn is a PhD in psychology, and she was equally horrified. Of course, it was fascinating to watch—the hook was deadly—but I think that day was a black mark in American history.

Its creator, Mark Burnett, as you undoubtedly know, bought the concept; it wasn't even his idea. Around that time, he also tried to put together a reality show with Vladimir Putin. I later had a meeting with Burnett, out of curiosity—CAA asked me to meet him because he was making noises about wanting to do scripted television—and I came away with an intuitive feeling he was one of the most dangerous people I'd ever met. He had no concept of what writing was, what drama was, how to tell a story—he literally knew nothing about any of it. So of course, he's the one who soon goes to Donald Trump and says, "You were my inspiration for coming to America and making something of myself," which we now know is based on a book Trump didn't write, that's 99.9% lies, fabrications, and exaggerations. That's the frog moth crawling into Sarah Palmer's mouth right there, and it's come full circle. Putting Donald Trump on television as a "billionaire" in *The Apprentice*—at a time he was flat broke, desperately in debt, and couldn't borrow a dime from any legitimate lender—brought us to where we are today. He's a grifter, a moral vacuum, and a sociopath, maybe the worst human being our country's produced on a lot of levels. Packaging him as a master-of-the-universe tycoon on reality television was the most damaging fraud ever committed by an American network, and I lay that squarely at Burnett's and NBC's feet. They knew exactly what they were doing—and who they were dealing with—and went ahead anyway. Because of greed.

They're responsible for his rise, and when the history books are finally written, they're going to be closely scrutinized for the role they played in this punk's resurrection.

You told me once you were inspired to write something about the O. J. trial, and then you wrote this post-9/11 piece for HBO, so I know you've taken stuff that's going on in society and affected you in a deeply emotional way and addressed it through narrative fiction. Are you inspired to address what's going on now?

The answer is yes, and my first impulse is to write a play about my great-uncle and F. D. R. That's the next thing I'm going to work on. So I'm trying to address it, not directly, but by talking about a more inspiring vision of ourselves as a people and a country, to see if we can find a way out of this.

Would you say that season three of *Twin Peaks* was in any way a reaction to it?

Yes, although more in retrospect, or maybe anticipation of where I sensed this was headed. We started writing in 2012, in the wake of the economic crash four years earlier. That was a huge component of where we went with it, writing about the social and economic disaffection of an entire group of people across the country. Many of them we would now typically identify as Trump supporters—white people in rural areas affected by the death of the manufacturing economy, their factories and way of life all fading away. We talked about that a lot with this piece and found ways to depict the aura of dread and despair that has unleashed.

I wanted to wrap up this period, before we move on to *The Return*, by talking about the Marvel movies, the *Fantastic Four* movies. If I'm placing them correctly, these also came during that same period of time, when you were trying to focus more on book writing, and you were looking not at TV shows, but at movies, because they wouldn't require the same level of commitment. Is that right?

Yes, so that I could pursue my own writing without conflict.

And how did you get those movies?

My agent asked me if I was interested in doing a Marvel movie. They'd had terrible trouble developing the Fantastic Four for a decade. They'd gone up, down, and sideways with it and never settled on a script they liked, but they still held the option on the material. It was one of the first comics I ever connected with and had a real fondness for. I read a couple of the scripts they'd developed, and they were all over the place. So we had a meeting and said, "Look, you need to return to the charm of the original, that of a dysfunctional family grounded in humor, more so than almost any other Marvel title." For better or worse, that's what I tried to do with the first one. The second was just a mess, a hodgepodge, and I didn't have all that much to do with what ended up on screen.

But the first one, to the extent that it worked, captured the comedy and humanity of four people who are put in this peculiar situation.

Why do you think the Fantastic Four have proved so difficult to adapt compared with other Marvel franchises?

Honestly, I think it's more the fact that Marvel themselves hasn't had a chance to develop one. The people who really understand that material are [Marvel president] Kevin Feige and the folks around him, and they weren't in a position to have much to say about this movie. Fox owned the title, and they were determined to do it their own way, the way a lot of studio movies get made now. They wanted a good trailer, a good poster, and they wanted to be able to sell it globally. Based on my interaction with their execs, they didn't particularly care what the content of the movie was. It was more about trying to milk the last dime out of a familiar title.

The first film wasn't a bad experience but the second film was?

The first film wasn't a bad experience because they were eager to make the movie, and they were happy they ended up with a script that they could shoot. The way this gets done now is they picked a distribution date for the second one without having an idea for the movie. And then it was a mad scramble to get something written they could put in front of a camera. The script never got there. And so that one was pretty brutally screwed up.

Someone told me you were a big Jack Kirby fan. Is that true? Did you have artists or writers whom you were particularly interested in or invested in as a kid?

I was a big fan of Marvel, so that made me a big fan of Jack Kirby and [Steve] Ditko. I really enjoyed his work. A friend of mine, Dick Cook, who used to run Disney, ended up with all of Kirby's library, and he had a bunch of other ideas that weren't owned by Marvel. I don't know if any of them have gotten off the ground as features. Kirby was one of those guys who was in the right place at the right time with the right material. And his contribution as a visual artist was central to Marvel's success.

Were you going down to the comic stop shop every week to pick up the latest releases?

Oh, yeah.

Were there particular characters you had to have every month?

There were, and there was a particular place to buy them—this was midsixties, '65 to '67. Comic book collecting wasn't really a thing yet. But there was one store in Hollywood, the Cherokee Bookstore, at the corner of Hollywood and Cherokee. Downstairs was an old used and rare bookstore, and upstairs was this big comic book room. Anybody who was a collector in Southern California made a beeline to that place. That's where I started buying older editions of all those Marvel characters that I'd come to like. Most were only a few years old at that point. Later on, it became a much bigger industry. Some of those books are over fifty years old now. I still have my collection.

Was there one specific character, or were there just a bunch of different ones?

A bunch of different ones. It was primarily Marvel. My favorites were Daredevil, Doctor Strange, X-Men, and Spider-Man. Fantastic Four was my first interest, but then I branched into the others because I found them ultimately more intriguing.

❧

10

"I Just Thought It Would Be Audacious"

(The Return + The Novels)

The seeds of *Twin Peaks* season three were planted over five years before its actual premiere on Showtime on May 21, 2017, when Mark Frost reached out to David Lynch to suggest they resurrect the show. A budget dispute between Lynch and Showtime nearly sank the project, but was eventually resolved; while many of the actors rallied behind Lynch, Frost was noticeably quiet during the brouhaha.

Some 500,000 people tuned in for the premiere—a "low" number, according to the website TV by the Numbers. Viewership dipped after that, ranging from about 200,000 to 350,000 over the remaining sixteen episodes (or "parts," as they were officially labeled, consistent with Lynch's insistence that he was making one eighteen-hour movie rather than an episodic television drama). The particularly provocative and creatively stunning Part 8 drew 246,000 viewers but created enough buzz that 100,000 more people tuned in two weeks later, when the following episode aired.

Ratings may not have been dazzling, but reviews were; twenty of the nation's TV critics crowned it the best show of 2017, tied for first with HBO's *The Leftovers*. *Sight & Sound* magazine's annual critics' poll named it second best *film* of the year, after *Get Out*, with Tom Charity crowing: "It blows up TV, creatively, and puts pop culture on a new wavelength. And it has so much to say about the legacy of 'the American century' that of course it's the most resonant, relevant 18-

hour movie at this time of meltdown and crisis."

The entire season was scripted by Frost and Lynch before even a single scene was shot, with Lynch directing. For much of the time that Lynch was shooting and postproducing, Frost was doing what he loves most, writing books—specifically two *Twin Peaks*–themed novels, *The Secret History of Twin Peaks* (published in October 2016, seven months before season three premiered) and *Twin Peaks: The Final Dossier* (released a year later, about two months after the season finale).

Secret History—the first freshly produced *Twin Peaks* material from either creator in twenty-four years (excluding scenes Lynch shot exclusively for *Twin Peaks: The Missing Pieces*, the DVD released in 2014)—generally steered clear of anything that was about to turn up in the series. Its publication was greeted rapturously by fans and received some terrific reviews, for both content and form, though some devotees were rankled by apparent narrative discrepancies between the book and the first two seasons of the television series.

The Final Dossier, a much slimmer volume, was freed from the constraints of having to avoid spoilers, and Frost took advantage of the occasion to address many of the burning questions fans had hoped would be answered in season three (though they should have known better). However, even *The Final Dossier* leaves many questions hanging—including, perhaps most urgently of all: Is this the end of *Twin Peaks*?

***

Here we are at the famous rebirth of *Twin Peaks*, beginning in October 2016 with the publication of *The Secret History of Twin Peaks*, leading into the Showtime series, known as *The Return*, and finally *The Final Dossier*, published in October 2017. By the way, I've heard reports that David Lynch doesn't like the term *The Return*. Do you share that opinion, or are you OK with it?

The Return was Showtime's way of distinguishing the new show from the old. That did not come from us.

How do you feel about it?

It's a label. A marketing idea that made it easier for people to identify what we were doing. I was neutral on it. The show was going to speak for itself no matter what it was called.

OK, so I'm wondering if this chronology is correct. This comes from *Room to Dream*, the book that David cowrote with Kristine McKenna. Right after Christmas Day 2011, you and David meet for lunch at Musso & Frank and start talking about doing *Twin Peaks* again. She's putting that right after Christmas Day 2011; I think I heard you somewhere say that it was August 2012.

That's my memory. Maybe we talked on the phone then. I know I reached out to him and suggested we have a chat. I could have the date wrong, but I don't remember it being right after Christmas. I remember it being a hot day; we walked out of the restaurant, and David was dressed all in black and looked uncomfortable in the heat. That's my memory of it.

In all the time between 1992, whenever you saw *Fire Walk With Me*, and 2011 or 2012, what kind of relationship did you and David have? Did you talk at all? Did you see each other socially at all?

Only occasionally, and only if there was some kind of business to discuss with *Twin Peaks*. For a long time, the show went kind of dormant. It ran on Bravo for a while. It wasn't until they released the first DVDs that we started to see it kick back up in people's consciousness. So we talked from time to time about issues relating to that. I remember we had a long conversation about the gold box set—that would have been around '06. I went over to his house, and we had a nice chat and a cup of coffee. The next time was when I called him and said, "I've got an idea."

That was the first time you had proposed bringing it back?

Yes. It didn't occur to me that was practical until the marketplace for the DVDs and online fan forums suggested there was a lot of interest.

This was well ahead of the reboot boom that was coming, particularly for network TV. I just thought it would be audacious to bring a show back after all that time, pick up the story however many years later—not try to re-create it or remake it—and continue with a different chapter.

Was it something that you sat on for a while, or you called him immediately?

I only called him once I felt I had a sound idea.

I've heard you talk about how you called him up, and you said either on the phone or at lunch that you think you have a way in. What was that way in?

I don't want to give away too much, but it had to do with what had happened to Cooper and how he might come back. Basically what you saw—after much discussion and shaping and writing—in *The Return*.

David's been quoted as saying, "This show is different from the *Twin Peaks* that's gone before, but it's still securely anchored in *Twin Peaks*."

I agree with that. The root of the story still flows from that place and ends up circling back there, so it's the alpha and omega. We rarely, if ever, went outside of the town on the old show, and from the beginning we were going to do that in season three. That's what I proposed, that we'd take the story other places. So it expanded upon—but ultimately was contained within—the world we'd created the first time, on a canvas that felt larger both in time and in place.

Did the fact that it had been twenty-five years and Laura had made that comment about seeing Cooper again in twenty-five years, did that factor in at all?

That came after we'd talked about it at that lunch. We sat down and looked at the final episode to see what it sparked for us. And it was at that point, when we heard that line, that we realized how close we were in terms of the calendar. There it was, and it'd been there from the beginning.

The two of you sat down in a room together and watched a DVD of the final episode?

He has a screening room in his office in Lookout Mountain, so we looked at it there.

Going back to Kristine McKenna's timeline: she says there were nine months of talks between the two of you before you actually started to sit down and write.

I think that's about right.

Nine months before you started writing?

Yes, but there was a lot of note-taking.

This was Skype the two of you were using?

Some of this was in person, but as soon as I moved up to Ojai in 2012, we started on Skype.

I see. So before you moved to Ojai, you were in LA, and you guys would meet in person at an office or somewhere?

Yes, usually at his place. He doesn't like to go out much. We still had our house in LA at that point, so I was going back and forth a lot.

She actually does say that in 2012—this might be Lynch's wife who says this—in 2012, you started visiting his house, and the two of you would sit in David's painting studio and write.

That was after we started writing. If I was in town, I'd come over, and we would sit and work the way we used to in the old days.

How many people knew this was going on, besides you and David?

No one, aside from the people who worked for him and our families. We didn't tell anybody.

Your wife, Lynn, for example—she knew?

Yes. But not any details

How would you describe the process of the two of you working together, compared with the original series?

Very similar to the first time around. I didn't see it as substantially all that different. Same kind of back and forth—like ping pong, batting things around and having a lot of laughs.

In anticipation of season three, a lot of people were speculating that we would see a decisive progression toward abstraction, given movies like *Inland Empire* and some of David's later work. Did that come up at all in your conversations—that issue of abstraction versus accessibility?

Yes, that was a line of discussion. Lynch doesn't like to be pinned down. He prefers to be provocative and likes putting something suggestive more than explicit out there and letting people react to it. I'm more narratively trained and believe more people respond to something that's internally cohesive. So that proved to be a point of departure in our separate work over the last twenty years.

Back to the timelime: By the beginning of 2014, according to Kristine, the two of you had completed enough of a script to begin looking for financing, and your first stop was Showtime. I also heard that David Nevins, who was president of Showtime Entertainment, had heard that you were thinking of reviving it and had reached out

to you guys.

No, that's not true. The first person we talked to was our friend Ken Ross, head of CBS Home Entertainment, who'd done a fantastic job with all the DVDs. Being well-placed at CBS and part of the same corporate family as Showtime, we reached out to Ken for his advice. He affirmed that Showtime should be the place to start. Because, obviously, having the same company do all the ancillaries made a lot of sense. I'd also known David Nevins since the nineties, and Gary Levine—who had been the network exec on the show at ABC way back in the early days—was his number two at Showtime. So I felt very comfortable, given the relationship I had with both those guys, that they might be a receptive audience. So that was the one and only meeting we took. We went to their office in person, told them we'd written a couple of hours and we'd like to see what they thought about moving this forward

"They" meaning Nevins and Levine?

Right.

You gave them the first two parts?

The first two hours—basically what ended up as the first two hours they televised.

And they read it?

And responded very favorably. They originally wanted to do a certain number of hours—I think nine hours all together, maybe ten with the two hours upfront. We said we just wanted to write it; we don't know how long it's going to be. It took a long time to negotiate the contract, and while they were negotiating, we kept writing. We just started writing the rest of the script.

You never met with anybody but Showtime about this?

Correct.

And then, going back to Kristine's timeline: On October 6, 2014, you guys both sent the tweet out that "It is happening again." Then in January 2015, you turned in a 334-page script to Showtime. That's all accurate?

I believe so, yeah. Although I think it was longer than that.

Was there any difference in the writing process between the first two hours and everything that followed? If you go back and look at the original series, you wrote the pilot in a certain way, then the rest of season one another way, and then season two as you were airing. Was there some dichotomy between the writing process for the first two parts and then the rest of the season?

Only in that we had a lot more architecture to build out before we could start drafting. Now that we knew we were going to be writing it fully, the blueprints had to expand beyond what we'd done for the first two hours.

You didn't have nearly as much time to write the rest of season three, though, did you?

I would say the first two hours were the slowest to write, because we had to forge the new world we were going into, and the pace picked up from there.

I had read somewhere that you and David had determined early in your conversations that you knew what the last line of season three was going to be. Is that true?

Who said that?

I don't remember exactly where I read it or heard it.

It might have been true at one time, but I don't know if it was true the way it ended up.

Meanwhile, negotiations are dragging on and off, and on April 6, after fourteen months of haggling, Showtime presents a budget that David at least thought was woefully inadequate. What were you thinking?

I felt it was a very low number given how much material we had, but I also thought that if he just shot what we wrote, we'd end up with so many more hours than they'd originally contracted for that it would all even out. But he had a budget in mind, and a budget is something you have to live with. I wasn't involved with the budgeting process, but having done plenty of them, I know you can't push the button unless you know you've got the time and resources you need. So he took that step of stepping away from the show, and always claimed it was never a stunt, not a negotiating ploy. He really just didn't feel he could do it, and so I take him at his word on that. And then it all worked out, because he drew a line in the sand and they said, "OK, I guess we still want the show," and they stepped up.

I wanted to talk about casting for a minute. You had this amazing cast in *The Return*, bringing in newcomers like Naomi Watts, Michael Cera, and so on. But I think some people were surprised that certain characters didn't come back, like Annie, for instance, first because Cooper's last words—or the doppelgänger's last words—had been, "How's Annie?" There were a lot of stories circulating about all these actors and actresses, like Joan Chen, wanting to come in. Was that just an organic thing, about who would be in it and who wouldn't?

It's where the story took us and who we could use to facilitate the story, and there were a few people we weren't able to accommodate.

Was there any discussion about bringing Chet Desmond [Chris Isaak] back, since he had disappeared in sort of the same way that Phillip Jeffries did?

I mentioned it to David a couple of times, but he didn't pursue it.

Once production started, how much time did you personally spend in Snoqualmie Valley?

We were up there for six or seven weeks. I went for the end of prep and three different times for about a week at a time. So at least half the time, we were in Snoqualmie, maybe two-thirds. I was there for more of it than when we came down and started shooting in LA.

How long was that for?

We started shooting early September 2015, and we didn't wrap until the end of April. We had a break over Christmas. We relocated to LA, and everything else was in and around LA until David decided he wanted to go shoot the Monica Bellucci scene in Paris.

Tell me about the Skype scene with your dad.

That was the first scene we shot. I was back East. My parents were there, my dad, my brother, my son, my wife, and we shot in our house on the lake in upstate New York. Thought it was a great scene for Dad to have as his valedictory, so I put a lot into that. Unfortunately, Dad didn't know what Skype was, so he thought somehow that it was all going to be on the phone. He didn't understand he was going to be on camera until the day we shot it. So we had to make cue cards for him, which my son was holding for him. Anyway, it was a special day for the family, and we all knew it was probably his last scene, so it was very poignant.

What a great scene. *Twin Peaks* fans were so happy to see him.

David directed it from LA, and he was terrific in getting a good performance from Warren, so it worked out really well.

Am I right that postproduction took about a year? What were you

doing during that time? Were you involved in post? I know you did a book tour for *The Secret History,* and then at some point you had to start writing *The Final Dossier.*

The first book came out in October of 2016. I had a big book tour— went all over the country, had a great response, a lot of fun meeting all of the fans. It was the first time I'd seen any of them in a long time.

Was this during postproduction?

Yes. Lynch disappeared in postproduction. I'd occasionally see a scene because the editor was a friend, and if I happened to be in the neighborhood he'd show me something, but Lynch never showed me a cut.

The first two parts were screened at Cannes in May 2017. Were you there for that?

No.

How come you didn't go?

Because I'd been to Cannes once. Horrible experience.

Before we get down to some of the nitty-gritty on season three, one weird, sort of out-of-the-blue question: Do you remember that insurance man who shows up in part one and asks for Sheriff Truman?

Yes.

Was that just a quirky little *Twin Peaks* thing, or was there some greater significance?

I don't recall there being anything specifically intended for that.

Well, I think we just made huge news in the fan community. Anyway, the whole tulpa concept, which was so important in season three: Can you tell me anything about where that came from?

It's part of Tibetan Buddhism. I came across it way back when I was doing research into some of the Tibetan concepts in laying out Cooper's character, who had an interest in those things.

In *The Final Dossier*, you cite Helena Blavatsky's references to sects that make use of tulpas, like the Brothers of the Shadow.

I may have come across that even earlier, because I was into Blavatsky well before the UFO stuff. I tried to read Blavatsky's *The Secret Doctrine* and *Isis Unveiled* at one point, and my brain still hurts. They're almost impenetrable. But there's a lot of interesting concepts.

I know you don't like to delineate creative responsibility, but that whole tulpa thing, was that Mark Frost?

We used it as a version of the doppelgänger, which was something Jung wrote about, as a universal archetype. The tulpa designation made it a bit more exotic and mystical. We did use the word doppelgänger at times, but they're close to interchangeable concepts.

How about all that Sumerian mythology—the different male and female forms of the demons. Was that something you had come across in your research as well?

That came from trying to find a way to incorporate the "Judy" reference in *Fire Walk With Me*.

Yeah, it was Bowie.

It's the Bowie character, but then it appears again at the end.

A monkey says it, yeah.

A monkey, right. So when we started talking about this, I asked him, "Who or what is Judy?" And Lynch said he had no idea. It was one of those things that came to him, so he threw it in there. So I tried to circle back and pin it into some underlying concepts in a way that made sense. By this time, the idea of the interdimensional demon that appears in the box was in play. I went through a list of Sumerian or Babylonian deities or demons and came across the name Joudy, and suggested we say it was distorted by Bowie's Southern accent and what he was really trying to say was "Joudy."

Do you have a favorite scene in season three? You've mentioned in the past that you are really fond of the diner scene between Bobby and Major Briggs in season two, and I'm just wondering if there was any equivalent to that in your mind in season three.

There were a lot of scenes I loved in season three. It's hard to pick one.

Can you pick more than one?

Michael Cera as Wally Brando. I nearly fell out of my chair laughing as we watched it being filmed. I loved all the work with the folks in the sheriff's station. Michael Horse was great throughout. Bob Forster was pitch-perfect. Harry and Kimmy, priceless. Everett eating soup alone in his garage. His moment with Peggy. What Russ did with the Dr. Amp monologues. Kyle's work from start to finish. Too much to name, because I don't want to leave anyone out.

Couple of questions about those scenes you just mentioned. In the scene with the soup, there was a lot of speculation because Ed's reflection doesn't match his movements. Do you remember that?

I don't know. Lynch may have made a dissolve between two takes that he liked. I haven't scrutinized it.

Another issue like that: I don't know how much attention you paid to the postairing chatter, but there was one episode where, at the

end, David's son comes into the diner and says—

Yelling somebody's name. I have no idea what that was about.

There was a lot of speculation after that episode aired. We saw one point of view of the diner. Then he cut to another, and the same patrons are sitting in completely different positions, as if there was some sort of dimensional shift. Any idea what that was about? Was that intentional?

That's probably overthinking it.

With Jacoby, you had mentioned to me at one point that in some ways season three reflected what had happened in 2008—the financial collapse.

We started writing in the aftermath of the collapse. So that housing project in Vegas was a stand-in for the abandoned, ghost-town neighborhoods of late-stage capitalism that popped up everywhere, and what that was doing to people, how this was hollowing out small towns. So that was anticipatory—the crash may have started in 2009, but it's pretty important background music that brought us to the Trump era.

And Jacoby was part of that as well?

Yes. Given everything that had happened once he lost his medical license, I liked the idea that Jacoby went into internet radio, not as a right-winger but an old-fashioned radical pirate radio program—trying to be a voice in the wilderness and bring us back to sanity.

A lot of people might choose something from Part 8 as their favorite scene. It certainly got a lot of attention at the time. I've always wondered what that looked like on the page—the whole flashback, the explosion, the birth of Bob.

It looked like a conventional screenplay. It was written in great detail.

We wrote a number of discrete episodes, few of which ended up airing exactly the way they were originally divvied up. Scenes shifted around or moved. Given the density of the visuals, we knew episode eight would play a lot longer than you'd normally attribute to page count. It wasn't originally written as a full, standalone episode, but all those designations were placeholders until he shot and edited. The thing was gonna be X number of hours long, so we just divided them to be able to conveniently show them, "Here's the original nine hours you contracted."

Here's the thing about Part 8: Most people I know interpret it as the birth of modern evil, and I think you've been quoted as saying that more or less—that Joudy somehow gave birth to Bob and spawned this frog moth that Sarah Palmer ingested. So does that mean that Sarah Palmer, from the time we meet her in season one, had been invaded by some sort of otherworldly evil spirit? And that the whole time that we thought she was this mentally unstable mother who was basically looking the other way while her husband was raping her child, does this mean that all of that is just not true anymore?

None of the things you saw in that episode are in any way directly contradictory to what you've seen before. They might be complementary, but I don't believe they're contradictory.

That's so cryptic, though.

I know, sorry. The entirety of those black and white scenes took only about ten pages.

That kind of strikes me as surprising, that it was so many pages.

It was pretty well fleshed out on the page.

It seems like Sarah Palmer had Joudy's frog moth inside of her from the time we first met her in season one, but it just was latent? And was Laura Palmer then the spawn of two evil entities, and yet she

was sent to Earth, it seemed, by the Fireman as some sort of golden orb to combat evil? Am I close?

I think you're in the ballpark.

That's all I'm getting, right?

That's all you're getting right now.

But this whole Sarah Palmer thing—I mean, I know that you like leaving some mystery to it, but you just said there was nothing that happened in season three that really changed what had happened previously. But I think one of the areas where people are most confused is that they never thought of Sarah Palmer as somebody who was inhabited by any sort of demon or spirit, and I think that possibility seems to be raised in season three.

Part of this was that Lynch couldn't let go of Laura Palmer as a character. There was something about her that just possessed him. That became a little bit more his obsession than mine.

I was listening to your interview with the writer-producer Sam Esmail on *Talkhouse Podcast*, which is just a great interview. The description of Part 8 seems to me like such a precise encapsulation of the way your partnership worked from a creative standpoint: the fact that this profound idea originated intellectually as a Mark Frost idea, which you scripted—the whole idea of the bomb as the original sin and so on—and then David came up with some unique and stunning way of visualizing it. Or, conversely, that David came up with some outré visual idea, and then you had to provide the narrative logic for it. So it could go both ways.

I think that's accurate. That's the process of creating. You create first on the page, and the director has to create and interpret that in their own unique way. For the most part, television is considered more a writer's medium than a director's, for that reason. It's not primarily visual; it's

CONVERSATIONS WITH MARK FROST

primarily conveyed through plot, story, and dialogue. *Twin Peaks* did change the way that that was perceived. But all those things for the most part—there are more than a few exceptions—had to be written first, so that's still the way it's done.

OK, but just to take one last stab at clarifying this point: a lot of people who saw *Fire Walk With Me* thought it wasn't even Bob who was raping Laura, but that it was Leland, and that the film was this very human story of a woman, Sarah Palmer, who just looked the other way because she couldn't deal with the reality of it and this father who was not really inhabited by an evil spirit but was inventing it to deny what he was doing. You said that what we saw in season three was not contrary to anything we'd seen before, but that does seem like a conflict.

It doesn't to me for some reason.

We talked about this before also, when we were discussing the ending of the original *Twin Peaks*, but I think it's relevant again here. A lot of people have no idea what happened in Part 18—who that Cooper was, what happened outside the Palmer house, why Cooper asked what year it was, and so on. But I have seen some really interesting fan theories about it. I don't know how you react when you hear these theories, whether you think they're crazy or not, but you know how in *Mulholland Dr.*, Diane Selwyn kills her girlfriend and then invents this imaginary life? And a similar thing happens in *Lost Highway*, with Fred Madison? So this theory by Tim Kreider maintains that Cooper—who is in reality not Cooper but someone named Richard—killed Laura and has invented this life so that he can live with the enormity of his crime. So the last thing that Laura whispers to him in the Red Room is "You killed me," which is what triggers that gasp.

Well, that part of the show is knitted loosely enough that it can be interpreted a lot of different ways. And I agree with your analysis about *Mulholland Dr.* and *Lost Highway*. They're both about protagonists who are disintegrating both psychologically and morally. I wouldn't stretch it that far for Agent Cooper, but that's what makes a horse race. Everybody has their own opinions.

Do you have an opinion? And is it necessarily the definitive opinion?

What I feel is it's not up to me to interpret it for other people. I've got my own thoughts and theories, but I prefer to keep them to myself, because I don't want to inhibit anybody from seeing what they see.

But your opinion and David's opinion—are they necessarily the same opinion?

I don't know the answer to that. There have been times I began to wonder about that.

Is there any possibility in your mind that almost the entire run of *Twin Peaks***—seasons one, two, and three, maybe up until Part 18—is a dream by someone? Like say the young Sarah Palmer? Or Cooper? Or Laura? You say you don't think anything in season three contradicts anything that happened previously, and I'm just wondering if maybe that is what you meant by that.**

The short answer is no. It never crossed my mind.

It seems like Cooper is always, in the end, failing in some way, whether getting trapped in the Black Lodge or the whole mess with bringing Laura, or Carrie, back to *Twin Peaks***, possibly as a result of a White Knight Syndrome.**

Yeah.

I mentioned this before, when we were talking about season two, but Joseph Campbell said that "the ultimate aim of the quest must be neither release nor ecstasy for oneself but the wisdom and power to serve others."

Yes.

And he said one of the differences between the celebrity and the hero is that one acts only for him- or herself while the other seeks to redeem society. So my question for you is, in your mind, was Cooper's White Knight Syndrome a character flaw or a characteristic of his heroism?

Both.

That's a great answer. But why a flaw?

It led to a lot of suffering, including his own.

But do you think he should have done something different from what he did?

No, I don't think he was capable of doing anything different.

But would you have done something different?

Probably.

What would you have done differently?

I haven't thought it through, so I don't want to answer glibly.

But wouldn't you have gone down into the Black Lodge to get Annie?

You mean Orpheus going into the underworld?

Sure. Or tried to save Laura?

I might have done that.

A lot of people accuse him of acting with hubris, but to me, he's doing exactly what Joseph Campbell said a hero should do.

He does what he thought was noble and good, but it has unintended consequences.

Did Homer's *Odyssey* play any role in the conception and construct of season three?

I did have *The Odyssey* in mind, but Lynch was not overly familiar with it, so I kept that to myself.

We talked earlier about your taste in music and what impact that has on your work. Was there something you were listening to during season three that might have influenced your writing? Obviously music played such a prominent role, with all those Roadhouse performances, like Nine Inch Nails.

I don't know if you've had this experience, but at a certain point, the musical RAM in my head felt like it was full, so there aren't a lot of people I go out of my way to listen to. Music is powerful because it seems to attach to emotional memories of particular times and places, and that part of your brain gets filled at a certain point. Most contemporary music says the same thing music for young people always has, and if you've already got your own version of that in your head, that need is fulfilled.

It's funny, though, watching [Frost's son] Travis's musical taste develop over the years, he listens to almost nothing that isn't from the fifties, sixties, seventies, early eighties. He's a big Sinatra fan. He'll say, "This is from the Columbia years, Dad, that's when he was really good." It's like, "Wow, who are you?" So it's kind of cool that's the music he's gravitated toward.

OK, so let's talk about the books—*The Secret History*, which came out in October 2016, before the show returned, and then *The Final*

Dossier, **published a year later, after the show had ended. I think the most pressing question here is, why Dougie Milford? I think that surprised a lot of people.**

I felt that in order to create a spine for that story I needed somebody who had been a minor character in the old show, who could guide us through a whole bunch of different twists and turns and different areas of the story, who didn't suffer from already having a firmly established backstory—and Dougie became a perfect tabula rasa for that. He was a character people remembered, so I worked outward from that little thumbnail we had of him originally and built what I thought was a pretty persuasive character.

Do you remember who created Dougie to begin with?

I'm guessing, but I probably suggested in a story conference that the mayor had a brother. I don't honestly remember.

At what point did you start thinking about writing the books?

I wasn't going to start writing the first book until we knew we were making the series—so they had to read the script, say we're in, then we had to agree on budget and schedule, and all these negotiations were long and protracted. So I didn't start writing the book until we rolled camera on the show. We'd negotiated a deal for the books, but it was all contingent on whether the series moved forward.

But if you turned in the script in January 2015, when did the idea pop into your head that you were going to write a novel? It was before you turned in the script, right?

Yeah, the idea had occurred to me by then.

Was there a discussion between you and David that you would write the book and he would direct the series? How that dichotomy would work? Or that there would even be a dichotomy?

We did. He wanted to direct all of them, so I said, "Fine, you should do that." And I said, "I'll write a book at the same time."

When you first thought about writing a book, I've read that the first book originally was going to be called *The Secret Lives of Twin Peaks*. Is that true?

That was a temporary title, a slugline for the contract. It wasn't set in stone.

Wasn't the subject matter of the first book somewhat dictated by the fact that you couldn't go in certain places because you and David had this agreement that the book wouldn't reveal anything that was going to happen in the series?

That made the most sense. I wanted something that deepened the world of *Twin Peaks* without giving anything away that was ahead of us, so I came up with the idea of two books, one that came out about seven months before the series debuted, and a second that came out after the series ended.

The one that came out seven months before the series debuted—*The Secret History*—was that completely written after production had wrapped?

No, I wrote it concurrent with production.

But did you finish it before they wrapped production?

A couple of months before.

Because the script was changing, right? That was something you probably needed to know as you were writing the book.

No, the first book wasn't affected by what was in the new show.

But you do sort of drop some hints here and there about stuff, all the interdimensionality. It does sort of seem to me that you are planting some hints about what we're gonna see.

Yes, but nothing changed that would have altered those things, because I wasn't disclosing anything that was particularly germane to the new show. There were thematic references, but nothing that was on the nose.

When you first floated the idea of a book, in your own mind were you immediately thinking that you were going to go back to Lewis and Clark, that that's where that book was going to start?

I'd always had this idea, actually way back when, but couldn't write it because I was running the show. I wanted to write a perverse James Michener version of the entire history of Twin Peaks, which is a lot like what *The Secret History* turned out to be.

Did you research Lewis and Clark and the Nez Indians at that time, or was that something you now had to sit down and do in order to write—

Tons of research. I wanted to ground it in a lot of real events and paper fiction over reality in a way that made it hard to discern which is which.

The website Pop Apostle almost page by page deconstructs both novels. They go out and try to find—they do basically what Tammy Preston was doing, only not fictionally. It's pretty impressive.

That might be interesting to anybody but me. I've already done all that.

You're right. So were you doing all this research from your computer, or were you traveling around the country and visiting different libraries and such?

No, you can do all that on the internet. I was reading books. Research that doesn't involve talking to people is relatively easy now.

Did you refer back at all to the access guide when you were writing *Secret History* **and later** *Final Dossier*?

I did for dates, times, and places. I tried to be consistent with what we'd originally set down for backstories. Names and obscure characters, it was helpful in that regard, and I kept a copy of it handy.

Pop Apostle actually compared the details in *Secret History* **with information from the access guide and the** *Twin Peaks* **cards— some of which was consistent, some of which wasn't. What about the old show and** *Fire Walk With Me*? **Did you have researchers or somebody—let's say you needed to know something that had happened in the show—did you have an assistant who would go watch it, or would you do it yourself?**

I was able to recall most of what I needed to know. I have the DVDs, so it was easy to call up something. And a lot was already online. The fans remember the old show much better than I do because they've watched it much more frequently over time. I don't know anybody who sits down and watches their own work.

When you're creating a world like this—and I did a lot of the world building away from the show, in print, with the books—there's no such thing as a perfect record. People keep saying, "But this doesn't agree with that." And I always say, "But that's how life is." People's opinions and memories differ, and that's what gets into the historical record, conflicting points of view. So I said, "Why not embrace that? Why be obsessively anal about having the record line up on every single issue? We're talking about a fictional world, so what does it matter? There's no final exam." We accept the fact that imperfections are always in the public record in small ways because they depend on the frailties of memory. That more accurately reflects the reality of how things are remembered and how they're passed down.

On some of these inconsistencies between the book and seasons one and two—like the whole backstory to Norma, Hank and Ed—was

that stuff that you deliberately put in?

Yes.

I wanted to talk to you about the Owl Cave ring, because that's something that seems to be important to both you and David, but to be honest, it's hard to tell if you are both on the same wavelength about it, or even what that wavelength is. The Owl Cave symbol started in season two, so I'd always considered it something that you, Harley, and Bob had introduced, but then David really went to town on it with the ring in *Fire Walk With Me*, and then in both *The Secret History* and *The Return* it plays such a huge role. Do you, in your own mind, have any clear idea what that ring signifies?

Yes. I don't like to explain things like that. But I like the ring. It was a clever addition in *Fire Walk With Me*, one of the elements I really liked, and I thought it would be useful, particularly in the book. I also knew we were going to use it extensively in the new series, so it made sense to wrap it back into the history as if it had always been there.

Yeah, it plays quite a prominent role in *The Secret History*. I understand that you don't want to put a name on it, but in your mind, do you have a concrete idea of what the ring means? And it may or may not be the same as what David thinks the ring means, or it is the same?

That's probably fair to say.

That it may or may not—

It's better left as something that can drift in your mind without a fixed, concrete meaning. It's a provocative symbol with all sorts of different associations, and since it's "supernatural," the more specific you get about it, the less effective it becomes.

Did you and David ever have a conversation about what the ring is?

Yes.

And do you think you're on the same page with respect to the ring?

Yeah, I think we were.

Because there's been a lot written and said about discrepancies between the different mythologies, and also among the characters' backstories between *The Secret History* and the first two seasons of the TV series. In one interview I read, you said that you don't like the word "canon," and that you think it's OK that sometimes there's more than one canon when more than one creator is involved. I think a lot of people had trouble accepting that, because they want everything to sync up, but the more I thought about it and the more that I watched season three and the more I read the books, the more I came to understand—I think—what you were saying: Basically that David has his own vision, and he doesn't care what anybody else thinks about it, so why should you be tied to that version of the canon when in fact you may have had something different in mind all along?

I agree. Lynch went off and did *Fire Walk With Me* entirely on his own. I was never consulted on it. The only way I could contribute was to try to fold some of that mythology back into season three and reverse-engineer it into a unified theory, but that's part of what makes the series interesting.

Right, but I think people are obsessed with trying to squeeze everything into a single unified theory. You had a lot of experience with reverse-engineering during the first two seasons anyway, right?

It's something you often do when working on a series.

Switching gears, but sticking with *The Secret History*, have you heard of the CBS All Access show *Strange Angel*, which is based on the book about Jack Parsons—a prominent character in your book?

I was made aware of it by a friend. I never read it and never saw any of it. That all happened after I'd already put the book to bed. I'd known about Jack Parsons for years, because one of my closest friends worked for many years at JPL [Jet Propulsion Laboratory].

He worked there after Parsons?

Long after, but he knew all about him and the peculiar history of the company—how they managed it, and how at various times they uncomfortably distanced themselves from him. Now they've come back to more or less embracing him as one of their founders.

It is one of the most incredible stories I've ever heard. Do you find it interesting at all that so many scientists are attracted to the paranormal?

If you go all the way back in history to the alchemists, you find people conducting experiments scientifically they thought brought them closer to the borderline between science and religion, or Satan and magic. That's a lineage you see all the way up to this group at JPL.

The reason I brought up Parsons was you spend a fair amount of time in *The Secret History* dealing with their trips to the desert and the Goddess of Babylon, and there's been a lot of speculation among fans that this concept of the Moonchild—Aleister Crowley's *Moonchild*—plays some role in season three, if not earlier than that even. But I don't know if that's the case or if you're just throwing out a million different possibilities without trying to establish anything definitively. So I'm wondering: Was the Moonchild concept relevant to *Twin Peaks*, or were you just interested in this story from a historical point of view?

I saw it as relevant to what we were working with on season three and used it in the book to foreshadow where we were headed, to suggest a way of interpreting what they were about to see.

So you've read Crowley?

I read him earlier in life and decided he was a freakin' lunatic, but it was an interesting theory in terms of the story in *The Secret History*, so I brought some of it forward as an influence in that story.

But you don't see a Moonchild in *Twin Peaks*, do you? Like Laura? Anyway, that book is impossible to read. I've tried like three times to get through it.

It is. He's a terrible writer, both labored and obvious. His books are pretty dreadful. He's more interesting as a portrait of mental illness run amok and the degree to which he influenced his time and society—he's the dark side of the Theosophists. He's often cited as a prototype for hedonism and narcissism in a cult leader. The guy was a mess, so he's an interesting character to study. The repression of the Victorian Era clearly produced Aleister Crowley. He was very much a product of, or a reaction against, his environment.

OK, you said you saw integrating Crowley as a way to "give people a way of interpreting what they were about to see." I understand that you and David both want to leave things open to interpretation, but does that mean—do you and David have your own interpretations?

I think so, but you never know with him. It seemed in concert when we were writing, but I can't vouch for what he was thinking or where he went with some of it afterward. You'd have to ask him.

But what I mean is, you're saying "to help people come to some interpretation in terms of what happened in season three"—and I assume you're talking mostly about Part 8—but is there one right interpretation of what happened in season three and does it matter what your interpretation—Mark Frost's interpretation—is, or is that just another point of view? Not just in season three, but in *Twin Peaks* in general, really.

I have my own interpretation, and I think we've covered it, but I also like to leave the door open for people to come up with their own. I've always encouraged them to do that, and that's where I'd like to leave it. There is no one way to interpret reality or a work of fiction, so why bother?

Do you ever read, when you come across a work that you find interesting and provocative—a film or a book—do you go research what the creator thinks about it? Do you afford that any particular weight, or is that just another interpretation? Do you look for a ~~definitive~~ itive interpretation as a consumer rather than as a creator?

If the work intrigues me enough that I want to dig deeper, I'll give that some thought. Varying artists assert varying levels of control or interpretation over what they've done. Some insist it can only be interpreted one way, but that seems like an exercise in futility to my mind. You have your own interpretation, so why not leave it at that? That shouldn't mean everybody needs to confirm it. That suggests your grasp of the material isn't quite as firm as you imagined it to be.

From a historian's perspective, if you look at the work of an artist, and you're trying to establish certain thematic preoccupations, then there's some value to knowing what that artist intended or thinks about something he or she created.

Yes, for a historian or a critic. My feeling is the work should speak for itself, and if it wasn't clear from what you were doing, what you were thinking or feeling or trying to say, then maybe you didn't do the job. As long as some people get something from it, if they take something away that's provocative to them and prompts either deeper examination of the work or self-examination, I think that's the most you can hope for.

While we're deconstructing—or not deconstructing—the mysteries in the series and the two books, who exactly do you think all these otherworldly entities are? Where do they come from? What do they want?

That gets into the hazy area of "What is this other reality we keep bumping up against?" I have an idea what it is, and can make suggestions, but none of us, short of absolute enlightenment, can assert we know the ultimate answer.

You are suggesting we pay particular attention to that speech by Douglas Milford—when he's talking about how they're not just one thing, but many different things?

Yes.

I see that speech as the key to *The Secret History*, because instead of asking questions you're actually trying to answer them—for a change!

I'd probably go along with that.

I read somewhere where somebody said the creature that Milford is shown by Nixon at the UFO facility bears a resemblance to the Experiment. Is that the way you see it as well?

You mean the thing in the box?

I do.

It's not unintentional.

Do you not call it the Experiment?

No, I've never heard that term before.

Really? What did you call the thing in the box?

I can't say, because we had a secret code for it.

Well, that's an interesting answer in and of itself. Now, with this

interdimensionality, were you guys aware of all the government research about that possibility, or was that just something you were just making up as you went along?

No, I knew about that research.

OK, next mystery. I've mentioned to you once before the Aaron Mento theory, with respect to the Bookhouse books.

Remind me again. With the titles?

Yup. This guy Aaron Mento, who's a fan, held up the picture of the books to a mirror and found what he decided was a secret code. He also argues that this explains the use of the letter I instead of the number 1 throughout the book, because I reflects back unchanged. So book one, which is Fear and Loathing on the *Campaign Trail*, two, *The Warren Report*, and eight, *Double Indemnity*, reflect back perfectly, and the first word of each spells Fear the Double. A warning from Briggs? That's just incredible, isn't it?

Well, it might not have been an accident.

You're not going on the record as saying whether or not that was intentional?

I'll just say I had some fun with it.

But there was some larger significance to those particular books being in the library?

Sure. I'd rather not say what each one means—I think it's fun for people to think about it. But in Lucy's case the idea was, well, this was about an ultimate showdown between good and evil, and Lucy has a fairly important part to play in that process at the end of the story. So in a way, it was like, "OK, that's how you come to understand why Lucy is able to do what she did."

Is there a reason why there's an "I" used throughout the book for the number one, which makes sense considering the way most typewriters were built at the time, but then the typewriter that you show in the book actually has the numeral 1? I know you're a typewriter enthusiast.

I hadn't thought of that. I took a picture of that typewriter because I thought it was supercool and looked like the one I imagined him using.

Where did you find that typewriter?

I'm trying to remember now.

Was it a German typewriter?

It might have been. I think I found it in a curio shop or a store in Santa Barbara.

Moving on to *The Final Dossier*, when did you start writing that?

I wrote it in the fall of 2016. The series came on in May of 2017. *The Secret History* came out in the fall of 2016, and I was writing *The Final Dossier* concurrent with that, in the fall of 2016.

Did you finish in the fall of '16?

I finished around Christmas.

At the time that you wrote that—

We published it in the fall of '17, right after the series ended.

Right, October—right around Halloween. So at the time that you wrote *The Final Dossier*, you had no idea how closely aligned the TV program would be with the script as you and David had written it? You didn't know exactly what was going to happen in the TV show

as Lynch was filming it yet?

I'd seen the scripts. I hadn't seen the finished version.

Your concept of the TV show at that time would have adhered very closely to the way the scripts were written?

Yes, correct. I didn't see the finished episodes until much later.

Because if I didn't know the timing, I would think that part of the purpose of writing *The Final Dossier* was to address questions that you knew were not going to be answered in the show. Is that right?

Yes. There wasn't a lot at that point—I'd seen all the pages for things that had been shot, so I knew what the contents of the show were, and I'd been on the set a fair amount. I just hadn't seen the final versions.

Part 18 aired in the summer of 2017. At that point, your book was already written. A lot of people who've read *The Final Dossier* were surprised that there was no mention of Richard and Linda, for example, or Carrie Page. The question is, when you wrote *The Final Dossier* did you know there was a Richard and a Linda and a Carrie Page?

I'd seen the pages they were mentioned in, and we had talked about Carrie—that part we'd mapped out—but he added the Richard and Linda references later and never explained his reasoning to me.

But Carrie doesn't show up till Part 18, right?

Yes, but we'd talked about those scenes in detail.

The scene of Cooper going through this portal or whatever?

And finding her in Texas.

Finding her as Carrie Page.

Yes. We'd worked that out conceptually. The Richard and Linda stuff, not so much.

This might strike you as kind of a crazy thought. It's either brilliant or crazy. You could tell me which. Is there any possibility that in the course of *The Final Dossier*, Tammy Preston is speaking for you, Mark Frost, in some sort of subtextual way? For instance, she says, "On a personal level, I will share with you, however, that regardless of the cost to my innocence or naiveté regarding these truths of the human condition, I emerged from this experience grateful for the wisdom it has given me and stronger of mind for the hard lessons learned." Is there any possibility that's also Mark Frost talking about *Twin Peaks*?

To an extent, yes, but that was about ninety percent the character.

Then by the same token, when you write—this is Chapter 14: "I mean honestly, are they cranking out these duplicate creatures in an alternate reality Kinko's with some kind of Lovecraft 3d printer?" or when you write, "So what do we do with all this information? How does it change the focus on what we're looking at here? If at all? What concrete leads was Jeffries on to? Are these just the insane ramblings of a man who, as you all know, swam in a sea filled with extravagant and esoteric conspiracy theories? Or do we calmly sit with this information and see whether and how it fits into what we already know?"—

As I hear it again, my voice is definitely a part of that perspective.

Is that an Easter egg?

To some extent. That's undoubtedly what I was thinking in the moment, working through the ideas, examining the themes.

I was going to ask you, is there material in *The Final Dossier* that was in the original script, but then somehow never made its way into *The Return*, like the stuff with Audrey or Major Briggs or Phillip Jeffries? But I guess we're saying at that point, when you were writing *The Final Dossier* you didn't know exactly what was going to be—

I knew everything that was going to be shot at this point. I was just trying to offer a little bit more perspective. Not spoilers, but clues about what it all might have meant. And it was appropriate because it was appropriate for the character. Tammy's assignment was to make sense of whatever she encountered. And frankly, some of those scenes are fairly enigmatic. I thought it might be interesting for her to offer her theories about where this was headed.

How did you decide what not to address? Like, just for example— and I don't know if this was in the original script—but the whole thing with Phillip Jeffries and whoever Mr. C is talking to in the motel room and what became of Phillip Jeffries and so on? How did you decide what not to address?

That all turned on David Bowie's availability. He was going to do the show, he wanted to, but sadly it didn't happen. And so Lynch was left with a choice about how to film or dramatize these scenes we'd written without access to the actor. We discussed it a lot, trying to find a way that would that serve that purpose, give you the sense that Mr. C was in some way talking to Phillip Jeffries, who appeared to have slipped into a crack in the space-time continuum. That would obviously have been more apprehensible had Bowie been on screen.

Do you have any idea who Mr. C was talking to in that motel room when he thinks it's Phillip Jeffries? And then it's not? Do you remember that scene where he takes out the machine?

Yes. It was someone pretending to be Phillip Jeffries to gain access to more information about someone else's location. I'll leave you to guess who it might be.

That stuff about Joudy, the explanation of Joudy when Tammy goes back and looks up the mythology, was that something that was conceived of for the show, even though you knew it wasn't going to actually be explained in the show? Was that already in your head that this was the background?

This started when David made this one enigmatic reference in *Fire Walk With Me* when he had the monkey say "Judy"—it was one of those things that just occurred to him. And he added it without fully knowing who or what that was. I thought putting it in some kind of context that made sense would be helpful, so I proposed the thing about, "Well, why don't we say that 'Joudy' is actually the underlying entity that's behind all this?" And that led to creating its backstory in Part 8.

In *The Final Dossier*, you sort of address this—obliquely of course—but was Laura Palmer killed by Bob/Leland or not? I mean, do you think Laura is dead or not, after Cooper goes back?

You mean by the end of season three?

Right.

It's sort of laborious to lay it out, but—I think we've talked about this—the idea was that by going back in time and having the hubris to think he could undo something, Cooper was following in the footsteps of Phillip Jeffries. He crossed a forbidden barrier, risked his existential existence to do it, and ended up hurling both he and Laura into a sideways, alternate reality.

We did talk about that, but about Annie and season two. I remember saying I understand where Cooper is coming from. I think Cooper is basically driven by a somewhat pure motive that's almost Joseph Campbell–like.

Yes, it is. It's the search for the Grail; he's searching for something pure, but risks altering the fabric of space and time for himself and the person he's trying to rescue and pays a terrible price. From a mythological standpoint, it all makes sense and is consistent with "Don't mess with the realm of the gods, or you'll risk your own damnation."

What do you think is the terrible price that he pays?

Just look where he ends up—standing outside that house, not knowing what year it is. He's lost and probably can't get back.

In *The Final Dossier*, you say this: "Is the evil in us real? Is it an intrinsic part of us, a force outside us, or nothing more than a reflection of the Void? How do we hold both fear and wonder in the mind at once? Does staring into the darkness offer up answers or resolution?" I mean, these are themes you've come back to over and over and over again in your work—evil, fear. We've talked pretty extensively about this. What are you ultimately trying to say about those themes?

Maybe it's better for someone else to decide that. For me, the resolution lies in letting go of the idea that they're any different from one another. That there is, in the final analysis, only the present moment. And the real challenge of living—the almost impossible task of it, but perhaps the path to something like enlightenment—lies in our ability to live in just the present moment, be alive to it, and actually see what's around you. That offers a solution to the question you posed because if you're able to master that, the rest of it melts together.

You also say in *The Final Dossier*—I think this is Tammy talking— "how easy it is to quit, give up. Lower our eyes." Is that in any way connected to the message at the beginning of *The List of Seven*—that "All the Devil asks is acquiescence—not conflict, not struggle"? Because in both cases, you seem to be saying that not struggling is some sort of sin in and of itself.

Yes, those two things are aligned. Let's use a contemporary example, with what we've seen in this country in the last three years. And it's not just here, it's worldwide—right-wing authoritarianism on the rise again, what appear to be international conspiracies of oligarchs and billionaires and criminals trying to rig the system permanently in their favor. That's tantamount to evil. And for all of us who are opposed to that, if we don't stand up and fight when they have the means and the power and the money—this feels like a pretty momentous struggle, and if we lose this one, it could be lights out.

How did it make you feel when David was quoted as saying he wasn't going to read the books?

That didn't surprise me. He's less interested in other people's work than most creative people I know. I almost never heard him talk about a contemporary film or somebody else's work. I don't know why. You'd have to ask him.

I'm going to put you on the spot here and ask if you have a favorite season of *Twin Peaks*.

No, I like them each for different reasons.

Can you elaborate on that?

Well, then I get into betraying bias, so it's a question I'd rather not delve into. I would say that the third season—twenty-five years later, when we were all different people—provided a more satisfying and richer feeling of appreciation.

Rightly or wrongly, I've got the sense that while a lot of people loved season three—certainly it was critically revered—certain fanatical fans of seasons one and two were not so happy with it. My theory is that if you really listen to what these people say, and you read between the lines, what they wanted was more Mark Frost. To them anyway, it lacked a lot of the warmth and charm of the first

two seasons. I really wonder if what they wanted was more of the best parts of seasons one and two, which happen to be the parts when David wasn't around so much. I think maybe they wanted more Mark Frost and Harley Peyton and Bob Engels.

That could well be. I haven't spoken to them much myself, but if you look at Lynch's body of work and establish he's going to be the driving force and less collaborative—as this was the case in season three—then it's going to be dark. That's where he works. Those are the colors on his palette. That's who he is.

Right, there's that, but maybe just a little less humanity and warmth to it, when you compare it with seasons one and two?

Let's just say I tried to get as much of that into the work as I could—

And then you stepped away.

That was contractual. It was always going to be more his rodeo than mine.

A writer at the online magazine Nylon called season three the Old Testament *Twin Peaks*: harder, colder, angrier, with less humor. Would you agree with that?

Yes.

Was that intentional? Was there a reason for it?

You'd have to ask him that. There were things he added after I stepped away, and scenes he wrote while he was shooting, all of which took it in that direction. That's more a result of his temperament, of his interests.

John Thorne wrote an editorial in *Wrapped in Plastic* where he said he didn't think fans really wanted Lynch to do a film that addressed the unanswered questions from seasons one and two because they

wouldn't like the way he addressed them. So John wrote that what fans really want is David Lynch directing a script by Mark Frost. I think a lot of fans felt that they didn't get that in season three, particularly with respect to the ending. How does that make you feel?

It's more politic if I don't express anything about that at all.

In retrospect, do you think Showtime was the right partner?

Absolutely. They presented it superbly, marketed it extremely well, and they are absolute pros in every department. I really like the people, they do consistently good work, and they take chances. They also gave us everything we asked for, so it's hard to feel anything other than a real sense of mutual respect.

It's interesting. Comparing season three to seasons one and two, I sometimes wonder whether you guys having to work around those broadcast-network constraints back in the day in some way lent the ABC show a certain charm that it might not have otherwise had. I don't know if you feel that or not.

I do, because it asks you to be more resourceful from a storytelling standpoint or even a character standpoint. You have to have a certain amount of restraint, like trying to write a sonnet within the parameters of the form. It's hard to argue that we're any better or worse off now. It's just a different world. We're talking about the way society has changed. Bochco used to be obsessed with this idea of breaking down broadcast standards—'cause he'd grown up a lot more than I did with rigid and ridiculous constraints on that kind of storytelling, so he was hell-bent on getting away with stuff, and that's why *NYPD Blue* was such a triumph for him. He was able to get them to curse and show a little bit of nudity. That was new ground he was really interested in breaking. I didn't care so much about bending the rules because I came of age at a time when the rules were changing so quickly that it was hard to know what they were from one week to the next.

In the end, would you judge the third season a success? Are you happy that you did it?

Yes. Number one, it's a success simply because we made it that far and got it done. That's extraordinary to begin with after all that time. It's a piece more attuned to the times we live in. The old show was attuned to its own time. Here we were on the rollercoaster that was taking us toward the Trump era, and I felt that it spoke to the darkness we're all living in now in a way that more work needs to be done.

OK, last *Twin Peaks* question, at least for now: you not so long ago told *Vanity Fair* that you hope the show will continue, which I imagine you probably just felt like you had to say, but do you feel like the story of *Twin Peaks* is complete? Or would you like to see more?

This is a mousetrap of a question, because you always like to leave hope alive for people who are hoping for more. So I never want to close the door on that entirely. I wrote 1,200 pages about *Twin Peaks* in this last go-round, between the script and the two books. It remains a wonderful, alive creation for people that I hope stays provocative and interesting and open to their various lines of inquiry for a long time to come. As far as I'm concerned, that means the story isn't over.

Can you address it on the record, even from a creative standpoint? I mean, do you feel like you have anything left to say about it? Or do you feel like, you know, considering all the time that you've spent on it in your life that there are other things you want to do? I mean, is there any on the record way you could say?

If there is, I haven't thought of it yet, but I'll be sure to let you know if I do.

11

"Believe in the Good"

(Final Thoughts)

O dds and ends . . .

***

I've been meaning to ask you, with all the moving around that you've done over the years, do you feel like an Angelino or a New Yorker or a Midwesterner, or do you feel like a gypsy?

I identify strongly at a primal level as a New Yorker. We've talked about *American Nations* by Colin Woodard. It's a brilliant book, a different lens for looking at the history of this country as a series of eleven separate and discrete immigrations that settled different parts of the country, in effect creating eleven different and distinct nations within the rubric of the United States. It goes farther toward explaining the difficulties we've had integrating them than anything I've ever read. One of the nations he identifies is the tristate area around New York City, which he calls New Amsterdam. The dominant influence here were the Dutch, who first settled that part of the world and brought with them an incredibly facile and flexible style of mercantile government. They were brilliant merchants and gave rise to a society like they had in Holland that was committed to trade, multiculturalism, and meritocracy, so that anybody who contributed to the great steam engine of New York in whatever discipline they practiced was more than welcome. It was the

Emerald City, Oz, but only for people willing to roll up their sleeves and go to work to make something happen. That's the same energy you feel in New York today, and it's why it became the world center of the diamond business, the publishing business, the trading business, the banking business, the entertainment business. There's a reason it all coalesced around New York, and to that extent my identification, at a base level, is primarily as a New Yorker.

Because of the formative years I spent in LA and the decades I've spent here since, at a personal level I'm a Californian—the ethos of the Western frontier, of remaking the Old World in a new way, which the West Coast has always been about, shaping a different identity that was not tied to or weighed down by who you were before you got here. People came here to reinvent themselves and look toward the future. That's still true today. When I finally moved back here, I realized this was where I was going to make my home. I'm a Californian who still feels, deep down, like a citizen of New York.

One of the things that's interesting to me as we review your career over the decades is this: a lot of people—like Richard Levinson and Bill Link, or Ryan Murphy and Brad Falchuk, or Ed Zwick and Marshall Herskovitz—have had these professional partnerships that lasted for years and years and have resulted in numerous shows, but that isn't really you and David Lynch. You guys are associated together with really just one successful show. And you at least have talked extensively about how comfortable you are working alone. So I'm just curious: what, in your opinion, made your partnership work, and what did each of you bring to it?

It's a complicated question. It was forged by the fact that the second or third time out we did something that was successful and took on a life of its own, and that was the glue that held us together. We didn't work together then for nearly twenty years, and we started again in 2012 when I went to him and said I thought I had a way to bring it back. The one thing we had in common was the success of *Twin Peaks*. We had little contact with each other for those twenty years, a handful of times. With something as uniquely successful as *Twin Peaks*, given the way it ended, I felt it deserved another act. That was the basis, on my part, for approaching him and moving it forward. In the larger scheme of things, it wasn't a long collaboration. It was actually pretty brief and concentrated.

But very successful. So from a creative standpoint, what made it successful, and what impact did each of you have on that?

We had a mutual interest in the subject matter—the idea of world building from a narrative standpoint, something that incorporated a lot of American mythology and American issues. That was what I wanted to pursue. I wanted it to feel uniquely American. I think that's why the show had a timeless quality to it. It drew on a lot of archetypes of American life from the last hundred years. The small town was in many ways the perfect vehicle for examining American life. A lot can get lost in the wash of a big city, but when you confine it to a small town, you're able to examine these archetypes with almost scientific precision and compassion, and a lot of interesting results came out of that exploration.

So what did we both bring to it? When you're writing, it's a tennis match, you're batting the ball back and forth. One of my tasks was to keep perspective in terms of the larger narrative. Lynch was then free to do what I would call jazz solos within that composition. That's one way I can visualize it for you. When he brought those flights back into the context of the overall sense of the music, that seemed to be a good place for the music that was inside him to reside, and it resulted in some of the best work of his career.

David has been described as a surrealist, rightly or wrongly, but he did that British television show where he introduced the work of surrealist filmmakers. Is it too reductivist to ask what "ist" Mark Frost is?

The term I come back to is "humanist." What interests me are the interior lives and moral dilemmas, jeopardies, and development of human beings, couched within a narrative framework. I don't really love plot for plot's sake. Plot is a tool you learn to work with and need to master in a writing career. It's like carpentry. You learn how to make solid joists, how to plane a door, how to bring out the best quality of the wood. Those things become second nature to you. That's craft. So plot is related more to craft for me. What then becomes the focus is, "What's in this story and this particular set of people that can help illuminate being human?" That's I think where I come down in terms of an ism.

When you read something like *The Passion of David Lynch*, do you ever feel like your contribution to the partnership is diminished?

Academics usually have a thesis they're trying to prove, and they're not usually looking for a dissenting opinion. That was my feeling about the people I've spoken to who were writing about him. They make assumptions about his work and tend to be more than charitable about his contributions and what they assume he's going after. He's, unqualified, a brilliant director. My experience is that his process as a writer is not as consciously directed as they assume. It's more inchoate and often as mysterious to him because he's anti-intellectual. He never had a liberal arts education, and he's not interested in psychology. Not to say there's anything wrong with that, but academics making cases about collaborative work are usually making assumptions that don't bear up to scrutiny.

When all is said and done, do you think *Twin Peaks* is what you'll be most remembered for? Of course, we don't know what's coming next.

It's a hard question to answer. It's usually the first thing people associate me with, and if that's the first line in my obituary, so be it. I thought about that when Steven [Bochco] passed away. I was wondering, "Which show are they going to most clearly associate him with?" *NYPD Blue* seemed to be the one most mentioned, perhaps because it was more recent and that had a recency/primacy impact on memory. It also ran for a longer period of time than his other shows. That's just how things get pigeonholed. Ultimately you can't worry about how you're going to be remembered or what your legacy is. All you can do is what you do, and the rest isn't up to you.

For whatever it's worth, as a TV historian, I will always associate him first with *Hill Street Blues*, because I think that was the most revolutionary and influential of his shows.

I tend to agree with you. I think *NYPD Blue* was a furtherance of many of the same themes and some of the same character types, but I think *Hill Street* ultimately had more impact. It's funny how shows that burn that bright in the moment years later barely leave a ripple in people's imagination. It's the nature of the beast in television, more a medium of the moment than one for the ages. *Hill Street* is a good case in point.

I'm pretty sure you and David are never going to have to worry about that with respect to *Twin Peaks*, though.

I think coming back and doing what we did helped. Whatever else might have been uncertain about the show or how it was received, it clearly wasn't a smash and grab for cash. It was strikingly different from the original, even demanding at times. So in the long run, that may help its reputation more than harm it. A lot of shows that try to come back sully the memory of the first time around, simply because it's such a hard thing to do. High bar of difficulty to make that work.

Arthur Conan Doyle—who appears as a character in two of your novels—famously grew so sick of Sherlock Holmes that he killed him off, but then brought him back. Is that something you as a writer can understand? Have you ever felt that way about *Twin Peaks* or, say, Dale Cooper?

It was something I understood, and I thought it was illuminating about Doyle, because he decided to come back to the character later out of popular demand. He made his peace with him. We touched on it earlier about Levinson and Link and Columbo, the character that made them famous, only to have the actor rebel and challenge them about their vision of it. Imagine what that must have been like. For authors who are particularly known for a single character, that's probably a common issue.

Do you see any parallel to your life and *Twin Peaks* here, being, you know, that you came back to it?

Only because of the stories that I thought were left undone way back when. That's now been satisfied for me. Speaking for myself, I'm satisfied with taking these people, these characters, to where they are now.

Have you ever felt that people would never stop asking you about *Twin Peaks*, or that people would never look past *Twin Peaks* in assessing your career?

I did a few times back in the early nineties. After the show went off the air, originally there were a few years where I just wanted to move on to the next thing, but never to the point where I felt resentful about having had the experience.

Would you say *Twin Peaks* is the project that has been most satisfying to you? What have you worked on that was most fulfilling creatively?

It may disappoint you for me to say this, but it's a project I'm working on right now, the Krishnamurti book. It's more a culmination of all of my interests, and it's one of the most rewarding things I've worked on in terms of how it's personally meaningful. I'm grateful to have had the freedom creativity has given me, telling stories that hopefully mean something to people. To live with that every day is a great reward. I can't imagine a better feeling than that. Now, that's prior to the marketplace having a vote on it, and that tends to color your view of your work, if only in retrospect.

Interesting that you would choose a book rather than a TV show. We've talked a lot about literature—both your own and the writers you admire. *The New York Times* does this thing where they ask an author, "If there's one book you could ask the president to read, what would it be?" So let me ask you a variation on that question: If I were to ask you if there was one book you would give your son, Travis, to read, what would that book be? Or is that an impossible question?

I don't know if I can think of one book that sums up everything to that extent. I don't know what it would be. I'd have to think about it.

Joseph Campbell, another person you have spoken of having great admiration and respect for, knew the Olympic sprinter Jackson Scholz—Campbell himself was a runner—and he said of him, "It's funny, when you get on in years and look back and realize the role that certain people played in your life, it's surprising, and Scholz, I think, was one of the major people. Sometimes it's just a little kick that brought you onto this path instead of that one." Who are those people in your life who played a major role in determining who you became?

It could even be someone you've only met once or twice, right? When when I was working at the Guthrie Theater in the late seventies, before I came back to LA, I was asked to write the narration and biography for a filmmaker who was coming to Minneapolis, Abel Gance. Gance had made an epochal film about Napoleon—a silent film in the twenties that had been lost for many years. And it had been found—Zoetrope had found and restored it. Gance actually shot portions of it in a system similar to Cinerama, shot with three cameras side by side, and when you get to the big action scenes in the movie, suddenly curtains opened and the screen widened to the panorama of a Cinerama-like frame ratio—you could still see lines that separated the three strips of film. But it was stunning, and Gance came to Minneapolis to show the movie. They played a new score for it with a small musical ensemble—if I'm not mistaken Carmine Coppola, Francis's father, wrote the score. So I got to meet Gance, interview him, and spend time with him throughout that week. He was in his late eighties at that point, but he had a kind of glow about him. I'd always been drawn to French film, both classic and New Wave—Truffaut, Godard, Chabrol—so it was akin to meeting Jean Renoir. Gance was still a proud, unrepentant artist; he was still looking to the next horizon, the next new piece of work. I found his attitude toward life and living as an artist utterly inspiring and felt honored to have met him. He died just a couple of years later. So he was somebody who really lit a spark for me.

I've talked with you about Fred Rogers, how inspiring he was as a human being. How compassionate and present he was. I finally got to see the wonderful documentary they did about him and realized I'm in it. There's a shot of me from the catwalks hoisting up a light. It was stunning, brought the whole period back, like looking into a time machine.

There've been a few others. Because I'd been an athlete, as a coach John Wooden was a role model. I was a huge fan of UCLA basketball during his run. I got to know him later in life, and he was one of those people who surpassed their reputation. The soul of decency and common sense.

I would say—and we've talked about him—that at a formative time of my life, Alan Arkin was a big inspiration. Watching him navigate Hollywood and his own career, and the inevitable ups and downs that people face, but staying true to his vision of things. Alan was a great role model in that regard.

Looking back over your career, how difficult has it been for you to balance the commercial demands—ratings, book sales, supporting your family—with whatever larger goals you have had as an artist?

It's always a struggle in a business like this, because it's really hard to do what you want to do and make a living. Earlier on, I tried to balance—and follow Schlesinger's Law—do one for them and then do one for yourself; that way you keep your currency in the business, but it gives you the freedom to do your own work if you're moved to do so. For a long time, I followed that strategy. I'm now at a point later in life where I don't need to do that as much, take jobs just for a paycheck. I can just concentrate on what I want to do and believe in. I'm fortunate to be here, and I've worked hard for it.

A lot of writers—novelists, TV writers, screenwriters—say their main responsibility is to entertain and engage, so that people consume their work, so that they can keep working. How do you see your role as a writer, whatever the medium of expression? Do you have some responsibility to leverage your gift to communicate a message, or do you basically just see yourself as an entertainer?

Twin Peaks was a vehicle through which I was first able to articulate and incorporate some of those thoughts, both before and the second time around. Having had that experience, the few times I went back into television, all those ancillary issues that get tangled up with the work—ratings, dollars, access, status—held less interest as time went by. That's why I turned to prose and nonfiction and solitary work, where I could explore themes and stories that held my attention without anybody else, other than a publisher, saying yea or nay about it. I've never thought of myself as a writer who specialized in any one genre or medium. That's how I'd prefer to be known: as a writer who works in whichever medium best conveys the story I'm working with.

When you sit down to write something—a book or film or TV show—are you simply concerned with telling a good story, or is it equally important to impart some philosophy of life?

My thinking has evolved in this direction. My goal is to take the reader or viewer on a journey, and where they think it takes them is up to them. I wouldn't characterize my work as dogmatic or ideological in any way. I'm trying to tell a story that takes them on a journey, and hope it leads them somewhere they find interesting or beneficial or entertaining, or all three. The best you can hope for is a willingness to go along on the ride, and those are the people you're going to reach.

Is there a message you want to leave them with? Like when people talk about Mark Frost as a writer—not just as the cocreator of *Twin Peaks*, but as a writer, spanning your whole career—what would you like them to say about you?

What you want to feel is that your vision of life and reality and people somehow resonated with others and led them to ask questions of their own reality, of themselves. That you imparted to them some small piece of hope or wisdom or a good laugh when they needed it, something that lights a candle about what life can hold for them. That's more than enough.

You and I have spoken a lot over the months about how so much of your work explores the existence of evil in the world. What do you think is the most important point you've been trying to make about that?

Believe in the good. Evil may seem attractive or frightening—even terrifying, overwhelming—but eventually, it always yields if enough people believe in the good. The arc of humanity, taken as a whole— I'm reading books about Napoleon and Caesar now, all the ruin and bloodshed they visited on so many ordinary people, that's worlds away from the one we live in now. Of course, there are still daily outrages and horrors, but we're generally living in a more civilized world, the current administration notwithstanding. So I would say, "You've got to hold on to hope, and if you feel something needs to be done, do it. Don't wait for anyone to do it for you." Take the next generation, for example, when they confront the full nightmare of what climate change appears to have in store for us. They're going to be fighting not just for their own survival, but the survival of life on Earth, so I wish them courage, and I wish them conviction.

Last question: Is there anything that you haven't accomplished professionally that you'd still like to do?

I'd like to write a play and get back into the theater again, and I'm working on that, but aside from that I don't feel thwarted in any way. I've had a lot of freedom, particularly in the last twenty-five years, to do what I'm drawn to and managed to find a way to do that to support my family at the same time. So it all worked out pretty well. No complaints, no regrets.

APPENDIX A

Mark Frost's Film and Television Credits

Sunshine (1973)
writer

Lucas Tanner (1974–1975)
writer

The Six Million Dollar Man (1975)
writer

The Road Back (1979)
writer, director, producer

Gavilan (1982)
writer

Hill Street Blues (1982–1985)
writer, director, story editor, executive story editor

The Equalizer (1986)
writer

The Believers (1987)
writer, associate producer

No Man's Land (1987)
writer (uncredited)

Scared Stiff (1987)
writer

American Chronicles (1990)
creator, writer, director, executive producer

Nightbreed (1990)
writer (uncredited)

Twin Peaks (1990–1991)
creator, writer, director, executive producer

On the Air (1992)
creator, writer, executive producer
Storyville (1992)
writer, director
Twin Peaks: Fire Walk with Me (1992)
executive producer
The Repair Shop (1998)
writer, executive producer
Buddy Faro (1998–2000)
creator, writer, executive producer
Forbidden Island (1999)
writer, executive producer
The Deadly Look of Love (2000)
writer, co-executive producer
All Souls (2001)
writer, executive producer
Fantastic Four (2005)
writer
The Greatest Game Ever Played (2005)
writer, producer
Fantastic Four: Rise of the Silver Surfer (2007)
writer
Twin Peaks: The Return (2017)
creator, writer, executive producer

APPENDIX B

Mark Frost's Fiction and Nonfiction Works

Fiction
The List of Seven (1993)
The Six Messiahs (1995)
Before I Wake (as Eric Bowman) (1997)
The Second Objective (2007)
The Paladin Prophecy Book I (2012)
Alliance: The Paladin Prophecy Book II (2013)
Rogue: The Paladin Prophecy Book III (2015)
The Secret History of Twin Peaks (2016)
Twin Peaks: The Final Dossier (2017)

Nonfiction
The Greatest Game Ever Played: Harry Vardon, Francis Ouimet, and the Birth of Modern Golf (2002)
The Grand Slam: Bobby Jones, America, and the Story of Golf (2004)
The Match: The Day the Game of Golf Changed Forever (2007)
Game Six: Cincinnati, Boston, and the 1975 World Series: The Triumph of America's Pastime (2009)

SELECTED BIBLIOGRAPHY

Bochco, Steven. *Truth Is a Total Defense: My Fifty Years in Television.* Self-published, CreateSpace, 2016.

Boulègue, Franck. *Twin Peaks: Unwrapping the Plastic.* With a foreword by David Bushman. Chicago: Intellect, 2017. Distributed by University of Chicago Press.

Bushman, David, and Arthur Smith. *Twin Peaks FAQ: All That's Left to Know About a Place Both Wonderful and Strange.* Milwaukee, WI: Applause Theatre & Cinema Books, 2016.

Condé, Nicholas. *The Religion.* New York: Dutton, 1982.

Dukes, Brad. *Reflections: An Oral History of Twin Peaks.* Nashville, TN: Short/Tall Press, 2014.

Galbally, Frank, and Robert Macklin. *Juryman.* Victoria, Australia: Currey O'Neil, 1982.

Lynch, David, and Kristine McKenna. *Room to Dream.* New York: Random House, 2018.

Nochimson, Martha P. *The Passion of David Lynch: Wild at Heart in Hollywood.* Austin: University of Texas Press, 1997.

———. *Television Rewired: The Rise of the Auteur Series.* Austin: University of Texas Press, 2019.

Rodley, Chris, ed. *Lynch on Lynch.* London: Faber & Faber, 1997.

Shaver, Richard S. *I Remember Lemuria.* Evanston, IL: Venture Press, 1948.

Thorne, John. *The Essential Wrapped in Plastic: Pathways to Twin Peaks.* Dallas, TX: John Thorne, 2016.

***

REFERENCE LIST

Introduction

Appleyard, Bryan. "David Lynch Interview: The Director on Film, TV Before *Twin Peaks*, Painting — and Fixing Toys." *Sunday Times* (London), June 23, 2019.

Nochimson, Martha P. *Television Rewired: The Rise of the Auteur Series.*

Austin: University of Texas Press, 2019.

Chapter 1
Campbell, Joseph. *The Hero's Journey: Joseph Campbell on His Life and Works*. Edited by Phil Cousineau. San Francisco: Harper & Row, 1990.

Chapter 3
Manly, Lorne. "Being Careful Out There? Hardly." *New York Times*, May 1, 2014.

Chapter 4
Canby, Vincent. "Film: *The Believers*, from John Schlesinger." *New York Times*, June 10, 1987.
Wilmington, Michael. "Movie Review: Father, Son Versus Evil Cult in *The Believers*." *Los Angeles Times*, June 10, 1987.

Chapter 6
Bochco, Steven, Tom Fontana, Marshall Herskovitz, David E. Kelley, Dick Wolf, and Edward Zwick. "The Television Author: Shaping Character and Conscience: Character Studies." Moderated by Robert M. Batscha, Museum of Television & Radio, Leonard H. Goldenson University Satellite Seminar Series, May 17, 1999.
Lynch, David, and Kristine McKenna. *Room to Dream*. New York: Random House, 2018.
Jackson, Kevin. "Higher Peaks in View: The Man Who Wrote *Twin Peaks* Has Plans to Get Weirder." *Independent* (London), August 22, 1992.
Nochimson, Martha P. *The Passion of David Lynch: Wild at Heart in Hollywood*. Austin: University of Texas Press, 1997.
Campbell, Bruce F. *Ancient Wisdom Revived: A History of the Theosophical Movement*. Berkeley: University of California Press, 1980.
Campbell, Joseph. *The Power of Myth with Bill Moyers*. Edited by Betty Sue Flowers. New York: Anchor Books, 1991.
Bushman, David. "Compassion Is the Key: An Interview with Jennifer Lynch." *Blue Rose* 1, no. 2 (June 2017).

Chapter 7
Murray, Noel. "*Twin Peaks* Season 3 Finale: The Curtain Call." *New*

York Times, September 4, 2017.

Cerone, Daniel. "Television of the Absurd: *Twin Peaks* Co-Creators Try Again with *On the Air*." Los Angeles Times, June 18, 1992.

Hinson, Hal. "*Storyville*." Washington Post, October 9, 1992.

Canby, Vincent. "Review/Film; Lust, Greed, Murder, Blackmail: Big Wrongs in the Big Easy." *New York Times*, April 26, 1992.

Ebert, Roger. "*Storyville*." *Chicago Sun-Times*, October 9, 1992.

Chapter 8

Lutyens, Mary. Krishnamurti: *The Years of Fulfillment*. London: John Murray, 1983.

Nochimson, Martha P. *The Passion of David Lynch: Wild at Heart in Hollywood*. Austin: University of Texas Press, 1997.

Bushman, David. "Angel: Vampire Noir: Cocreator David Greenwalt Shines a Light on the Vampire with a Soul." PaleyMatters, June 20, 2017. https://paleymatters.org/angel-vampire-noir-e4eacd39dc4a.

Frost, Mark. *The Second Objective*. New York: Hyperion, 2007.

Russell, Craig. *The Devil Aspect*. New York: Doubleday, 2019.

Jackson, Kevin. "Higher Peaks in View: The Man Who Wrote *Twin Peaks* Has Plans to Get Weirder." *Independent* (London), August 22, 1992.

Frost, Mark. *The Match*. New York: Hyperion, 2007.

Chapter 10

James, Nick. "Films of the Year." Sight & Sound 28, no. 1 (January 2018). https://www.bfi.org.uk/features/best-films-2017.

Lynch, David, and Kristine McKenna. *Room to Dream*. New York: Random House, 2018.

Frost, Mark. *The Final Dossier*. New York: Flatiron Books, 2017.

Chapter 11

Campbell, Joseph. *The Hero's Journey: Joseph Campbell on His Life and Works*. Edited by Phil Cousineau. San Francisco: Harper & Row, 1990.

APPENDIX C

Letter from Mark Frost to his literary agent, Ed Victor, about his original plans to write a *Twin Peaks* novel, in the early days of the original serie*s (courtesy of Mischa Cronin).*

Dear Ed,

Some thoughts regarding our conversation the other day.

As the chronicle of the contempory life of an isolated, self-sustaining rural community, "Twin Peaks" dwells in a present that is hazily moored in time, a portrait of a rapidly vanishing genus of American life.

This town is alive in my mind, its borders extending far beyond the edges of the small screen for which we've produced the series. The breadth and depth of the storytelling in our first nine hours are already pushing the limits of what film narrative can sustain and there are still countless undeliniated details, people, places and things events going begging for expression. As the town accretes one layer of reality after another, so grows my frustration at our inability to present "Twin Peaks" in its richest, fullest form.

Your suggestion that fiction is the answer to this frustration rang clearer than the bells of St. Louis cathedral outside my window. The complexities of the stories and the brooding, conflicted interior lives of these characters would I believe superbly lend themselves to extended treatment on the printed page.

As you also suggested, rather than attempt a novelization of the existing material, at best a bastardized child with no discernible resemblance to either parent, why not dig down into the rich loam of the town's foundation? Not so much prequel or preamble, there's relevant history here arcing back to the region's geological genesis: the formation of the twin peaks and their idiosyncratic magnetic polarities, the net effect of which has been the attraction of a procession of deep mysteries to this particular landscape.

There would follow the development of flora and fauna, the arrival of early man and the birth of the legends and lore that abound in the region, ala Michener if you will, but filtered through a darker lens of considerably different cut and hue; this isn't Texas or Chesapeake, it's Twin Peaks. Anecdotal, macabre, gruesomely humorous, strange events are the norm in this remote corner of the world, and it's been that way since the first amphibian grew lungs and crawled up out of the primordial ooze.

We'd spend some time tracing the development of the area's Native American culture and again the focus is on the deviant, the oblique and the odd. The tribes that settled here were drawn by an obscure, intuitive, mystical impulse that led them far from their traditional home. Whether it was the spiritual-emotional effects of the dislocation, their new, drastically different diet or those disorienting magnetic resonances, the migration eventually resulted in disaster, madness and self-destruction. The remnants of the last tribe still live near Twin Peaks, in greatly reduced circumstances, a living reminder of the region's enduring and prevailing wierdness.

With the arrival of Anglo-Saxon hunters and trappers from the east, Twin Peaks enters its most crucial developmental era. Here resides the main body of the story. Without going into too much detail at this stage, I see the focus narrowing down to three families, each central to the birth of the town and its growth from a ramshackle wayfaring station to the city of 50,000 we find at the start of the series.

The Horne family, beginning with the arrival of Benjamin Horne's paternal grandfather. A hard, uneducated man, who drives his sons to better themselves and eventually wrest control of the area, a kind of backwoods Joe Kennedy. This story thread culminates in the triumph of the third Horne generation, as Ben and brother Jerry Horne realize their forebearer's dream, at perilous cost to their personal happiness.

Their chief rivals are the Packard clan, who we trace back to the late Andrew Packard's father, a sea captain driven by religious visions to build a city between the Peaks. His son, Andrew, and daughter Catherine, carry the family legacy forward, with Andrew assuming epic importance in the town's development. A man of tremendous will and charisma, Andrew leads the local logging industry into the 20th century, amassing a huge personal fortune, while making good on his father's hopes for the civilizing influences of culture and prosperity on a dark and inhospitable landscape.

Andrew's three local marriages and his fourth to a mysterious Asian girl he brings back from a trip to Hong Kong are good grist for the mill, as is the Freudian torch his sister Catherine carries for him. An equally strong-willed woman with a steel-trap mind and temperment of a cornered wolverine, Catherine's disastrous marriage to the mill foreman, Pete Martell, and her eventual dalliance with arch-enemy Ben Horne are right at the heart of this story.

Other people of key interest include the Hurley family, an introspective succession of writers and artists, with a fatal proclivity for the bottle, and the Hayward clan, two generations of general practice doctors, who tend to the town's physical ills, while humbly concealing their own spiritual crises.

Another constant is the presence of the Bookhouse Boys, a loose coalition of right-minded citizens, shrouded in secrey and dedicated to combat the occasional manifestations of darkness that emanate from the surrounding woods. Named for the small shack which serves as their headquarters and library, founded by Andrew Packard, three generations of Bookhouse Boys have stood a lonely sentry at the border of good and evil.

Ending the book with the events leading up to the death of Laura Palmer, the last frame we'll see before the first frame of the film comes up from black, remains a solid, sound destination for this journey.

AVAILABLE NOW FROM FMP

ORDER AT FAYETTEVILLEMAFIAPRESS.COM

The Last Days of Letterman by Scott Ryan
ISBN: 9781949024005

The Women of David Lynch
ISBN: 9781949024029

The Women of Amy Sherman-Palladino
ISBN: 9781949024043

Flight 7 Is Missing: The Search for My Father's Killer by Ken Fortenberry
ISBN: 9781949024067

COMING SOON

Laura's Ghost: Women Speak About Twin Peaks by Courtenay Stallings
(August 28, 2020) ISBN: 9781949024081

The Massillon Tigers: 15 for 15 by David Lee Morgan, Jr. (September 8, 2020) IBSN: 9781949024166

Moonlighting: Cases, Chases and Conversations by Scott Ryan & E. J. Kishpaugh (2021) ISBN: 9781949024128